Visions of

The New Jerusalem

Visions of

The New Jerusalem
Religious settlement on the prairies

Edited by
Benjamin G. Smillie

NeWest Press
Edmonton

Canadian Cataloguing in Publication Data

Main entry under title

Visions of the New Jerusalem

ISBN 0-920316-72-7 (bound). — ISBN 0-920316-70-0 (pbk.)

1. Prairie Provinces - Religion - History - Addresses, essays, lectures.
2. Prairie Provinces - Population - History - Addresses, essays, lectures.
3. Prairie Provinces - Emigration and immigration - Religious aspects - History - Addresses, essays, lectures. I. Smillie, Benjamin G. (Benjamin Galletly), 1923-

| FC3242.9.I4V58 | 971.2'02 | C83-091260-6 | F1060.9.V58 |

C,2

40,049

Credits:
Cover and book design: *M. Chung, I. DeCoursey*
Printing and binding: *Friesen Printers, Altona, Manitoba*
Financial assistance: *Alberta Culture*
The Canada Council
Multiculturalism Program: Government
of Canada

NeWest Publishers Ltd.
#204, 8631 - 109 Street
Edmonton, Alberta
Canada T6G 1E8

for Adele

Contents

Preface *ix*

I   **Introduction:** Religious Settlement on the Prairies *1*
      B. G. Smillie

II   **Historical background to prairie settlement** *13*
      J. N. McCrorie

III   **Two faces of the New Jerusalem:** Indian-Metis reaction to the missionary *27*
      Marjorie Beaucage, Emma LaRoque

IV   **Gestae Dei Per Francos:** The French Catholic experience in western Canada *39*
      Raymond J. A. Huel

V   **Anglicanism on the prairies:** Continuity and flexibility *55*
      Frank Peake

VI   **Protestants—Prairie visionaries of the New Jerusalem:** The United and Lutheran Churches in western Canada *69*
      B. G. Smillie, N. J. Threinen

VII   **New Jerusalem on the prairies:** Welcoming the Jews *91*
      Abraham Arnold

VIII   **Mennonites and the New Jerusalem in western Canada** *109*
      T. D. Regehr

IX   **The western settlement of Canadian Doukhobors** *121*
      Koozma J. Tarasoff

X   **Building the New Jerusalem on the prairies:** The Ukrainian experience *137*
      Stella Hryniuk, Roman Yereniuk

XI   **St. Peter's:** A German-American marriage of monastery and colony *153*
      Bede Hubbard

XII   **Hutterites:** An interview with Michael Entz *165*
      Gail McConnell

XIII   **Conclusion** *177*
      B. G. Smillie

Contributors *193*

Notes *195*

Preface

The idea for this book originated in a public lecture series sponsored by the Saskatoon Public library in the fall of 1978. Originally the title intended for the book was "Building the New Jerusalem," chosen because I wanted to focus on the optimism of some of the pioneer Protestant groups who came to the prairie with the hope of building a new society, a New Jerusalem which would be a just society. Protestants who became involved in the Progressive Movement in politics were dedicated to building the alternative future on the Pelagian doctrine of works, which proclaimed that "God helped those who helped themselves."[1]

However, many of the pioneer religious groups understood the "New Jerusalem" as it was depicted in the Book of Revelation which was written in the midst of one of the major persecutions of Christians in the Roman Empire. Because the hope of a new society came to immigrants in the midst of drought, grasshoppers, hail, and economic servitude to banks, railways and line elevators, and because the material surroundings on the prairie in the first two decades of this century did not produce a city where the streets were paved with gold, the title "Visions of the New Jerusalem" more accurately depicts the religious experience and the historical reality of the early settlers.

Considering the many and varied religious groups that settled the prairie, the editor faced the difficult task of selecting which groups to include in this book and which to exclude. Many that are excluded have left their mark on religious settlement. Mormons, Seventh Day Adventists, The Church of Christ Scientists, the Russellites (later called the Jehovah Witnesses) have not been included.[2] There are two main reasons for this: the first is the limitation of space, the second is the bias of the editor who has tried, not with complete success, to concentrate on writers from religious denominations that represent either, as in the case of the Indian-Metis, the first citizens of the country, or those who stand in the main Judeo-Christian tradition.

All groups had a sense of their destiny on the prairie. For some, like the Hutterites, Mennonites, and Doukhobors, their hope was in a peaceable kingdom with no war. The "Holiness" movement groups with high hopes of human perfection found a catalyst for action in temperance causes. This brought common action from Methodists, Presbyterians, Baptists and Evangelical Anglicans. Catholics and Orthodox Christians saw the vision of a New Jerusalem in worshipping God in the "beauty of holiness." This vision, which was perhaps the oldest, caught the joy of the Israelite pilgrim who, returning from the Babylonian captivity in the sixth century B.C., saw Jerusalem as the city of worship: "I was glad when they said to me, 'Let us go to the house of the Lord!' Our feet have been standing within your gates, O Jerusalem!" (Psalms 122:1) The twelve selected for inclusion were chosen mainly because the writers fulfill the intention of the book which is to give a perspective on religious settlements and provide a sense of the theological and historical commitment of the religious communities they represent. These writers do not speak with the official voice of their denomination, but all are well respected within their church.

Many books and journal articles written on western Canadian immigration have explained the motivation for settlement as the seeking of economic prosperity or political freedom. While these reasons are undeniably important, we feel that this outlook often looks upon religious beliefs as strange, bizarre phenomena and, therefore, downplays the primacy of faith as motivation.

In analyzing settlement history, it is apparent that the settlers, in many cases, did not achieve economic prosperity. They also suffered from a racism that curtailed their political freedom, but nevertheless they persevered with great tenacity. My contention is that the theological roots of many settlers, particularly their biblical hope in a New Jerusalem, was an intangible but strong motivation which helped them to survive, in spite of financial hardship and political manipulation.

Susan Langer explains how great metaphors (and the "New Jerusalem" is an example of such a great metaphor) provide potency to people in shaping their language and action.[3] Langer goes on to explain that the formulating of life through these symbols produces a "mythic consciousness" which becomes a way of breaking with old attitudes and providing a cohesive force to move people toward the new. A powerful contemporary example of this mythic consciousness is outlined by the liberation theologians of Latin America and the feminist theologians of North America who use the Exodus story in the Bible to show how subjugated groups can get out of the symbolic "Egypt" that circumscribes their lives to the freedom of an open future in which they take responsibility for their own liberation. Langer explains that too frequently metaphors die and are replaced by literal statements while mythology gives way to science. For the pioneer settlers described in this book, "New Jerusalem" evoked a vision sometimes embodied in the struggle for justice, sometimes in worship, but for all, the vision of a better future was grounded in their faith.

Where possible, a map is provided with each chapter to show the places of settlement of each religious group. There is no map in the chapter on Indian-Metis as their migratory form of settlement makes the task complicated. As well, the chapter on Protestants presented the difficulty of locating United Churches and Lutheran Churches which are predominantly congregated in the cities. Therefore, instead of maps, there are bar graphs of all Protestant religious affiliations on the prairies. For the excellent maps and bar graphs, I am indebted to Mr. Keith Bigelow and his supervisor, Professor K. I. Fung of the Geography Department of the University of Saskatchewan.

The photographs were selected and arranged by Anne Smart, program co-ordinator of the Saskatoon Public library. I am also indebted to Ms. Smart for her encouragement in getting this writing project launched.

Gail McConnell, former publications editor of the University of Saskatchewan and writer of the chapter on Hutterites, also gave me valuable editorial advice. Professor Don Kerr gave me excellent suggestions in preparing the manuscript for final publication.

The most generous editorial assistance was provided by Professor Faye Kernan, Western College of Veterinary Medicine, who made excellent revision suggestions on all the manuscripts. Her wise proposals about deletions and amplifications of my own writing convinces me that through Mrs. Kernan (nee Popoff, a Doukhobor family), I have met the "informed reader" for whom this book is written.

A special word of thanks goes to Margaret Laing who typed and retyped manuscripts many times.

I dedicate this book to my wife, Adele, who, like myself, is a late-comer to the prairie. She personifies both the patience of those who understand and the impatience of those who love. She has given leadership through church and environmental groups to causes that seek to protect God's creation for future generations. For us and our five children, she makes a home where we continually see some of the dimensions of the New Jerusalem.

Over the twenty years on the prairie during which I have served as chaplain, and then as professor, I have been made aware that many prairie people who may or may not have held on to their religious beliefs, are nevertheless seeking to identify their roots. It is my hope that this book will help to rekindle their vision of the rich legacy we have all received from those early prairie settlers who "have fought the good fight and kept the faith."

I am grateful to the Multiculturalism Programme, Government of Canada, and the Department of Culture and Youth of the

Government of Saskatchewan for their financial support of this
writing project.

B.G. Smillie
St. Andrew's College, Saskatoon
March, 1983

I Introduction: Religious settlement on the prairies

B.G. Smillie

The power of ideas to shape lives was graphically described by the Scottish literary historian Thomas Carlyle (1795 - 1881). Carlyle was derided by a business acquaintance for his enthusiasm for the romantic philosopher, Jean Jacques Rousseau. The business man scoffed, "Ideas, Mr. Carlyle, ideas, nothing but ideas." Carlyle replied, "There was once a man called Rousseau who wrote a book containing nothing but ideas. The second edition was bound in the skins of those who laughed at the first."[1] Carlyle was referring to the French Revolution which broke out in 1789. It arose from criticism of an incompetent government controlled by a prodigally effete King Louis XVI and Queen Marie Antoinette. When confronted with the starving poor, the Queen said, "Let them eat cake." During the Reign of Terror, hundreds of the French nobility, including the King and the Queen, were guillotined. Carlyle's comment is a gory reminder of the worst excesses of the French Revolution. It is also a healthy corrective to those who see history as a catalogue of incidents in which impersonal forces become the sole explanation of events. **Ideas have had, and continue to have, control over people's lives.**

This is a book about religious ideas that influenced the period of settlement in western Canada, predominantly on the prairies. When looking at the maps included in this book, the reader might wonder how one area of the vast Canadian continent could produce such a large number of religious communities. This in fact was not an accident, and was in part the result of one small clause in an abridgement to the Dominion Lands Act.

The government of Canada did everything in its power to

encourage rapid settlement on the prairie after Confederation in 1867, preferably settlement by individuals. The Dominion Lands Act of 1872 "entitled a settler to secure entry to a quarter-section of land on payment of a ten-dollar fee. A homesteader could obtain an adjoining quarter-section and could purchase it at a price set by government as soon as he had secured the patent for his homestead quarter."[2] But one vital exception to this method of individual settlement was contained in an abridgement to the Dominion Lands Act (called the hamlet or village clause) which stated:

> If a number of homestead settlers involving at least twenty families with a view to greater convenience in the establishment of schools and churches, and to the attainment of social advantage ask to be allowed to settle together in a hamlet or village, the Minister may, in his discretion, vary or dispense with the foregoing requirements as to residence . . .[3]

This abridgement annulled the necessity of limiting each settler to title deed to only a quarter-section, located within a checkerboard area. The provision was made particularly to encourage groups of settlers to engage in co-operative farming. But more significantly, this clause made it possible for numbers of families to homestead as religious colonies—groups of settlers who often had a vision of the New Jerusalem.

This vision was not a private religious experience but a shared belief among ethnic religious communities who saw themselves as a religious covenant people establishing the kingdom of God in virgin country. Some government officials and members of parliament, caught up in the euphoria of the Minister of Immigration, Clifford Sifton, saw the new western immigrants primarily as a strongly zealous and docile population who could be economically exploited to provide markets for central Canada's industrial base. The phrase "peasants in sheepskin coats" epitomized this condescension. The exploitative immigration policy towards the settlers who came from Eastern Europe proved highly successful in populating the west. Between 1901 and 1931 the population of the prairie provinces increased five-fold, from 419,512 to 2,353,529. In 1901, total Canadian production of wheat was 52 million bushels; in 1911 the volume had grown to 208 million bushels on the prairie alone, and by 1928 it had peaked at 504 million bushels from the three prairie provinces.[4] The chapters that follow describe the rapid expansion of religious settlement over the same period of time. In many cases religious identity helped to contribute to the rich cultural diversity of the prairie, but the religious settlements in many cases could not resist the onslaught of assimilation and the greedy self-centredness of liberal possessive individualism.

While there was a great variety of lifestyles amongst the religious settlements the biblical vision of a New Jerusalem was often retained. There were four main themes of the New Israelites that crystalized their faith, and they will appear in various guises in this book: the New Jerusalem as a political reality; as a heavenly city; as a centre of worship; and as a gift from God.

Jerusalem as a political reality

Jerusalem in the Bible was a symbol of political cohesiveness because King David (970 B.C.) chose this city as a place to weld together a loose confederation of twelve tribes into the nation, Israel. Before David made Jerusalem the capital, there were many regional religious and political centres in Palestine. As David came to be called God's holy anointed king, his kingdom began to take on Messianic proportions so that Jerusalem was known not only as the residence of the king, but also as the residence of God where an ideal society based on justice and righteousness might be built. During David's reign, Jerusalem became the Holy City, the centre of worship. But the political kingdom of David became threatened with national division (particularly after the reign of his son, Solomon) and with invasion by powerful neighbours. Paradoxically, as the nation state of Israel shrank, the hope of establishing the kingdom of God expanded.

The New Testament Christian Church believed that the saviour would come from the royal line of David, that Christ's reign was God's hope for the world, and that God's headquarters would be in a New Jerusalem. Furthermore, both Christians and Hebrews believed in an eschatology (doctrine of last things) which almost rejoiced in persecution. This doctrine became chiliastic—it spoke about a millenium, not necessarily limited to a thousand years, when the world would be inhabited by a humanity both perfectly good and perfectly happy. Subsequently throughout history, the vision of a New Jerusalem recurred and continues to recur (always with a political dimension), particularly in times of disaster when people expect and tensely await a miraculous event. At such times, it is not surprising that the needy and discontented masses have continued to be captured by millenial prophets promising God's kingdom of righteousness and justice.

An historical period that characterizes the political dimension of the New Jerusalem especially well is the period of the Crusades

(1095-1464). This was a time of revolutionary discontent that found its seed bed in the terrible deprivation of the poor. It was a time that produced unofficial charismatic leaders. It was a time when the zeal for a cause of righteousness became a religious crusade.

The first Crusade (1095), according to British medieval historian Norman Cohn,[5] was an epoch that evoked a spiritual rapture combined with a military crusade to recapture the Holy Land, particularly Jerusalem, from the Moslems.   Adding fuel to this religious zeal was the stirring preaching of an ascetic monk, Peter the Hermit (1050-1115).   Even before Pope Urban (1088-1099) had officially sanctioned the Crusade, Peter had been to Jerusalem and Cohn describes his magnetic appeal:

> In the Church of the Holy Sepulchre, Christ had appeared to [Peter the Hermit] and had given him a letter commissioning him to summon the Crusade. Peter seemed to have contributed to the myth by carrying the heavenly letter with him wherever he preached. His success as a propagandist was immense. As he passed through northern France an army of crusaders sprang into being. People hastened to sell their belongings to buy weapons and travelling kit; then having no longer any means of subsistence they began to move off.[6]

Norman Cohn explains that these hordes who followed Peter the Hermit and other *prophetae* were invariably poor with little military training, but this lack of competence in the military arts was more than compensated for by their enthusiasm. The areas of Europe they had come from had suffered droughts and famine. Added to this, they lived in constant terror of the devastating plague which brought an agonizing death to the majority of the population in towns and villages of eastern France and western Germany.[7]

It was not surprising that this mass expedition of paupers, uncontrolled by the feudal knights and religious leaders, indentified with the "host of witnesses" of the early Christian martyrs who were "destitute, afflicted, ill-treated, of whom the world was not worthy— wandering over deserts and mountains and in dens and caves of the earth" (Hebrews 11:37-38). Like the early apostles, they "looked forward to the city which had foundations, whose builder and maker is God" (Hebrews 11:10).

In the eyes of succeeding generations of Christians, some of the experiences of the Crusades have lingered. There is still the vision of an earthly Jerusalem intermingled with the heavenly Jerusalem, so that this Palestinian city has become a miraculous realm abounding both in spiritual and material blessings.   Cohn conveyed the excitement of the children in the vagabond armies of the eleventh century: ". . . no wonder that when the masses of the poor set off on their long pilgrimage the children cried out at every town and castle: 'Is that Jerusalem?'—while high in the heavens there was seen a mysterious city with vast multitudes hurrying towards it."[8]

In the nineteenth and twentieth centuries, the symbolic power of the vision of a New Jerusalem did not fade. It is still rooted both in history and in the hopes and dreams of the people who live a sordid daily existence and who seek liberation from their present oppression. It is ironical that the political scientist, Karl Marx, who considered religion as an opiate and scornfully accused religious socialists of dreaming their "editions of the New Jerusalem" with "castles in the air" (which compelled them to appeal to the feelings and purses of the bourgeois")[9] nevertheless had his own Jerusalem dream in the classless society he espoused. In his "edition of the New Jerusalem" personified in the classless society (which has given hope to millions of people, particularly in oppressed colonial areas of the world), Marx pointed to the future:

> when labour is no longer merely a means of life but has become life's principle need; when the productive forces have also increased with the all round development of the individual and all the springs of co-operative wealth flow more abundantly . . .only then will society by able to inscribe on its banners from each according to his ability to each according to his need.[10]

Although Marx's philosophy was rooted in historical materialism, many of the Social Gospel leaders in western Canada incorporated the Marxist hope because they were aware that much of the theology that they had inherited was an inadequate opiate.

Analysis of the political dimension of the New Jerusalem on the prairies as a symbol of new hope for immigrants indicates that it was a major theme for church leaders who were aware of overcrowded housing in the cities and marginal farming amidst grasshoppers, drought, bitter cold and fluctuating grain markets. This alternative vision (amplified by Ben Smillie in Chapter 6, "Protestants: Prairie Visionaries of the New Jerusalem") is represented in the writings of J. S. Woodsworth, Methodist minister, prophetic politician, and first leader of the Cooperative Commonwealth Federation party.

Some of Woodsworth's vision was caught up in the idealism of the period, particularly in the idea of bringing to Canada William Blake's dream of "building Jerusalem in England's green and pleasant land" while living in the midst of the "dark Satanic mills" of the industrial revolution. Woodsworth pictured the New Jerusalem as arising through community planning. While working for the Methodist Temperance League, he envisioned Regina as an ideal city[11] (a vision that requires some poetic license). But while on a visit to Montreal, after climbing Mount Royal and seeing the beauty of the lights below, Woodsworth had a glimpse of the future "Holy City" which combined the Biblical and the Marxist vision:

> In this city of homes I thought I could discern the indistinct outlines of the work places of the future . . . They worked throughout the day not as masters and slaves, not as jealous rivals, but as partners in a common enterprise.[12]

Woodsworth's bench partner in the House of Commons, William Irvine (Presbyterian and Unitarian minister elected in 1921 from the Independent Labor Party), had an agrarian version of the Social Gospel hope. In his book *Farmers in Politics*, Irvine saw the ideal city not as Jerusalem but as Jesus' home town, Nazareth. Seeing the United Farmers as the vanguard of the new day, Irvine wrote:

> Objectionable as it may be to some, the new leaders are coming from the ranks of those who have been up till now the 'despised and rejected of men.' The agrarian and urban industrial organizations are the Nazareth from which are coming the prophets of a new day . . . To those who doubt the reality of the New Nazareth, I say, 'Come and see.'[13]

But the most theologically articulate of the Canadian Social Gospel writers was Salem Bland, Professor of Church History at Winnipeg Wesley College and influential teacher of many young prairie ministers during the western settlement period. Conscious of faith having to bear fruit in the political arena, Bland's vision of the New Jerusalem came from an ideal "New Christianity" of the future. He singled out the tough resilient faith of the Ukrainian immigrants as having within it the dynamics of a new religion of the frontier. What makes Bland's example interesting is that Ukrainians in the West have so frequently been treated in a condescending manner by the Anglo-Saxon Protestant leadership. Although Bland's tone hints of a patronizing outlook, he nevertheless captures the new hope represented by these immigrants.

Accusing the Anglo-Saxon of being so practical that it is hard for such a person to believe in a Holy City, Bland added:

> But the Slav instinctively believes in a Holy City, and only needs

to be told where it is to be found to set out forthwith over rivers, bogs, and rugged mountain ranges . . . it is just this religious faith the western world needs in this crisis—the spirit of the little child, the spirit of brotherhood, the sense of the preeminence of religion, the idealism that will risk everything for a dream.[14]

Such religious idealism has been highly criticized by Canadian historians and theologians who react against the theological and political naivety of those who espouse this dream of an ideal society. These criticisms are discussed in the concluding chapter. However, the Social Gospel of the New Jerusalem militantly supported protest leaders who believed that God was calling people into the political arena to transform the world. Although this theology may have been unorthodox and reduced major Christian doctrines into humanistic homilies, it did produce a progressive spirit in prairie politics which has worked miracles in social justice for deprived people. James McCrorie in Chapter 2, "Historical Background to Prairie Settlement," suggests that the prairie radicals who led both the labour and agrarian revolt to win important legislation have lost their impact in a resource-extraction, state-capitalist economy. This challenging statement is also discussed in the conclusion of the book.

Jerusalem as a heavenly city

There is a chorus to a stirring old hymn by Isaac Watts which gave a setting for religious pilgrims who saw themselves with a heavenly destination:

We're marching to Zion
Beautiful, beautiful Zion
We're marching upward to Zion,
The beautiful city of God.[15]

Many of the groups who immigrated to the West identified themselves as a pilgrim people not with an earthly but a heavenly destination. This vision is made clear by the writer of the Epistle to the Hebrews who summons Christians to stand firm in the faith in times of persecution. "So Jesus also suffered outside the gate in order to sanctify the people through his own Word. Therefore let us go forth to him outside the camp, bearing abuse for him. For here we have no lasting city, but we seek the city which is to come" (Hebrews 12: 12-14).

The New Jerusalem focus in this Hebrews passage is on the importance of being a colony of heaven in the midst of a perishing world. In Chapter 12, "The Hutterites," Gail McConnell quotes the Hutterite elder, Michael Entz, who explains the reason why Hutterites live a communal life in religious colonies. "In the outside world there are too many temptations . . . You can easily fall there, do things that are not right, nor in accordance with your beliefs. It is easier to maintain what you believe in within the colony. You have more watch. Pete watches me and I can watch Pete . . . You have got to have a watchman around you in order to be a good Christian. It's a narrow path; we call it a narrow path to heaven (Matt. 7:14). And it's got to be narrow, if you want to enter the gates of the New Jerusalem."

However, it must be noted that this theme of a colony of heaven in the midst of a perishing world does not in all cases presuppose colonies completely ostracized from the world around them. This is illustrated in Chapter 11 in Bede Hubbard's description of St. Peter's German Catholic colony at Muenster, Saskatchewan. Hubbard attributes the courageous journalism of the *Prairie Messenger* (which has won many awards for outstanding religious journalism) to the fact that the publishers have political independence within the Roman Catholic ecclesiastical structure.

An essential characteristic of the immigrants who came to Canada with the pilgrim outlook (living in the world but not of it) was the strong feeling of solidarity with fellow pilgrims of the same religious group.   Norman Threinen, who describes Lutheran settlement in the West through work with refugees (Chapter 6 on "Protestants: Prairie Visionaries of the New Jerusalem"), explains the enormous logistical task of settling ten million refugee Lutherans from Europe. Lutherans in Canada who knew the experience of being pilgrims in a strange land "did bring hope to many dispossessed people, particularly Germans uprooted after two world wars. Their support is remarkable in that it covers every facet of these people's lives, which includes opportunities for gainful employment."

In Chapter 9, Koozma Tarasoff describes the hostility suffered by Doukhobors because they were "pacifists of Slavic origin, speaking Russian and leading a lifestyle which competed with the dominant mode of private enterprise." Tarasoff says that the only way Doukhobors survived amongst Canadians of "British stock" was by retaining their Doukhobor colony identity. He points out that with the growth of multiculturalism in the 1970s, the climate of acceptance for Doukhobors greatly improved so that there was less need for the protection of separateness.

Ted Regehr, in Chapter 8, explains that Mennonites who came to western Canada also saw themselves as a colony of heaven living by the radical ethics of Jesus in the midst of a perishing world. But among the Mennonites this produced two quite different responses, says Regehr: "As the physical and geographical boundaries of the Mennonite Utopia became more indistinct, some resorted to the historic response of the Mennonites. . . . They packed their goods and removed themselves to new and more isolated frontiers, first in Saskatchewan, northern Alberta, and British Columbia, and later in Mexico, Paraguay and British Honduras. Others began to redefine the nature and characteristics of the kingdom of God . . . vertically rather than spatially. Mennonites are occupants of both a lower physical or secular kingdom and of a superior spiritual or godly kingdom."

Somewhat surprising is Frank Peake's account of Anglican settlement. In Chapter 5, Peake qualifies the Anglican experience of the New Jerusalem. "Certainly [the Anglican] was engaged in a pilgrimage. It was not however a pilgrimage which had begun when he first stepped on the prairie soil; it had begun in a distant past. . . . The Anglican was aware of the precious gift of the vision of the New Jerusalem; he was aware of his vocation as a pilgrim but also saw himself as part of a long procession of history and tradition transcending locality and time."

Jerusalem as a centre of worship

The New Jerusalem theme was often expressed in worship. Jerusalem was a Holy City and pilgrims, often living under persecution, travelled long distances to worship in its temple. The one hundred and twenty-second Psalm (quoted in the Preface) expresses the joy of the pilgrim coming within sight of the city.

Jerusalem was thus seen as God's central residence and also the place from which God would establish his kingdom of justice and righteousness. But in the book of Revelation, Jerusalem is no longer the centre of worship for a small insignificant nation; its temple has been removed and the city represents the centre of hope for all humankind: "By its light shall all the nations walk; and the kings of the earth shall bring their glory into it, and its gates shall never be shut by day—and there shall be no night there . . ." (Rev. 21: 24-25).

It is in the setting of Jerusalem as a centre of worship that Abraham Arnold in Chapter 7, "New Jerusalem on the Prairies— Welcoming the Jews," describes the devout Jewish worshippers of the Diaspora scattered over the world: "For religious Jews, the synagogue is a constant reminder of Jerusalem, and at every service the entire congregation is called upon to rise and face eastward in ritual reminder of the Holy City."

Similarly Raymond Huel, describing "The French Catholic Experience in Western Canada," stresses this same view of Jerusalem in Chapter 4. Huel says: "The Catholic New Jerusalem was not a city on a hill to be imitated by others nor was it centred on an imminent coming of the kingdom of God. Unlike Protestant eschatology which stresses the presence of God in history, the Catholic experience takes the form of a liturgical vision in which history becomes complete in the mass, the ultimate form of worship."

It is in the "Ukrainian Experience of Building the New Jerusalem on the Prairie," Chapter 10, that we see the most transcendent description of Jerusalem as a theme of worship. Stella Hryniuk and Roman Yereniuk explain: "Through participation in the liturgy, the believer experiences a journey or a procession that leads the worshipper to the final destination—the New Jerusalem. Even as the priest commences the liturgy with the words, 'Blessed is the kingdom of the Father, the Son and the Holy Spirit,' the believer is reminded of the New Jerusalem as the final destination."

Jerusalem as a gift from God

To some groups it was crucial to see the New Jerusalem as a gift from God, not something created by human ingenuity. The harmony between human beings and the world of nature came from those who saw not just the ideal of a New Jerusalem, but the whole created order as a gift. The theme is poignantly expressed in Chapter 3, "Two faces of the New Jerusalem," by Marjorie Beaucage and Emma La Roque who write from a Metis-Indian religious orientation: "The cries of the Northland are echoed across the land in the suffering powerless people who are not to be satisfied with the consumer society." Those who see life as a circle await the day when they "can again be a people, a race that knows in its bones that the covenant is with God, that life is a gift, that earth is a gift and that we are bound to this earth-woman in life." The prophet Isaiah captures the same theme in his image of the peaceable Kingdom:

> Righteousness shall be the girdle of his waist, and faithfulness the girdle of his loins, the wolf shall dwell with the lamb. And the leopard shall lie down with the kid, and the calf and fatling together, and a little child shall lead them . . . they shall not hurt or destroy in all my holy mountain for the earth shall be full of the knowledge of the Lord as the waters cover the sea. (Isaiah 11:5-6, 9)

This harmony between human beings and the world of nature emphasizes gentleness rather than power, smallness rather than bigness. This view stands in stark contrast to those settlers who felt called to build an ideal society within the political arena. Many assumed that the earthbound kingdom of God centred on their own political activity. The criteria required for God's action, they believed, was dependent on their own programmes to establish the kingdom. One result was the self-righteousness that developed particularly in the progressive movement on the prairie which had considerable religious motivation.

The most important thing to learn from the theme of Jerusalem as a symbol of hope is the increasing awareness that the future is given to us by God as a gift. This will be a theme explored more fully in the conclusion where it will be pointed out that the changing vision of the New Jerusalem is bringing religiously motivated people, particularly those caught up in social political action, to be more relaxed about their accomplishments because they see that God calls them not to be successful but faithful. Nor are there illusions in the minds of most people who work for the Judeo-Christian tradition that the kingdom of God is going to be established based on the political power of the church. There is not the facile optimism of the Social Gospel which suggested that the world is getting better and better because of our progressive accomplishments. Yet across denominational boundaries there is a political toughness that sees the political arena as a major centre of God's activity. Witness the recent involvement of many churches in environmental issues, particularly those related to uranium mining, or in peace and disarmament issues. In all of these issues, which invariably are politically linked, the people of faith hold a vision of a New Jerusalem—a vision which emphasizes that it is God's promise to give us the gift of a new world. This promise, this sense of the world as a gift, motivates people to change the world, and to retain their faith. It also links them with the pioneers of the past, who in their covenant with God believed God would be with them in all the changing scenes of life in trouble and in joy. This book is the story of their dreams.

II Historical background to prairie settlement

J.N. McCrorie

During the past 300 years, the prairie region of Canada has undergone two fundamental transformations of its political economy and society. It is in the process of undergoing a third.

Beginning with the seventeenth century, the European fur trade transformed the subsistence economy and society of the plains Indians. By the close of the nineteenth century, cattle and wheat were well on their way to replacing furs, displacing Indians and Metis with farmers and ranchers of European ancestry. In each instance, the impetus to change was initiated by needs and interests residing beyond and outside the region and concerned with the exploitation and development of indigenous natural resources. Successive prairie populations responded by creating and developing new, appropriate communities. And all to no avail.

The era in which wheat, cattle, and agrarian rural communities dominated the region is coming to a close. In their place, new communities based on the exploitation and processing of nonrenewable resources—coal, natural gas, oil, potash and uranium—are attracting new population, providing new investment and employment opportunities, laying but another foundation for a future with no future.

These transformations have not been nor are they now the result of some inexorable law of economic development and progress. They have been initiated and developed through human endeavour and struggle—endeavours and struggles in which people within and beyond the region have divided and clashed over questions of class, ethnicity and community: that is to say, over fundamental questions of making a living and fashioning a social existence and human community.

The era of the fur trade

On May 2, 1670, King Charles II of England granted to Prince Rupert, the Duke of York, Lord Shaftesbury and the remaining, well-bred share-holders in the Company of Adventurers Trading into Hudson's Bay, a monopoly in trade over a region now encompassed by the provinces of Manitoba, Saskatchewan, and Alberta, part of the Northwest Territories, northern Ontario and the northwest corner of Quebec.   The charter which granted the monopoly in trade provided:

> . . . the sole trade and commerce of all those seas, straits, bays, rivers, lakes, creeks and sounds, in whatsoever latitude they shall be, that lie within the entrance of the straits, commonly called Hudson's Straits, together with all the lands and territories upon the countries, coasts and confines of the seas, bays, lakes, rivers, creeks and sounds aforesaid that are not actually possessed by or granted to any of our subjects, or possessed by the subjects of any other Christian Prince or State . . . [The] said land be from henceforth reckoned and reputed as one of our plantations or colonies in America called "Rupert's Land" and further, we do . . . make create and constitute the said Governor and Company for the time being, and their successor, the true and absolute lords and proprietors of the same territory, limits and places aforesaid . . .

The powers and privileges so enumerated were sweeping and awesome. Surely it is not impertinent to inquire by what right the English King indulged his relatives, and friends so generously. The fact that the King of France had long before laid claim to the same territorial domain might tempt one to conclude that Charles was merely exercising the divine right of kings, a privilege over which his father lost his head. The evidence appears otherwise. The land was there for the taking, French Roman Catholic views and claims notwithstanding. Nor is there any evidence to suggest that it ever occurred to Charles that the territory in question might—under the provisions and customs of English common law—belong to those who from time immemorial had occupied it. They were, in respect of the demands of English private property, dismissed as mere "savages" and as such not entitled to the considerations and privileges of law appropriate to a "civil" population.

A convenient, but not an obvious conclusion, for the "savages" from whom the land was stolen became the very population upon which the future and prosperity of the fur trade was to rest. It is well known that the Indian tribes and populations provided the principal sources of labour for the prosecution of the English fur trade. What is perhaps forgotten is the desperate degree to which the English, Scottish, Orkney and Shetland employees of the Company—factors, explorers, warehousemen, bookkeepers, carpenters, gunsmiths— were dependent on the indigenous "savages" for instruction and guidance in the most fundamental acts of survival in a harsh and demanding environment.

To be dispossessed of one's land and territory in the interests of satisfying the commercial demands for fur across the North Atlantic was but one of several adjustments faced by the indigenous, native populations. Contrary to popular opinion, the superior technological accomplishments of the English did not in every instance induce the Indians to interrupt the economic rhythm and routine of centuries in order to harvest furs in exchange for guns, powder, hatchets, knives, kettles, tobacco, blankets. The records of the Company bear ample testimony of the lengths to which the English traders had to resort in order to involve and entrap an ever widening circle of the territorial populations in the trade.

True, one cannot gainsay the advantage of possessing specific items of superior European technology. But a price was exacted beyond the mere, and I would suggest, uneven exchange of commodities. Fur-bearing animals, once pursued in keeping with the requirements of a subsistence economy, were now harvested with systematic vengeance to which the Indians were unaccustomed. Hunting and trading acquired a value and importance that was as novel as it was demanding and disruptive of an older pattern of family life. The rapid depletion of fur-bearing animals obliged Indians in one locale to compete for supply in territory occupied by others with whom they had hitherto only a passing and often co-operative relationship.

Most important of all, integration with the political economy of the fur trade resulted in the reciprocal loss of independence and a correspondent dependency on Europeans for goods and technology the Indian populations had once produced and provided for themselves. If, to repeat, some of the goods were superior, dependence and the loss of self-sufficiency were no less real—a development that was as challenging to the survival of the native populations as the introduction of alcohol and European viral diseases hitherto unknown in the region.

These challenges notwithstanding, the native populations adapted, and if one carefully considers the specific changes and adjustments they undertook in the short span of 200 years, one may indeed marvel at their resilience, imagination, and tenacity. And all in vain.

The New Jerusalem

In 1869 the new Canadian government purchased Rupert's Land from the Hudson's Bay Company. It will come as a surprise to some today that the senior civil servants involved in the negotiations questioned the legality of the Bay's claim to the territory, arguing that the land in question had been claimed by Louis XIV as a "right of discovery," rendering the charter granted by Charles II null and void by its very provisions. The Colonial Office was loath to accept this interpretation and claim and obliged the Hudson's Bay Company and the new Dominion Government to negotiate a sale and transfer of land.

In return for the transfer of ownership of Rupert's Land to the Government of Canada, the Hudson's Bay Company was paid 300,000 pounds. In addition, it received a land grant of 1/20 of the land within the fertile belt, and allocations of land in the vicinity of trading posts in the amount of 50,000 acres. It is of some historical interest—for those with a sense of humour—to note that a minority of the share-holders viewed the terms of sale and transfer as "involving too great a sacrifice of their interests" and the agreement with the Dominion Government was accepted with reluctance.

The reasons for the purchase of Rupert's Land were several. First, westward expansion of American settlement promised in time to turn northward. The Canadian government believed the Hudson's Bay Company lacked the resources and political power to defend its so-called private property against the encroachment of settlers bent on homesteading and displacing a political economy predicated on furs with one rooted in agriculture.

Second, the government was convinced that should American settlers invade Rupert's Land, they would demand that the territory encompassed by their homesteads be politically incorporated with the United States.

Their conclusion has merit if one considers the uncontestable fact that since 1866—one year before Confederation and three years before the purchase—the American Congress had given every indication of favouring the economic and the eventual political union of British North America and the U.S.A. on American terms.

But their conclusion is nevertheless shocking and revealing if one acknowledges that it was drawn without consultation with the indigenous populations of Indians and Metis. To add insult to injury, it was clear from the record that the new Dominion Government viewed the plains Indians and Metis as both unsuitable and unreliable stewards of the very territory they had occupied and worked, in the case of Metis, for at least 200 years.

Having purchased Rupert's Land and written off the Indian and Metis populations, the Dominion Government was faced with the task of economically and politically disposing of both.

Insofar as the Indians were concerned, Macdonald's government moved with a degree of haste and sense of purpose uncharacteristic of "old tomorrow," as the Prime Minister was often called. The final solution—if one may use that term—was to integrate the Indians into white society. In the meantime, it was deemed wise to relocate them in temporary holding areas, to be known as reserves, and to prepare and have signed a set of treaties which would give the ceremonial appearance of legality to an act which, when one thinks carefully and thoroughly about it, was quite common in the worst of the British legal tradition. As for the Metis, they were already halfway along the road to integration. Their claims and their most modest and responsible statements of their needs were *never* taken seriously.

The Metis and some of the plains Indians, upon discovering the real intent and determination of the federal government to so dismiss them, would revolt, and enjoy the fleeting moment of making fools out of General Middleton and his eager, Protestant, Ontario volunteers. Their rebellion would cost the Conservative Party its national political hegemony and help reduce its status to the pathetic one it still enjoys today. Their rebellion and the government's response would alert and strengthen French Roman Catholic resistance to Anglo-Protestant schemes of assimilation. But the rebellion would fail, leaving civil disobedience and calculated acts of drunken and disorderly behaviour as the only means of registering their historic grief and defiance.

The disposition of the land and territory so decisively and cynically expropriated from the Indians and Metis proved more difficult to resolve. The decade of the 1870s was one of considerable uncertainty. The economic promise of Confederation had failed, raising the question as to whether Canada could maintain and build a viable political society, independent of the United States, on an economy based on the exploitation of and trade in natural resources. The general view of the period was that the prairies had to be

PRESENT DAY MAJOR SETTLEMENTS

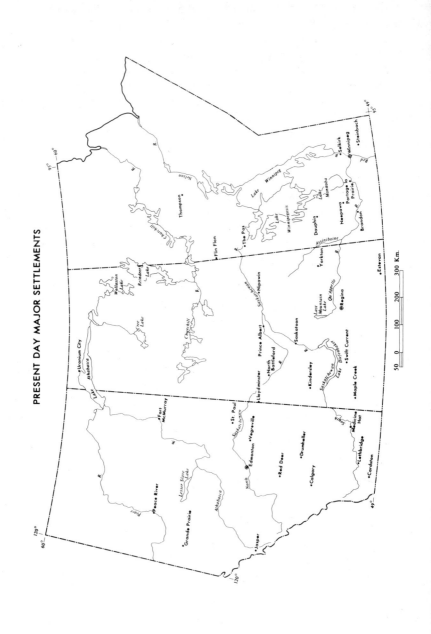

occupied by settlers of British, if not European, extraction, politically committed and loyal to the new Dominion. But what would they do for a living? Farm? Perhaps. But under what conditions? This was the vexing question.

For the first time, a small but growing group of manufacturers in central Canada proposed that national salvation was to be found in a policy of industrialization and urbanization. The proposition was not greeted with the kind of unquestioning, unwarranted, and naive support it enjoys today. Canada, in the decade of the 1870s, was still predominantly a rural society. Many English-speaking immigrants had ventured across the North Atlantic to escape the worst ravages of industrialization and urbanization in Great Britain. French Canada saw the preservation of its language, religion and culture in rural, resource-based, and not urban, industrial communities. Moreover, urban men of commerce tied to overseas trade in natural resources became alarmed when manufacturers began to plea for protective tariffs as a necessary condition for successful industrialization. To all of these, industrialization was not a self-evident panacea.

John A. Macdonald and the Conservatives, however, were convinced that the political future of the country hinged on the development of a more "appropriate" and "promising" economic base. They adopted the proposition of industrialization and protective tariffs as an election issue. The battle was fought in the federal general election of 1878, and with typical Canadian decisiveness, the electorate divided on the question.

Fortunately for Macdonald and the central Canadian manufacturers, the popular vote doesn't necessarily determine the composition of the House of Commons. Despite the real division in the country, the Tories gained sufficient seats to form a majority government in the Commons, and accordingly set about to plan and inaugurate what became known as Macdonald's "national policy."

Of the various ingredients that went into the National Policy including the construction of the Canadian Pacific transcontinental railroad and protective tariffs, one is most significant—the settlement of the prairie region and the development therein of a rural, agrarian society.

Ten years had elapsed since the purchase of Rupert's Land, and the federal government had proved singularly inept in arranging for the resettlement of the territories. The task was nevertheless viewed as urgent and the new national policy of industrialization offered a fresh framework within which to consider and assess options.

Capitalism, indeed industrial capitalism, requires a market, preferably a captive market. In time, the captains of Canadian industry discovered that capitalism requires, in addition, a noncompetitive expanding market. The tariff legislation of 1879 guaranteed a captive market, protecting goods manufactured in central Canada from the importation of cheaper goods from either Great Britain or the United States. Or so it seemed. The proposal to settle the prairies and develop therein an agrarian, rural rather than an industrial, urban society promised to provide a noncompetitive, expanding market for goods and technology manufactured in central Canada.

As the nineteenth century drew to a close, the possibilities of such a market boggled the mind. How many hammers, saws, nails, plows, wagons, harnesses, binders and threshing machines would be required? Surely the sky was the limit. And who was going to finance settlement, provide credit, construct storage facilities for grain, expand the slender railway network, market grain, provide timber for barns, fences and homes? Surely, ambitious men of trade and commerce, not those men and women who would be foolish enough to homestead and settle these inhospitable and foreboding prairies.

The stage was set. Breaking with tradition, Clifford Sifton, Laurier's Minister of the Interior, inaugurated an ambitious programme of immigration that reached beyond the shores of Britain to Iceland, Denmark, Sweden, Norway, Finland, Germany, the Ukraine, Russia, Romania, and the Austro-Hungarian Empire. The Homestead Act was skilfully employed to attract applications for "free land" and convert public domain once again to units of private property.

The act of homesteading, of breaking sod and converting a semi-arid plain into a fertile bread basket, of enduring extremes of climate, of defying setbacks and rejecting failure, is perhaps one of the most dramatic and heroic moments of modern Canadian history. Like the Indians and Metis they replaced, the pioneers displayed instances of courage, imagination and resolve seldom evident among their more affluent and complacent grandchildren.

The physical difficulties and hardship of homesteading, however, were but a prelude to an even more important struggle that would dominate the economic and political life of the prairies for more than a century. As early as the 1890s, the more radical pioneers had discovered that the economic and political rules of the game were stacked against them; that the building of a viable, prosperous agrarian economy and society was functional, yet subordinate to the creation of an urban, industrial society in central Canada. The early attacks on the line elevator companies and the CPR were broadened

Saskatchewan Archives Board

Wheat blockade at Wolseley, Saskatchewan.
108 loads of grain, February 22, 1902.

As early as the 1890's, the more radical pioneers had discovered that the economic and political rules of the game were stacked against them; that the building of a viable, prosperous agrarian economy and society was functional, yet subordinate to the creation of an urban, industrial society in central Canada. The early attacks on the line elevator companies and the CPR were broadened...

to include the Winnipeg Grain Exchange, the banks and mortgage companies, the farm machine companies, retail and wholesale merchants, the tariff policies of the Conservatives and Liberals, and eventually the "old line" political parties themselves. By the 1930s, the very efficacy of capitalism itself was called into question and a minority of agrarian radicals were calling for socialism.

It would be incorrect and irresponsible to suggest that the agrarian community was united and in accord over these questions and issues. The pioneers had come west from a diversity of backgrounds and experiences, and they had settled the prairies for a variety of reasons. Some saw farming as a challenging, but attractive opportunity to accumulate capital, invest it in more profitable, non-agrarian ventures, and move on. Others—through luck, good management and/or unscrupulous business practices— had, in a short period of time, become large and prosperous farm operators. A speculative system of marketing grain, combined with energetic, if not ruthless, enterprise had yielded handsome dividends. For these, the economic and political rules of the game were more than satisfactory. Moreover, Clifford Sifton, Minister of Immigration, had seen to it that agrarian prairie communities would

First information tent entered by the Saskatchewan Wheat Pool in provincial fairs. Weyburn, Saskatchewan, 1927.

To the lasting credit of so many nameless, pioneering men and women, bigotry did not in every instance prevail, and the impetus to challenge, reform, and change the economic and political institutions governing prairie life — springing as it did from the ranks of the rural, agrarian middle class — came in time to cut across ethnic and religious barriers.

be divided, at least initially, along ethnic and religious lines. To the lasting credit of so many nameless pioneering men and women, bigotry did not in every instance prevail, and the impetus to challenge, reform, and change the economic and political institutions governing prairie life, springing as it did from the ranks of the rural, agrarian middle class, came in time to cut across ethnic and religious barriers.

In view of the opposition within the agrarian community, the effort of the prairie radicals to build a New Jerusalem is all the more arresting. They created, in opposition to the line elevator companies and the Winnipeg Grain Exchange, the Grain Growers Grain Company (1906), later known as the United Grain Growers, the Saskatchewan Co-operative Elevator Company (1911), and the Wheat Pools in 1923 and 1924. When the Pools failed as effective international marketing agencies in the crash of 1929, the more radical farm men and women agitated for the establishment of a compulsory government marketing board, a struggle that eventually resulted in the establishment of the Canadian Wheat Board.

The retail trade within and the wholesale trade between

provinces were challenged by the organization of local consumer co-operatives and provincial co-operative wholesale societies which eventually amalgamated to form Federated Co-operatives. Banks and finance companies were confronted with the organization of credit unions and in time, particularly during the 1930s, co-operatives were organized to invade the private preserves of farm machinery manufacturing (CCIL) and oil refining (Consumers Co-operative Refineries, now part of Federated Co-operatives).

When the prairie region joined Confederation (Manitoba in 1870 and Saskatchewan and Alberta in 1905), the parliamentary traditions and two-party system already established in the older, more settled provinces to the east, were conveniently imposed on the west. For a time, the Liberals in Alberta and Saskatchewan and the Tories in Manitoba were able to articulate and represent agrarian discontent—at least at the provincial level. But the coming of the Non-Partisan League in 1917 and the electoral victories of the Progressive Party in 1921 challenged the hegemony formerly enjoyed by the two old line parties. In the same year, the farmers in Alberta were successful in electing a provincial government made up of candidates sponsored by the United Farmers of Alberta; in Saskatchewan, the Liberal government of Premier Martin hastily disassociated itself from its federal counterpart, and a new coalition known as the Liberal Progressive Party was led to power in Manitoba in 1922 by John Bracken. The depression of the 1930s further heightened agrarian mistrust of established political parties, giving rise to the formation of the Co-operative Commonwealth Federation in 1933 and the Social Credit Party in 1935.

There can be no question but that taken together, the creation of these political and economic counter-institutional arrangements made a difference to prairie life. The power of the private grain trade to extract wealth from the prairie provinces was momentarily checked. Banks, finance companies, independent retail merchants, retail wholesale chains, etc. were at last forced to take into account the presence of an alternative outlet and modify their business practices accordingly.[1] The rise of "third" parties effectively disrupted the hegemony of the Liberals and Conservatives and resulted on more than one occasion in the enactment of enlightened, legislative precedents. Perhaps most striking of all, the values and ideological claims of capitalism were themselves questioned, if not totally discredited, leaving many an apologist for capital to wonder over the political stability of the remote west.

But sweeping and awesome as these accomplishments undoubtedly were, they failed to change the fundamental principles and rules that govern a dynamic, changing capitalist society. If they slowed down and made more bearable the transformation of an agriculture based on small, independent, labour intensive family farms to one predicated on large, capital intensive corporate units, they did not prevent it. How many thoughtful farm men and women today share, with any confidence, the dream of their forebearers to build, maintain and perpetuate a healthy, prosperous rural community, based on large numbers of relatively small, family-owned and operated farm units? The process of farm enlargement, the decline in rural population, the abandonment of rural communities, the intensification of capital investment in production have progressed too far to encourage such wishful thinking. These trends, together with a renewed assault upon the Crowsnest rates, the rail transportation network, and the orderly system of marketing grain have at once signalled the end of yet another era and reaffirmed an earlier assessment by prairie provincial governments that a secure and lasting future for the west was not to be based on agriculture.

A future with no future

It is important to recognize that agriculture and the rural community of *relatively* small family farmers which it sustained was found wanting long before the advent of the major changes which are transforming the industry today.[2]

The seeds of misgiving were sown in the 1930s and cultivated in the reconstruction period following the Second World War. In Manitoba, Saskatchewan, and Alberta, governments of different political persuasions concluded—some more decisively than others—that the boom-bust character of the wheat economy could not provide the basis for a stable and prosperous future. The pursuit of additional and alternative sources of development such as oil, natural gas, potash, timber, uranium processing and manufacturing as a means of broadening and diversifying the economic base of the region was begun in earnest.

The case of Saskatchewan is perhaps the most instructive. Here the provincial government of the day was nominally in favour of socialism and committed in principal to public ownership and democratic planning of the economy. But as early as 1944, it was clear that the leaders of the CCF and the dominant figures in the provincial cabinet had no intention of honouring the decisions of their party's conventions and fulfilling the dreams of their more courageous and dedicated followers. They recognized that massive public involvement in and transformation of the provincial economy along genuine socialist lines would result in a prolonged, intense, and disruptive political struggle. They were not prepared to initiate such a struggle; they did not believe the population either desired, or was prepared to endure such a struggle; and they had no intention of relinquishing office in the pursuit of cultivating and promoting such a struggle.

They chose instead to confine their reforms to the safer, shallower waters of education, health and social welfare, nationalizing the odd public utility in the bargain. These reforms troubled, but did not fundamentally offend capital—particularly monopoly capital. And the intensity of the struggle that attended each and all of these reforms—important and valuable as they have been—was sufficient to reassure the leadership and more timid members of the CCF of their wisdom in leaving the principal initiatives and responsibilities for the development of the economy where they had always been, in private hands.

In each province therefore, governments committed to the expansion and diversification of the regional economy awaited the response of the private sector in the redevelopment of the region. True, the CCF and later the New Democratic Party governments of Saskatchewan exacted and continue to demand a price, preventing at least the worst excesses of capitalism so evident during the permissive days of the Roblin-Weir administration in Manitoba. But even in the case of potash—first developed by the private sector and later partially nationalized with the assistance and blessing of Wall Street—one is dealing in the last analysis with an instance of state capitalism, not socialism.

Once again, we are witnessing the effective abandonment of an established industry in favour of the redevelopment of the prairie region in response to nonregional demands for natural resources other than food. And once again, the impetus and agenda for development are in the hands and control of foreign capital. There is, however, an important difference. Unlike furs and wheat, potash, coal, oil, natural gas and uranium are nonrenewable resources. We are creating new investment and employment opportunities on a resource base with a limited future.

It is too early to predict, with assurance, the manner in which the agrarian population will react to their new role in the scheme of things. The pressures on farm men and women to adapt and accept the transformation and diminution of their industry are considerable, and in some respects, rewarding. To date, an effective attempt to "fight back" and modify, if not arrest these trends, has not materialized.

In the meantime, new resource-based communities are replacing the old, providing a new and different range of job opportunities. They will not last. It remains to be seen if a younger generation, confronted with the denial of a future, will profit from the lessons of history and build with their own hands, a New Jerusalem on the prairies.

III Two faces of the New Jerusalem: Indian—Metis reaction to the missionary

Marjorie Beaucage
Emma LaRoque

Jerusalem has always been a political and religious reality. In the context of the missionary coming into Indian land, the new Jerusalem can be viewed as having two faces. On the one side is the confusion between civilization and Christianity, and on the other side is the sacred activity of caring for the place where God dwells— the Creation.

Missionary zeal motivated the overtaking of a land and its race of people under the guise of bringing them into the kingdom of God. The missionaries came to the new land to claim it in God's name, not realizing that the land was already under the sovereignty of the Creator as viewed by the people who inhabited it.

Building the New Jerusalem on the prairies meant the "civilization" and Christianization of the Indians. The missionaries came from Europe believing in development and progress. Their goal was the conversion of the "heathen from the darkness to light, from superstitious idolatry to sincere Christianity."[1] The assumptions and philosophies underlying missionary societies seemed to be that Western civilization and the Christian message were superior. Colonization and the missionary movement were seen as necessary vehicles of the Lord to reach the "heathen". The secular faith in progress combined well with the missionary faith in the inevitable and ultimate success of the Gospel. Progress and teleology nurtured each other. This marriage between Christianity and State was repeated again and again by most missionaries involved in "Indian work" across the prairies. With few exceptions, missionaries clearly wished not only to convert the Indian to Christ

Saskatchewan Archives Board

Boys at work at the Regina (Indian) Industrial School, 1905

With few exceptions, missionaries clearly wished not only to convert the Indian to Christ but also to change the Indian way of organizing society into the European way. Education and agriculture were the means used to achieve this end.

but to change the Indian way of organizing society to the European way. Education and agriculture were the means used to achieve this end.

The Oblates of Mary Immaculate arrived in the Red River District in 1818 when Father Provencher was sent from Quebec to establish a mission among the Metis and Indians.

In 1820, the Reverend John West came to the Red River settlement as a chaplain to the Hudson Bay Company and as a missionary to the natives. Soon after his arrival, he embarked upon an elementary school program for Indian and half-breed boys. He believed that there was little hope for adult Indians, but the children offered a "wide and most extensive field for cultivation," he wrote in his journal. Evident here is the germ of the boarding school mentality of the missionaries.

Wherever the missionaries visited or resided, they usually set up places of instruction. The establishment of schools for Indian children mushroomed in many parts of the land. Most of these schools were operated by various missionary societies (representing different denominations) and often financed by the Department of Indian Affairs.

The curriculum consisted of reading and writing with the Bible as the main textbook. Or, as someone else has written, it could be said the Indian education was traditionally based on the four R's—reading, 'riting, 'rithmetic and religion.

Many, if not most, of the Indian tribes hunted and gathered on a seasonal basis. Consequently, the children would miss school according to seasons. To combat the irregular attendance, missionaries set up boarding schools for the children. The Grey Nuns started a school in 1844, but it was recorded that "the Indians did not like to be taught by women." The school served essentially two purposes: it kept the parents under the influence of the church concerned, and it gave more power to the churches in the formation of government policy with respect to the Indians.

Harold Cardinal, an Indian leader from Alberta, bitingly critiques the residential schools:

> They alienated the child from his own family; they alienated him from his own way of life without preparing him for a different society; they alienated the child from his own religion and turned his head resolutely against the confusing substitute the missionaries offered.

The discipline that was enforced in a typical boarding school from the 1840s to the 1950s looked something like the following:

> The bell rings at 5:00 A.M. when the children rise, wash, dress and are made ready for breakfast. At 5:30 they breakfast; after which they all assemble in the large schoolroom and unite in reading the Scriptures, singing and prayer. From 6:00 - 9:00 A.M. the boys are employed and taught to work on the farm, and the girls in the house, at nine, they enter their schools, at twelve they dine . . . At one they enter school, where they are taught till 3:30 after which they resume their manual employment till six. At six they sup and again unite in reading the Scripture, singing and prayer. In the winter season the boys are engaged in the Evening school and girls are taught needle work until nine, when all retire to rest. They are never left alone, but are constantly under the eye of some of those engaged in this arduous work.[2]

Missionaries controlled Indian education until the 1950s, at which time the government took over.

Along with foreign education, the missionaries also encouraged the Indians to settle down and become farmers. Their identification with and promotion of Western values provided a pacification program for the government. By encouraging agriculture, setting up residential schools and constructing churches, the missionaries paved the way for reservations.

Missionaries also often acted as middlemen between government and natives on various issues. In 1869, when the Metis people protested against an arbitrary takeover of their semi-agricultural Red River settlement by the Canadian government, Bishops Tache and Machray "both offered their services to the Canadian government in facilitating the transfer."[3]   Again in 1885, when the same people for the same reason openly resisted the Canadian troops (this time in Saskatchewan), Bishop Tache sided with the law and order position of the Crown, though he expressed some sympathy for the Metis grievances.

In the same era, Methodist George McDougall negotiated two treaties for the government of Canada with prairie tribes. He gathered Indians on the prairies, preparing them for the coming of the white man's "civilization."

Father Albert Lacombe, usually cited for his peace-making efforts between the Blackfeet and Crees, "persuaded the Blackfoot tribe of Alberta to allow the Canadian Pacific Railway to run through their territory."[4]

Another result of Western invasion of Indian territory is the "de-historization" of the Indian. Both primary sources (fur traders and missionary journals) and Canadian historians have distorted the Indian's experience and place in the settlement and development of Canada. The Indian in history has been cast as a "savage" or a "noble child of nature"; the epithets describing his savagery are considerably longer than those describing his nobility! A survey of history books, ranging in publication dates from 1829 to 1970 reveals contradictory and incomplete portraits of the Indian as a human being with derogatory comments predominating. Indians were described as "treacherous," "dirty," "barbaric," "grotesque," "superstitious," "red devils." Not only is the Indian treated in a negative way, but the telling of the story of native life is dependent on the story of the European in Canada. The early travel narratives of the white man give only the explorers' and fur traders' descriptions. The use of their diaries along with missionary journals have often been the only source of information for modern historians. By uncritically relying on these sources, modern writers perpetuate the stereotypes and jaundiced attitudes about Indian life. For example, Monseigneur Grandin, in a letter dated March 5, 1900, judged their "natural weakness was a too great lack of self-confidence," and Father Riou writes that the "Blackfeet, although intelligent, were extremely proud and immoral." These quotes were used as an explanation in "*Etudes des Oblats*" for why there were no vocations among native folk. It was with the coming of Western man that, for the Indian, time and history became a line of chronological events rather than a circle of ongoing life.

There is very little documentation concerning native response to the missionary presence. Only recently has Indian participation in history begun to be documented. Missionaries usually assumed that natives had no beliefs, and were bereft of culture and traditions, history and religion. Although Indian tribes did not produce a systematic theology in Western terms, most of them were deeply committed to religious attitudes, beliefs, and practices. Indian religion was based on a communion with nature and a connectedness with all of life. There were many rituals among native peoples—the sacred pipe-stem, the sweat lodge, the vision quest—but perhaps the highest religious expression among the Plains people is found in the Sundance. As early as 1882, attempts were made by missionaries and police to suppress the dance. Reasons given were: work suffered, the self-infliction was of 'heathenish' origin and it promoted a spirit of insubordination. To the charge of work suffering, it is interesting to note that the Roman Catholic Indians could leave work for pilgrimages. And there was little chance that insubordination would result from a Sundance since the dance required inward and outward discipline. As to self-infliction, its practice is found in all great religions. In its aim to "bring the compassion of Manitou and to mortify the flesh and subdue it to His will,"[5] the Sundance may be akin to the stigmata of St. Francis.

The whites could not understand its meaning, hence in 1895 the Sundance was outlawed by Section 114 of the Indian Act. The words of Thunderchild about the dance and its prohibition give further insight:

> The Sundance is a sacred institution. Through it, prayer is made for all people . . . When a man gives of himself to those who are unfortunate, when his heart says, 'I thank thee Great Spirit,' can one believe that nothing comes of it? White people have not understood and they condemn the dance. I see only blessing from it . . . Today the dance is forbidden; those who

have made their vows cannot fulfill them, and it is heart-rending
. . . Can things go well in a land where freedom of worship is a
lie? To each nation is given the light by which it knows God, and
each finds its own way to express the longing to serve that One.
It is astounding to me that a man should be stopped from trying
in his own way to express his need or his thankfulness to God. If
a nation does not do what is right according to its own
understanding, its power is worthless. I have listened to the talk
of the white man's clergy, and it is the same in principle as the
talk of our Old Men, whose wisdom came not from books, but
from life and from God's earth. Why has the white man no
respect for the religion that was given to us, when we respect the
faith of other nations?[6]

Thunderchild (1849-1927) was a Plains Cree Chief whose people
finally reserved near Turtle Lake, Saskatchewan. In 1923, Indian
Anglican missionary, Edward Ahenekew, wrote down the chief's
stories. Thunderchild's life had spanned the days of freedom to the
days of the reserve fences. As a non-Christian, this was how he
assessed the white religious invasion.

It seems to me that since we have been fenced into reserves, the
Cree nation has shrunk, that there are fewer of us. The white
men have offered us two forms of religion: the Roman Catholic
and the Protestant. But we in our Indian lands have our own
religion. Why is that not accepted too? It is the worship of one
God, and it was the strength of our people for centuries. I do
not want to fight the white man's religion. I believe in freedom
of worship, and though I am not a Christian, I have never
forgotten God. What is it that has helped me and will help my
grandchildren but belief in God? This country lasted long with
only Indians here, and then the white man came and they came
with might. That was permitted by God. Yet see how they
treated the nation that is weaker. Surely our nation is not to be
wiped out.[7]

In direct contrast to Thunderchild's dignified rejection of
Christianity was Chief Pequis' fawning acceptance of it. In 1831,
Archdeacon William Cockran of Red River cajoled Pequis and his
followers to a settled agricultural life. On August 9, 1838, Chief
Pequis is supposed to have handed a letter to Reverend David Jones
upon his last visit to the "Indian Settlement." It is uncertain who
actually wrote this letter or whether it expressed Pequis' real
sentiments. But the historical value of the letter is that it expresses a

typical brainwashed response, not unlike that of colonized peoples elsewhere. The letter is self-explanatory:

> Servants of the Great God: We once more call to you for protection and assistance; and hope it will not be altogether unavailing. You sent us what you call the Word of God and the Word of Life. We left our hunting grounds and came to the Word of Life. When we heard the Word of God, we did not altogether like it; for it told us to keep only one wife, to cast away our idols, our rattles, drums and gods, and all our bad heathen ways; but the Word of God repeatingly telling us, that if we did not leave off our bad devils . . . that the Great God would send us all to the great devil's fire . . . we now like the Word of God. Mr. Jones is now going to leave us. Mr. Cockran is talking of leaving us. Must we turn to our idols again? Or must we turn to the French Praying-Masters for protection and assistance, where a good few of our children and relations have gone to? We see not less than three French Praying-Masters have arrived in the River, and not one for us. What is this, our friends? The Word of God says that one soul is worth more than all the world. Surely then, 300 souls is worthy of one Praying-Master. Can it be expected that once or twice teaching to a child can be sufficient to make him wise, or to enable him to guide himself through life? No . . . and we are the same. . . . As Mr. Jones is to be the bearer of this letter, we leave him to explain our case more fully. We once more beg you to consider our case . . . to send us a Father to reside with us here, to teach us, our wives and our children, the Word of God. We thank you all for what you have done for us and our children . . . We all wish to let you know, as Mr. Cockran began with us, we wish him to end with us; he is now well accustomed with our oily and fishy smell, and all our bad habits. May the Great God be kind to you all . . . that you may do good to all the poor Indians. . . .[8]

Plains Cree Edward Ahenekew (1885-1961) was born in Sandy Lake, Saskatchewan. In 1910 he was ordained as an Anglican deacon. He spent many of his years teaching in mission schools. In 1918-1919, an epidemic of influenza devastated numerous Indian people. Deeply affected by the suffering of his people, Ahenekew (at the age of thirty-five) entered medical school in Edmonton. Unfortunately he had to leave his studies because of illness and financial troubles. It was while he was in a state of discouragement that the Reverend Canon Edward Matheson of Battleford encouraged him to collect Cree legends and stories. In 1923 Ahenekew interviewed Chief Thunderchild. As well, he spoke through his literary creation, "Old Keyam." "Keyam" is a Cree word with many shades of meaning; Ahenekew interpreted it as "I do not care," but explained:

> Old Keyam had tried in his youth to fit himself into the new life; he had thought that he would conquer; and he had been defeated instead. If we listen to what he has to say, perhaps we may understand those like him, who know not what to do, and in their bewilderment and their hurt, seem not to care.[9]

Through Old Keyam, Ahenekew expressed his doubts, his hurts, his apologetic anger and even guilt feelings about being a Christian. He was an Indian man full of agony—understanding his people's ways yet committed to Anglican Christianity. He spoke against the boarding schools, but in apologetic tones. He espoused Christian tenets but even here he added a poignantly beautiful description of the Sundance. Whatever position he took, he was treading a hazardous road. Yet he always accepted Christian civilization as superior, for after all, he had learned to do well in this context (another typical response of colonized peoples).

As shown in the reactions of these three men, the Indian response to Christianity varied from rejection to acceptance to struggle and tension.

Contrary to mythology, Indians were not passive children of darkness waiting with glazed eyes for light or for baubles. There were probably many reasons why native peoples chose to show interest in the newcomers. Interest in the missionaries was not uniform, but a natural curiosity and diversion from routine motivated some, while commercial interests—getting a credit rating with the fur company by befriending a missionary—drew others. A factor not often considered was the native belief that Manitou reveals messages through guardian spirits; Indians were open to those who claimed to have received a revelation from God. Foresighted Indian leaders also requested education for their people so that they might learn the white man's ways, but they did not ask for the Christian indoctrination that came with it. Chief Star Blanket of Saskatchewan, foreseeing the coming shortage of the buffalo, asked for missionaries to teach them agricultural life.

Today, various native authors approach the system and history with keen perception and prophetic insight. The struggle continues. White Christian folk should not be surprised when native peoples express hostility or skepticism towards them. Although the churches have changed and are changing their missionary thrust, the

Ken Wolfe, Saskatoon Separate School Board

Saskatoon Native Survival School, organized by native parents and sponsored by the Saskatoon Separate School Board, Saskatoon, Saskatchewan, 1980.

The struggle continues. White Christian folk should not be surprised when native peoples express hostility or skepticism towards them. Although the churches have changed and are changing their missionary thrust, the ambiguity of their roles is deep within the memory of the native populace.

ambiguity of their roles is deep within the memory of the native populace.

There is not one historical event more significant than another in this dynamic of oppression that has been lived out on the prairies. There is no measuring whether Anglicans or Catholics had the most serious impact. In any time or place when a dominant group imposes its values, its traditions, its educational biases, its economic and political systems over another group, there is oppression. This is the sort of relationship that has gone on and continues to go on between the white society and Indian peoples. The vibrations of the initial impact of invasion and uprootedness reverberate still. Oppression recycles itself from generation to generation. This process of oppression has a domino effect: when a race is invaded or uprooted, traditions are either destroyed or extensively changed. This means the disintegration of culture which leads to instability, insecurity, and hostility. It means losing the cultural livelihood which really means losing self-sufficiency. Having lost independence, self-confidence and self-respect go too: and people no longer believe in their ability to survive as a people.

In all fairness to the missionaries, it must be said that, in retrospect, their role poses questions that did not occur to them. On the whole, they were men and women of integrity and devotion to Christ. Their labours and self-sacrifice were often heroic. From our perspective, we can charge them with uprooting Indian culture. This they did, but they were convinced that the triumph of the white man's ways was inevitable and right. This unconsciousness may well be the most frightening aspect of their role. Sincerity is not necessarily the ultimate criteria of the Christian calling to serve others.

It is true also that, while Christian education helped destroy Indian culture to a severe extent, it also provided a sense of stability to Indian communities. Many Indian leaders in the past (1920s and 1930s) and of today were trained in missionary schools.

Today, native people may be the prophets of the New Jerusalem — the land of justice and faithfulness where a scattered people can be gathered. The native philosophy of life and land holds the vision of the New Jerusalem which the missionaries failed to see. "Let those who have ears to hear, listen to what the Spirit is saying. . . ."

The dream, the tradition, the now voiceless vision (buried beneath the destructive growth patterns that pollute the air, foul the water, rape the land) is emerging. Even as it is expressed, it is attacked by giant pipelines driving into the guts of the earth. The corporate giants are the savages, hostile to the dignity of the earth and its creatures. One anguished minister expressed the

contradiction when he saw the terrible effects of the James Bay
Hydro Development on the Cree of Waswanapi:

MOVE OVER Indian
You are primitive, backward and
uncivilized
You have committed the unpardonable
sin:
You have left your land as it was
in all its untamed beauty
You have not developed it.

We are coming
and we shall strangle the rivers. . .
and we shall slash the trees. . .
and we shall drown the land
and we shall kill the game
and rip the rocks apart. . .
and carve our initials all over the land;
in roads and railways and hydro
right of ways. . . .
for we are civilized and you are backward.
—Hugo Muller

The attack is not only on the land, but on the soul too. There is
already too little spirit left in our lives. The cries of the Northland are
echoed across the land in the suffering of powerless people—people
who are not to be satisfied with the consumer society. Happiness is
not just what you buy or own or possess. The cry for rebirth is not
crushed.

The woman, Mother Earth, still struggles with the Beast, so that
her children will not be devoured, so that the harmony of the Circle
of Life will be restored. Perhaps the new earth is like the teaching of
Black Elk:

You have noticed that everything an Indian does is in a circle,
and that is because the Power of the World always works in
circles, and everything tries to be round. In the old days we were
a strong and happy people, all our power came to us from the
sacred hoop of the nation, and so long as the hoop was
unbroken, the people flourished. The flowering tree was the
living centre of the hoop, and the circle of the four quarters
nourished it. The east gave peace and light, the south gave
warmth, the west gave rain, and the north with its cold and
mighty wind gave strength and endurance. This knowledge

came to us from the outer world with our religion. Everything the Power of the World does is done in a circle. The sky is round, and I have heard that the earth is round like a ball, and so are all the stars. The wind in its greatest powers, whirls. Birds make their nests in circles, for theirs is the same religion as ours. The sun comes forth and goes down again in a circle. The moon does the same, and both are round. Even the seasons form a great circle in their changing, and always come back again to where they were. The life of a man is a circle from childhood to childhood, and so it is in everything where power moves. Our tepees were round like the nests of birds, and these were always set in a circle, the nation's hoop, a nest of many nests, where the Great Spirit meant for us to hatch our children.

We can again be a people, a race that knows in its bones the convenant is with God, that Life is a gift, that the Earth is a gift and that we are bound to this earth-woman in life, that we need to be chastised and purified when the harmony of right relations is broken. But we need to be reconciled with the earth. A balance of needs and rights, for the whole human race, and not just parts of it, needs to be created. We must learn to nurture our earthly garden once again.

> . . . the man who sat on the ground in his tepee meditating on life and its meaning, accepting the kinship of all things, was infusing into his being the true essence of civilization. And when native man left off this form of development, his humanization was retarded in growth.
> —Chief Luther Standing Bear.

Not until the white Westerner comes to an appreciation and affirmation of the spiritual qualities, lifestyle, and culture of those whom he has looked down upon as "underdeveloped" or "savage" can he discover the common humanity which binds them together.

IV Gestae Dei Per Francos:
The French Canadian experience in western Canada

Raymond J. A. Huel [1]

On first appearance it would seem that the establishment of a New Jerusalem is a concept usually associated with the activities of Protestant and evangelical groups. However, a closer examination of the motives and goals inherent in this concept reveals that the French-speaking element within the Roman Catholic Church in Canada held views that were somewhat analogous. While they did not popularize the term, French-speaking Catholics were generally convinced that they had been singled out by God to fulfill a special mission in North America. This consciousness of being a covenant people was a legacy of monarchical and Catholic France and it had been apparent in the works of the early chroniclers of France, for example, Godfrey of Tours who related the extraordinary conversion of Clovis during the momentous battle of Tolbiac in 496.[2] However, it was Jacques Bongars, in the early seventeenth century, who captured the essence of France's contribution to the development of Catholicism in the title of his study of the Crusade historians, *Gestae Dei per Francos* — the deeds of God through the actions of the French.[3]

Early religious endeavours in New France were motivated by a religious revival in the mother country. The Jesuits, for example, attempted to establish the *Regnum* in Huronia where they hoped not only to Christianize the native population but also to protect its culture against the detrimental effects of contact with Europeans.[4] Although politics and the exigencies of the fur trade frustrated the "great design" of the Jesuits, they and those who followed them solidly entrenched Catholicism in New France. After the Conquest, the Church became a dominant institution and its clergy a social and cultural elite. This status, superior to that enjoyed under the kings of France, was enhanced by the absence of conflict between gallican and ultramontane[5] which had characterized the Church of France. Because of its isolation from France, the Catholic Church in Quebec escaped the anti-clericalism which accompanied the Enlightenment and the French Revolution, although the Revolution profoundly influenced the ideology of the French Canadian clergy by reinforcing its ultramontane views. The Quebec clergy came to regard French Canada as the source of a revitalized Catholicism which would spread across North America and continue the glorious mission of France, the eldest daughter of the Church.

Roman Catholicism in Quebec became associated with ethnic survival and, consequently, religion and language became interdependent. The clergy taught that if the French Canadian lost his language he would soon lose his faith and his national identity; hence, assimilation was the spectre from which the faithful had to be protected at all costs. The hierarchy regarded the preservation and cultivation of the French language as the most effective weapon in the struggle to maintain not only the heritage of New France but also the Roman Catholic community and its faith.

The Catholic Church in the West propagated in the interior the ideals and ambitions of its eastern parent. It was from Quebec City that Bishop Joseph-Octave Plessis sent Father Joseph-Norbert Provencher and his companions to Red River in 1818 to evangelize the Indians, educate the young and, in so doing, establish the Church of St. Boniface. Two years later, Provencher was named titular Bishop of Juliopolis and coadjutor of the Bishop of Quebec in the North-West. The See of St. Boniface, created in 1847, extended from Lake Superior to the Rocky Mountains. To serve this vast area where priests were scarce, Provencher sought the assistance of a missionary order. His appeals were subsequently answered by the Oblates of Mary Immaculate, a congregation founded in 1818 by Bishop Charles de Mazenod of Marseilles, France. The Oblates, who had come to Canada in 1841, were the first Catholic missionaries to enter the country after the Conquest.[6] In 1845, the arrival in Red River of Father Pierre Aubert, Oblates of Mary Immaculate (O.M.I.), with his young companion, Brother Alexandre Tache, marked the beginning of an important period in the history of the Oblate Order.

The Oblates were to western Canada what the Jesuits had been to New France. As missionaries among the Indian Tribes, the Oblates lived up to the expectations implied in their motto — *Evangilizare*

Saskatchewan Archives Board
Societe historique de la Saskatchewan Collection

Un souvenir de mon voyage a Lebret, Saskatchewan.
G.R. Girard O.M.I. 2 Juillet, 1921.

The Oblates of Mary Immaculate (O.M.I.) were to western Canada what the Jesuits had been to New France. As missionaries among the Indian tribes... they suffered isolation, deprivation and physical hardship in bringing the cross to "the great lone land". As French-speaking Catholics, the Oblates also reinforced the uncompromising ultramontane Catholicism of Quebec with all that entailed in terms of zealously guarding and enhancing the prerogatives of the Church.

pauperibus misit me[7] as they suffered isolation, deprivation and physical hardship in bringing the cross to "the great lone land." As French-speaking Catholics, the Oblates also reinforced the uncompromising ultramontane Catholicism of Quebec with all that entailed in terms of zealously guarding and enhancing the prerogative of the Church.

From its very humble beginnings as a mission, the Church of St. Boniface slowly spread across the Canadian northwest to Saskatchewan, Alberta, and the Northwest Territories. The Canadian West was an excellent area in which to establish the French Catholic equivalent of the New Jerusalem because, after fulfilling the precepts of the Church, the French-speaking clergy regarded the agrarian vocation as the surest guarantee of eternal salvation. Since the clergy also considered this attachment to the land as an essential requisite for ethnic survival, the prairies were also an ideal *milieu* in which to preserve and enhance French Canada's patrimony. French Canadians could regard the West as an extension of their *patrie* because it had been explored by their ancestors and evangelized by their missionaries.

Furthermore, the legislation enacted for the government of the Northwest Territories was well disposed toward Catholic interests in general and French Catholic ones in particular. The Northwest Territories Act of 1875 stipulated that a majority of ratepayers in any district could "establish such schools therein as they may think fit" and tax themselves accordingly. The minority in the district, whether Catholic or Protestant, could establish a separate school and be liable only for the support of that school.[8] An amendment to this Act provided for the official use of both French and English languages in the debates of the Legislative council and in proceedings before the courts of the Northwest Territories.[9] An ordinance passed by the territorial council in 1884 entrusted school management to a Board of Education comprising a Catholic and Protestant section. Each section was responsible for the administration of its own schools and this bifurcation bore a marked resemblance to the dual school system existing in Quebec.

Despite these positive attributes, French Canadian attitudes towards the North-West and its settlement were sharply divided. In Quebec, there was widespread scepticism regarding the agricultural potential of the prairies. Fifty years of appeals for charity and stories of privation from missionaries had done little to erase the conviction that the prairies were synonymous with hardship and desolation.[10]

In addition, public opinion in Quebec refused to be swayed by the concept that the West was a French Canadian *patrie*. Much to its dismay, Quebec was beginning to realize that it was not an equal partner in confederation and that Quebec alone belonged to the French element. Consequently, *la vieille province* argued that nothing should be done to weaken the French fact within its borders. Migration to the West could cause such weakening and result in expatriation with eventual assimilation by an Anglo-Protestant majority. The conclusion was obvious: it was preferable to remain in Quebec and contribute to enhancing the influence of that province in Confederation.

Even the French-speaking hierarchy was divided on the issue of western settlement. The metropolitan of the Catholic Church appealed for colonists from Quebec in the hope of saving Franco-Americans from certain assimilation by repatriating them to western Canada. However, Quebec clergy preferred to devote its energies to the settlement of northern Quebec and northern Ontario. Hence, Tache had to dispatch missionary-colonizers and form lay societies to promote French-Canadian emigration to western Canada.[11] Since the stand adopted by the Quebec episcopacy supported the belief that emigration meant expatriation and subsequent assimilation, many prospective colonists decided that it was to their advantage to remain in Quebec where they constituted the majority.

Tache's policy was continued and intensified by his successor, Archbishop L.P. Adelard Langevin, O.M.I., under whose leadership the missionary-colonizers had the dual role of attracting new colonists and administering the sacraments to their parish settlers. These intrepid colonizers greatly influenced the existence of western Canada's French Catholic settlements. They publicized the advantages of the prairies in special reports and in their correspondence to friends and relatives in eastern Canada and Europe. Also, they sought out colonists and settled them in communities across the West.

In addition to seeking out settlers, the clergy of St. Boniface desired to reproduce the traditional institution of Quebec on the western plains. Central in this concept was the establishment of the parish as the unit around which all communal life revolved. Following the example of Quebec, responsibility for education and health care would be delegated to religious communities. If New France had provided fertile ground for the spiritual energies of mystical France, the West would do the same for those of Quebec. *La vieille province* responded to the appeals for assistance from St. Boniface and the other dioceses that were established later. In 1844, for example, the Sisters of Charity of Montreal, more popularly known as the Grey Nuns, sent the first members of their order to Red

River. In the West, these heroic sisters were destined to play an important role as missionaries and educators, as well as caring for the sick and infirm. Other female orders came later to take charge of convents and schools. These religious communities provided services of incalculable value. Not only did they perform functions that were indispensable in a developing society, they did so for little cost in accordance with their vow of poverty. In propagating the ideals of *Gestae Dei per Francos* these religious communities also contributed to the cultural survival of the French-speaking communities in the West.

Despite these dedicated efforts, the large wave of French-Canadian, Franco-American and French emigration envisaged by the St. Boniface clergy failed to materialize. In 1891, out of 66,799 people who inhabited the four provisional territorial districts, 13,008 were Roman Catholics and only 1,543 of these were French-speaking.[12] Furthermore, the status of the French and Catholic elements in the western population did not improve with time.[13] The French became a minority not only within the population at large but also within the Roman Catholic community. It was obvious that French-speaking Catholics would never become a significant force in western politics. Henceforth, the clergy could no longer hope to assert French Catholic rights in the West by mere force of numbers. This would require moral suasion and appeals to historical precedents—arguments which the majority did not consider seriously.

In the absence of a significant Roman Catholic population in the West, the original confessional school system became redundant. The English-speaking majority favoured a non-denominational school system (similar to the one in Ontario) with British character and traditions. Consequently, the territorial authorities began to modify the school system so that by 1901 its confessional features had almost disappeared.

In 1892, the French-speaking element received a serious blow when the Legislative Assembly of the Northwest Territories adopted the motion that, henceforth, proceedings of the assembly would be recorded and published only in English.[14] In 1905, amid great controversy, Sir Wilfred Laurier was able to maintain the principle of separate schools in the new provinces of Saskatchewan and Alberta. But the importance of this principle was decidedly restrained. Roman Catholics no longer had the right to administer an autonomous educational system; they had only the privilege of erecting separate schools, of electing their own trustees in such districts and of employing Catholic teachers. In the final analysis, the distinction between separate and public schools existed in name only because both systems were subject to the same statutory legislation and regulations of the Department of Education. This was a radical transformation of the bifurcated system of 1875 in which Catholic and Protestant schools had been completely distinct and autonomous.

The maintenance of this system of separate non-confessional schools in Alberta and Saskatchewan was a disappointment to Archbishop Langevin because it confirmed the spoliation of French and Catholic rights in the territorial era. (The territorial era refers to the period of time prior to 1905, when both provinces were part of the Northwest Territories). Equally disheartening to Langevin was that only six Catholic Members of Parliament from Quebec had voted against the legislation which formed the new Provinces.[15] This fact indicated that the "Quebec bloc" in Parliament would not or could not protect the interests of the French Catholic minority elsewhere in Canada.

Nevertheless, Langevin and his clergy were resolute in their determination to maintain and enhance French Catholic rights in the West. Basing their view on the premise that whatever promoted the interests of the French language was *ipso facto* advantageous to the interests of Roman Catholicism, the hierarchy of St. Boniface took the initiative of promoting the union of French-speaking groups in the West. Developments in Manitoba and the Territories made the hierarchy realize that it was not sufficient to establish schools and convents. These institutions had to be protected against legislation detrimental to their interests. The archdiocese's official organ, *Les Cloches de St. Boniface*, reminded the faithful that laws were enacted by elected representatives and, consequently, Catholic voters had to unite not only to defend but also to assert their rights. *Les Cloches* stressed the necessity of a *cercle* or club in each centre to bring Catholics together.[16]

In 1908, Langevin urged a federation of all the *Societes St. Jean-Baptiste* in the French-speaking centres of Manitoba. Units of the *Societe St. Jean-Baptiste* had also been established in Saskatchewan and Alberta. In Saskatchewan, existing local groups federated in 1909, but the movement did not expand to the extent anticipated.[17] Later, more formal organizations were established either in response to a controversy affecting French minorities and their schools (l'Association d'Education des Canadiens-Francais du Manitoba, 1916), or in response to the need for greater solidarity (l'Association Catholique Franco-Canadienne de la Saskatchewan, 1912; l'Association Canadienne-Francaise de l'Alberta, 1925).

In addition to encouraging the organization and union of French
enclaves in the West, the clergy also promoted establishment of a
French language press. This press, *L'oeuvre de la bonne presse*, had
a double goal: to propagate Roman Catholic ideals and further the
interests of the Church (especially in educational matters), and to
promote the interests and defend the rights of the French language.
As well, French Catholic newspapers would provide a means of
communication among the French groups and thus reinforce the
sense of national solidarity.[18]   The paper established in 1901 by
Archbishop Langevin to serve his diocese was *Les Cloches de
St.Boniface*. A few years later, a regional press developed to meet
more specific needs of more distinct areas. For example, *Le Patriote
de l'Ouest* appeared in 1910 in Saskatchewan; in Manitoba, *La
Liberte* began publishing in 1913 and *La Survivance* began to serve
Alberta in 1928.

Despite their zealous efforts on behalf of immigration and
organization, the French-speaking clergy realized that the struggle to
protect French-language and Roman Catholic interests in the West
had suffered serious reverses. This was evidenced by the small
number of western French-speaking Catholics, the lack of a
substantial emigration from Quebec, and the unlikelihood of much
tangible Quebec support. Hence, the western hierarchy recognized
the need to use more effective weapons than appeals to historic
precedents and the British sense of fair play. To redress the balance
in their favour, the French-speaking clergy called for a union of all
Catholic ethnic groups. They hoped that French and other ethnic
associations (such as the *Deutsche Katholische Volksverein*) would
work together, without ethnic distinction for the "reconquest" of
Catholic rights in educational matters.[19] Considering the prairie
immigration pattern, the concept of a pan-Catholic federation was
practical. But more important, it was justified on the grounds that
the Catholic Church had always respected differences of race and
language among nations because they were based on natural law
which was regarded as the expression of "fundamental relations
constituted by God."[20]

During the period of large-scale immigration to the West, the
Archdiocese of St. Boniface and its suffragan bishops followed the
practice of the Apostles and utilized the language of those whom they
evangelized. This use of national language was also a reflection of
the pattern of group settlement that had developed in the West.
Where the faithful were grouped in sufficient numbers, they were
constituted into a parish and provided with a priest of their own
nationality (or at least one who spoke their language). In addition,

the bishops also provided religious orders and teaching communities recruited along national lines (for example, *Les Filles de la Providence* among the French, the Order of St. Benedict among the Germans, the Order of St. Basil the Great among the Ruthenians).[21]

To complement their efforts on behalf of European Catholic immigrants, the hierarchy also promoted the establishment of ethnic newspapers. West Canada Publishing Co., directed by the Oblate order in Winnipeg, published four weekly journals: the English *North-West Review*, the German *West Kanada*, the Polish *Gazeta Katolicka* and the Ukrainian *Kanadyskyj Rusyn (Canadian Ruthenian)*. By 1911, West Canada Publishing had spent over $50,000 to promote a Catholic press in the West.[22] In Alberta and Saskatchewan, the Oblates published *La Survivance* and *Le Patriote de l'Ouest* and subsidized both journals.

It was no easy task to minister to the needs of multicultural flock. Some European Catholics, suspicious of the motives of the French clergy (even when they spoke their language) insisted on priests of their own nationality.[23] Because priests of other nationalities had to be called, their presence weakened the dominant position of the French element in the western Canadian Church. To complicate matters, English-speaking Catholics scattered throughout the prairies and also demanded services in their own language.

More serious and significant, however, were the Ruthenians who immigrated from east central Europe. Since in Canada no separate church organization existed for Catholics who belonged to the Greek rite, it was appropriate for them to come under the jurisdiction of the existing administrative units of the Roman Catholic Church. Based on previous developments in Europe, many Ruthenians suspected the Latin-rite clergy of attempting to detach Ruthenians from their traditional ways of worship.[24] In addition to differences in rite, the problem of language, the zealous activities of Protestant denominations, and the confusion over ecclesiastical jurisdiction among members of the Eastern rite further complicated the Ruthenian situation in western Canada. Archbishop Langevin, who had over 32,000 Catholic Ruthenians in his diocese by 1911, was quick to realize the detrimental effects resulting from the lack of religious authority and clergy.[25] In 1899, in an attempt to alleviate the scarcity of clergy, Langevin visited the Redemptorist monastery in Rotterdam, Netherlands, in search of missionaries to work among the Ruthenians in his diocese. Only one candidate, Father A. Delaere, answered the Archbishop's call and, after studying Ukrainian at the Redemptorist monastery in Brandon, he began his missionary work in the Riding Mountain Park area.[26] As a result of Langevin's efforts, other French-speaking priests studied Ukrainian and established themselves among the Ruthenians until a sufficient number of national clergy were available.   Langevin also collaborated in negotiations which resulted in the establishment of the Ukrainian Catholic Church and the appointment, in 1912, of Nycyta Budka as its first prelate.

The settlement of the West intensified a polemic indigenous to the Catholic Church in Canada. This was the controversy between French and English-speaking Catholics (the latter were often contemptuously referred to as *"les irlandais,"* "the Irish", by the former). This ethnic rivalry was, in fact, a part of the larger polemic surrounding the nature of the Canadian identity—it reflected the extent of bilingualism and biculturalism across the Dominion. Given the rapid rate of growth and development in the prairies at the turn of the century, many people envisaged the day when the West would hold the balance of power in Confederation. Within the Church, there were groups who realized that the ethnic balance within the hierarchy would be decided by the creation of new dioceses in the West. Traditionally, French-speaking prelates had been in the hierarchy majority and, in 1900, all bishops in the West were French-speaking and suffragans of the Ecclesiastical Province of St. Boniface.

Unlike the French-speaking clergy, "the Irish" had not been missionaries, colonizers, or explorers but their lack of endeavour was offset by their knowledge of the English language which helped to reconcile Catholicism and British citizenship. In Canada, Roman Catholicism had become associated with Quebec and, consequently, it had been viewed as an alien force by staunch Anglo-Saxon Protestants schooled in the traditions of the Reformation and an "anti-papist" bias. In sharing the same language and political traditions as the majority, "the Irish" made Catholicism more compatible with North American conditions and institutions— provided one was an English-speaking Catholic. This proviso would be significant in western Canadian politics where it was suspected that Quebec, through its bloc in Ottawa, was attempting to gain control of the West. Furthermore, Canadian statesmen and parliamentarians preferred to deal with "Irish" (English-speaking) prelates, especially when controversial issues such as separate schools and language were being discussed. To French Catholics, separate schools and linguistic schools were synonymous and this peculiar status added fuel to any controversy surrounding separate schools. As Roman Catholics, "the Irish" naturally defended separate schools but they were, nevertheless, outspoken opponents of French or foreign-language instruction in these schools and were thus considered the lesser of two evils.

Although they were a minority within the Catholic Church in Canada, "the Irish" were, nevertheless, the most vociferous and activist element. In many instances they considered themselves to be superior to Canadian-born English-speaking Catholics and they delegated themselves the responsibility of being the voice of the English-speaking Catholic population at large. The fact that they were dispersed and numerically weak did not prevent "the Irish" from pressing their claims for separate parishes, clergymen and prelates. For example, in December, 1906, a delegation of eleven Irish Catholics waited on Archbishop Langevin to request for St. Mary's Parish (the English-speaking parish in Winnipeg) English-speaking priests, the creation of new English parishes in Winnipeg, and the establishment of an exclusively Catholic college. The delegates also requested the appointment of an English-speaking bishop for Winnipeg.[27] The Irish element later petitioned Pope Benedict XV, stating that English was becoming the dominant language in the West and that changes in church organization and administration had to be made to keep up with the times. The agitation continued in Rome and Canada and, in December 1915, Winnipeg was removed from the jurisdiction of the Ecclesiastical Province of St. Boniface and erected as a separate archdiocese.[28]

In the meantime, Irish-French rivalries developed in other areas. In 1910, "the Irish" proposed a candidate for bishop of the newly created Diocese of Regina but, through Langevin's efforts, French Canadian Olivier-Elzear Mathieu was appointed. Two years later, however, "the Irish" succeeded in having James Thomas McNally named first Bishop of Calgary. McNally was the first English-speaking bishop to be appointed in the old Ecclesiastical Province of St. Boniface and his nomination marked the beginning of the end of the ascendancy of the French-speaking clergy in the hierarchy of the West. The erection of Winnipeg as a separate archdiocese in 1915 confirmed this trend.

Such was the fate that Providence had ordained for the descendants of Catholic France in western Canada. Their goals of continuing ancient traditions and establishing the perfect Catholic Society were not to be realized—at least not to the degree envisaged by their French-speaking clergy. A French Catholic West did not materialize because French Canadians and other French-speaking Catholics did not come in sufficient numbers. It could also be argued that the western hierarchy, by its recognition and acceptance of the need for ethnic clergy and parishes, weakened not only the position of the French element in the West but also its own position within the governing councils of the Church.[29]

In some respects, the French Catholic experience in the West resembled the biblical vision of the New Jerusalem. The Catholic New Jerusalem, however, was not a city on a hill to be imitated by others nor was it centered on an imminent coming of the Kingdom of God. Unlike Protestant eschatology which stresses the presence of God in history, the Catholic experience takes the form of a liturgical vision in which history becomes complete in the mass, the ultimate form of worship. In coming together to worship, the Catholic community—through its historical past—is united with the apostolic tradition. For French-speaking Catholics in Canada this liturgical vision was even more significant because through it, they communicated spiritually with the contributions their French ancestors had made on behalf of the Roman Catholic Church. The liturgy also served to remind them that while Christian France had fallen in 1789, the Kingdom of God would continue to be extended by French-speaking Catholics in Canada. *Gestae Dei per Francos* represents that unity of race and language which French Catholic Canadians struggled so valiantly to preserve. Viewed in this perspective, the efforts on behalf of *la survivance* were not merely attempts to maintain a particular idiom. These efforts were a struggle to preserve the French language in order to better preserve the Roman Catholic faith, which for these believers was the true channel of grace and salvation.[30]

This conviction of being a pilgrim people provided French-speaking Catholics in Canada with the strength and willingness to resist North American persecution which was manifested in official suppression of the French language in Manitoba and the Northwest Territories, in restrictive legislation affecting the teaching of French, and in the status of schools in French Catholic districts. The schools and language crises in Manitoba, in the Northwest Territories and later in Saskatchewan galvanized the French Catholic minority in Canada and made this minority more conscious of its past, its identity and its destiny. The consequent persecution complex made French-speaking Catholics more determined to resist assimilation and (by implication) the loss of their faith.

There is, however, one fundamental difference between the French Roman Catholic Canadians and the Canadian Protestant examples of establishing the New Jerusalem. Within Canada's French-speaking body and within the entire Catholic community, there were no doctrinal or theological differences which would cause a group to break away and establish what it deemed to be the true

Christian city free from corruption and degradation. Even Riel's attempt to establish a new social order and religion in the Northwest in 1885 was not as radical a departure from the tenets of the French Catholic tradition in Canada as a cursory observation might suggest. Riel adopted and refined the ideas of the Quebec ultramontanes. Central to his ideology was the concept "that the metis would continue, expand and perfect the evangelical mission of New France in America."[31] As a prophet, Riel's "task was to found the third and the last era of the Kingdom of God—French-Canadian-Metis Catholicism, following Roman Catholicism as the latter had succeeded Judaism."[32]

Riel's new religion was the product of his troubled mind and personality; it was also a nativist-millenarian response to the difficulties which the Metis society faced in its confrontation with the advancing agricultural frontier. His religious views were denounced by the clergy and, if he had become a martyr, it would have been because his execution produced a political upheaval in Quebec. It was a secular and political Quebec that took up Riel's cause, overlooked his religious heresies and, because of his racial origin, regarded him as a compatriot unjustly condemned by the English-speaking majority. Riel's execution, therefore, was viewed as a blow directed against the entire French-Canadian community.

The French-speaking minorities in the West were a microcosm of Quebec society and its institutions. The differences that arose in the Catholic tradition on the prairies were cultural and they were related to the very essence of the Canadian identity. Within this context French Canadians were victims of their historical past and they were doubly suspect in the eyes of the dominant English-speaking elite. Being French-speaking, they were a reminder that Canada could not be a true British dominion until they were assimilated or their influence limited to Quebec. As Catholics, they revived old anti-Catholic prejudices and gave them new meaning and thrust. Thus, it was no small wonder that the dominant elite responded with such alarm to the French Catholic presence in the West. This elite was convinced that a second Quebec was being established on the prairies and, to prevent this calamity, it pressed for legislation to enhance the role of the school as a guardian of Anglo-Protestant values and traditions.

Although their numbers and influence dwindled with the advance of the twentieth century, it cannot be denied that the French-speaking clergy fulfilled an apostolic mission in western Canada. During the missionary era, they established the church over a vast area and, during the settlement period, they consolidated its

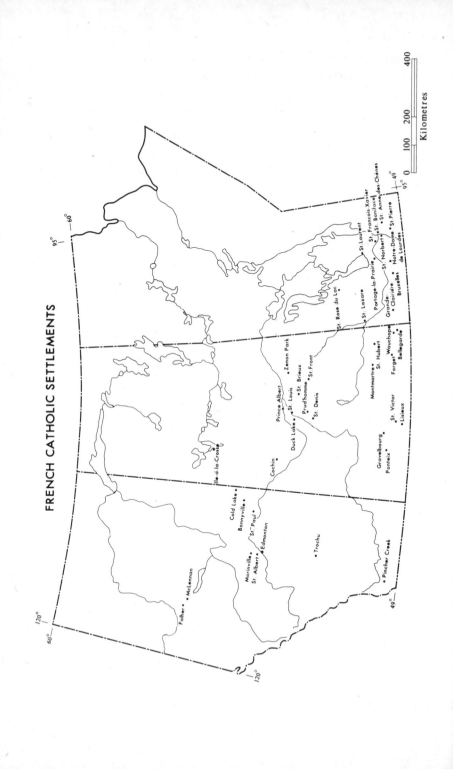

FRENCH CATHOLIC SETTLEMENTS

Kilometres
0   100   200   400

Falher• •McLennan

Morinville•
St. Albert• •Edmonton
•St. Paul
Bonnyville•
Cold Lake•

•Trochu

•Pincher Creek

Cochin

•Île-à-la-Crosse

Prince Albert•
Duck Lake•
•St. Louis
Prudhomme• •St. Brieux
•St. Denis •St. Front
•Zenon Park

•St. Rose du Lac

•St. Lazare

St. Laurent•
St. François-Xavier•
Portage-la-Prairie•   •St. Boniface•
•St. Norbert• •St. Anne-des-Chênes
Grande   • St. Pierre•
Clairière• Notre-Dame•
Bruxelles•   de Lourdes

Montmartre•
•St. Hubert
Forget• •Wauchope
Bellegarde•

Gravelbourg•
Ponteix•   •St. Victor
•Lisieux

60°   95°

120°
60°

49°   95°

49°

120°

The sound room of the French radio station CFNS, Saskatoon, Saskatchewan. A. de Marjerie *left,* Rev. R. Ducharme *centre* and R. Pinsonneault *right.*

The existence of communities in western Canada speaking le doux parler *and practising the Catholic faith of their ancestors is a tribute to the efforts of the French-speaking clergy and proof that their efforts were not in vain.*

structure.   However, more important than their contribution as pioneers and builders was their role as pastors. Among the French-speaking minorities, they inculcated ethics and values that reflected the finest flowering of the sincere and deep-rooted Catholicism of Quebec. As the steward of Catholicism, the French-speaking clergy in the West assumed a dominant role in the struggle to ensure *la survivance.* They maintained that status in the educational and cultural activities of the French Canadian minorities until they were slowly replaced by a lay elite in the post-World War II era. The existence of communities in western Canada speaking *le doux parler* and practising the Catholic faith of their ancestors is a tribute to the efforts of the French-speaking clergy and proof that their efforts were not in vain.

V Anglicanism on the prairies:
Continuity and flexibility

Frank Peake

The first point to be made in considering Anglican settlement on the prairies is that rarely was it undertaken for its own sake. That Anglicans came to the prairies in the seventeenth, eighteenth and nineteenth centuries for the purpose of establishing a New Jerusalem is a suggestion which probably would have filled them with amazement.

Early settlement was undertaken for social and economic advantage. The Hudson's Bay Company, whose agents were among the first white men to penetrate the prairies, was in business to make profits from the fur trade. It is true that, in the absence of any other public agency, the Company was also charged with the maintenance of public order and a degree of pastoral oversight. In the heady days of the Restoration it was assumed that these would be carried on in an atmosphere that was both monarchical and Anglican. Although the charter of the Company contains no reference to any religious obligations, the accompanying instructions did contain the following injunctions:

> Forasmuch as most of our colonies do border upon the Indians, and peace is not to be expected without due observance and preservation of justice to them, you are, in our name, to command all *Governors* that they at no time give any just provocation to any of the said Indians that are at peace with us, ...And you are to consider how the Indians and slaves may be best *instructed in and united to the Christian religion*; it being both for the honour of the Crown and of the Protestant [i.e. Anglican] religion itself, that all persons within any of our

territories, *though never so remote*, should be taught the knowledge of God, and be made acquainted with the mysteries of salvation.[1]

Regardless of such injunctions, the Company sought to restrain both settlement and missionary expansion.

In England, the end of the eighteenth century saw the onset of the Evangelical Revival. This was largely an Anglican response to the earlier Methodist revival and found its focus and centre in the "Clapham Sect," a group of friends, most of whom lived at Clapham, then a village outside London.[2] Under the leadership of John Venn, rector of Clapham, the group of people included numbers of people who were prominent in government and commerce. Among them were William Wilberforce, a member of parliament from 1784 until 1833, the friend of Pitt the Younger and a strong advocate for the abolition of slavery and the slave trade; Charles Grant, a director of the East India Company and Zachary Macaulay, the father of the historian. Members of the Clapham Sect were also active in missionary enterprise, especially in India. The sect was the driving force behind the formation of the Church Missionary Society (C.M.S.) in 1799. Some of the members of the society and those who served on its committees were also directors of the Hudson's Bay Company which made them aware of the need and possibility of missions in British North America.

Through this combination of circumstances, John West was despatched to serve as the Company's chaplain at Red River. Soon after his arrival, however, he made it clear that he was more interested in the spiritual well-being of the Indians than in ministering to the servants of the Company. This incurred the displeasure of the Company and probably contributed to the shortness of his stay. Nevertheless, other missionaries followed him and by the 1840s there were half a dozen at work in Rupert's Land. It should be noted that this missionary work was not undertaken by the Church itself which had no facilities for such a task but by societies within the Church, chiefly, the Society for the Propagation of the Gospel (S.P.G.), the Church Missionary Society (C.M.S.), and the Colonial and Continental Church Society (C. & C.C.S.).

The oldest of these societies, the S.P.G., was founded in 1701 to supplement the work of the earlier Society for Promoting Christian Knowledge (S.P.C.K.) which had been formed to support and encourage the building of schools and the distribution of Bibles and tracts. The primary purpose of the S.P.G. was to support chaplaincies in providing the ministrations of the Church to British

Clergy and students on the doorstep of Archdeacon MacKay School, The Pas, Manitoba, July 1916.

During the nineteenth century Anglican missions to the Indians extended through the prairies and beyond. The C.M.S. (Church Missionary Society) was committed with single-minded devotion to the evangelization and conversion of native peoples.

people overseas, although it also undertook evangelistic work among native peoples. It had been founded to meet the needs of settlers in New England but expanded its work to all parts of the world. The society maintained some missionaries on the prairies and actively supported Emmanuel College in its early days at Prince Albert as a training school for native catechists and teachers.[3]

The C.M.S. was founded in 1799 as "The Missions Society." Not until 1812 did it adopt the formal title, "The Church Missionary Society for Africa and the East."[4] It was concerned exclusively with the evangelization of native peoples initially in India but later in British North America.

The third society, the C. & C.C.S., was an outgrowth of the Newfoundland School Society, formed in 1823. Commonly known as the 'Col. & Con.', the C. & C.C.S., with its monthly magazine significantly named *The Greater Britain Messenger*, saw its primary responsibility as directed to Anglo-Saxon settlers.[5] No one exemplified this view better than George Exton Lloyd of Barr Colony fame[6] and later, Bishop of Saskatchewan. The most important contribution by the C. & C.C.S. was its support of Emmanuel College, Saskatoon. Both the C.M.S. and the C. & C.C.S. were strongly evangelical in outlook.

The major burden of the work on the prairies was undertaken by the C.M.S. and later, by its support of Emmanuel College, by the C. & C.C.S. Both were distinctly evangelical or low-church societies, whose origins lie in the eighteenth century when the practise of Christianity in the Church of England had degenerated to the point where, at its worst, it was little more than a gentlemanly nod in the direction of Christian ethics. Both the Wesleyan and the Evangelical revivals were attempts to combat this by an insistence upon personal commitment to Jesus Christ, marked by an experience of conversion and followed by a rigorously disciplined, if somewhat narrow, way of life. Although this was not the intention of John Wesley, such an approach tended to lay great emphasis upon the relationship of the individual soul with God at the expense of the church and sacraments. Hence the name "low Church," meaning that those so named took a low view of the importance of the church. With the Oxford Movement or Catholic Revival, which began in the 1830s, a new emphasis appeared which continued to insist upon personal devotion but also affirmed that the spiritual life which followed could only be adequately nurtured and fed within the Church, which was seen as the Body of Christ, and by the divinely instituted sacraments. The supporters of this view were known as "High Churchmen". To many low churchmen this was seen as playing into the hands of Roman Catholicism and for more than a century there was conflict, sometimes bitter, between the holders of the two views.

In these circumstances it is not surprising that, in the eyes of the C.M.S., bishops were almost regarded as a necessary evil. But the society conceded that they were necessary and from the 1820s there was pressure for the creation of a bishopric on the prairies. This hope was realized in 1849 with the consecration of David Anderson as the first Lord Bishop of Rupert's Land.[7] Anderson and his clergy soon realized the vastness of the undertaking before them and the need for more living agents. They also noted with alarm the growing number of Roman Catholic missionaries, including bishops, most of whom belonged to the Oblates of Mary Immaculate (O.M.I.), a French mission order. Anderson and his colleagues continued to badger the C.M.S. for the appointment of more missionaries and by the 1860s, the number at work in the diocese had risen to about fifteen. Realizing the impossibility of giving episcopal oversight to such a large area, Anderson began to think of possible future divisions of the diocese. As he looked at the map he concluded that three bishops would be needed. The area surrounding the Red River settlement he saw as one diocese, but the northwest and northeast would be two other areas requiring bishops. Exploratory work in the northwest was undertaken by James Hunter, a C.M.S. missionary who had been in the field since 1844 and whom Anderson made Archdeacon of Cumberland.[8] Anderson himself investigated the possibilities of the area between the Red River and James Bay.[9] His hopes were realized when John Horden, who had come as a missionary to Moose Factory in 1852, was consecrated Bishop of Moosonee twenty years later. In 1874 John McLean and William Carpenter Bompas became Bishops of Saskatchewan and Athabasca respectively.

It is probably fair to say that nineteenth-century missionary motives and methods were not always, at least by more recent criteria, as enlightened as they might have been. There was a tendency on the part of the missionary to see himself as the emissary of a superior civilization sent to those living in pagan darkness that he might bring to them the benefits of gracious living, houses, trousers, soap and Sunday, together with the rather less obvious benefits of the Gospel. This tendency is clearly implied in the writing of Reginald Heger who, although referring to another continent, had said:

> The heathen in his blindness
>   Bows down to wood and stone
> Can we, whose souls are lighted
>   With wisdom from on high,
> Can we to men benighted
>   The lamp of life deny?[10]

Is it surprising that the native peoples were not always able to distinguish between the flag and the Cross, between the practices of civilization and the precepts of the Gospel? It was this confusion which aroused the ire of Stefansson, the Arctic ethnologist and explorer, who wrote:

> The three commandments, 'love they neighbour as thyself,' 'thou shalt keep the Sabbath holy,' and 'thou shalt eat thy potatoes with thy fork,' impress themselves with equal vividness upon the aborigines and are likely to be seen by them to be means of grace of co-ordinate value.[11]

Something of that same attitude was demonstrated by James Hunter when in 1847, he wrote home to the secretaries of the C.M.S. saying:

> The children in our schools are taught nothing but English which they readily acquire and read very fluently; I hope that in

a few years the English language will altogether supersede Indian at this station as it has already done at the Indian Settlement. Translations are therefore required for the old Indians and for stations recently formed but as the stations become more fully established the Cree language will give place to the English. . .[12]

In the report which accompanied the letter he added:

> Attitudes towards Civilization
>
> During my absence . . . the frames of four . . . houses were put up by the Indians . . . Several Indians are now cutting off wood for houses which they intend to raft down the river. On their farms they are growing excellent crops of wheat, barley, potatoes and turnips, and some of them have horses, cattle and pigs. They are now dressed in European clothes and are abandoning their native indolent ways and adopting active and industrious habits. Many of them are now excellent Sawyers and Squarers and are able very materially to assist the Carpenter in the erection of our new buildings.

Half a century later, C.E. Whittaker wrote in the same vein about the Eskimos of the western Arctic. This does not mean that the missionaries completely ignored the native languages. They could not afford to do so for obvious and practical reasons. Whether they saw them as part of a culture to be preserved is another matter. In many instances it is probable that they did not. At the same time most of the nineteenth century missionaries were assiduous in their efforts to meet the native people in their own language and, in spite of a frequently limited educational background, they were suprisingly successful although some found the task impossible. In spite of what he had said, Hunter could claim to have been the first of his contemporaries to minister to the Cree Indians in their own language. In this he was helped by the fact that his second wife, a daughter of Chief Factor Donald Ross, was partly Cree. Others were equally determined. Many of their published translations and dictionaries were intended primarily for educational purposes, and St. John's school at Red River was founded by John West for the purpose of educating promising Indian boys. Developed as a theological college by David Anderson, the first bishop, many of its students were Indians or of mixed race. Emmanuel College, founded at Prince Albert in 1879 by John McLean, the first Bishop of Saskatchewan, was also intended for the training of a native ministry. Included in its curriculum was the teaching of native languages.

It is not the purpose of this study to trace the ecclesiastical organization of Anglicanism on the prairies since this has been done elsewhere.[13] Suffice it to say that by 1900 the ecclesiastical province comprised eight dioceses and today includes ten.

Large scale European settlement did not begin until the end of the nineteenth century with the coming of the railways. Here again the motives of the settlers were probably as much social and economic as they were religious. Most of those who acknowledged Anglican allegiance came from the British Isles, some of them by way of the United States, but in all likelihood their motives and hopes were little different from those of other settlers. The landless labourer of the agricultural revolution saw the possibility of becoming the 'squire' or 'lord of the manor' of several hundred acres of free or nearly free land. The urban worker of the industrial revolution saw the possibility of becoming his own master, free from the regimentation of the factory whistle and the servitude of the mill. That he did not know the horns from the tail of a cow did not seem important.

It is generally agreed that urbanization, the concomitant of industrialization, militated against institutional religion. The growth of the factory system often required workers to move from the community in which they had grown up and where they were surrounded by friends and relatives. The move might be no more than a few miles but familial links were broken and the constraints of behaviour, including habits of public worship, were removed. Moreover, vast new urban areas in the first few decades of the nineteenth century were often devoid of churches and chapels. There was neither incentive nor opportunity for the industrial migrants to take part in public worship even if they had been so inclined.[14] Blake could sing in vain of "building Jerusalem in England's green and pleasant land". For most industrial workers the land was anything but green and pleasant and the hope of a New Jerusalem seemed very remote indeed. Although churches and chapels were built in large numbers during the middle of the nineteenth century, it was too late to win back many of those who had drifted away. It was from people such as these, or from their children, that many of the immigrants to the prairies were recruited.

Once they had arrived on their prairie homesteads, these new settlers found that the rigours of the climate and the chores incidental to survival left little time for anything else. Schools, churches and other cultural luxuries would inevitably have to be left until the proverbial "next year". Moreover, from an Anglican point of view, the conduct of public worship seemed to require the presence of a clergyman. Even when the settlers were religiously inclined, as no doubt some were, they could not administer the sacraments for themselves and it would have dawned on few to read the prayer book offices of morning and evening prayer for themselves and their neighbours. One settler, who later became a clergyman,[15] has left an idealized description of an immigrant ministering in this way to his neighbours but it seems unlikely that the practice was widespread. There was undoubtedly a measure of disillusionment and frustration among the settlers for whom the reality seemed so different from the promise. What kept most of them on their homesteads was not so much tenacity and determination as the sheer inability to raise the fare home. The idea that the settlers saw themselves primarily or even nominally as builders of the New Jerusalem accords ill with the evidence. Not only were many of them indifferent, and occasionally even hostile, to matters of religion, but often they were without pastoral ministrations for a decade or more after their arrival. Vernon's comment of half a century ago is not without its truth:

> There is an interesting difference between the coming of the Church to the Mother lands and the coming of the Church to Canada. There, some great apostle, some great missionary bishop or faithful clergy, came and preached Christ crucified to people who had never heard his name, and then ministered the sacraments of his grace and established his Church. No missionary bishop was the herald of the Church to this Dominion. The Church came to Canada with the coming of ordinary churchpeople, not of Church leaders . . .[16]

How far the settlers on the prairies could be seen to be "ordinary churchpeople" is therefore open to question. There are two interesting variations of this theme. One was the Brotherhood of Labour initiated by Adalbert Anson, the first Bishop of Assiniboia (Qu'Appelle) in 1885. The other was the Barr Colony established in the vicinity of Lloydminister in 1903. Both were attempts to transplant what was best in English society and religion to the Canadian prairies.

The Brotherhood of Labour was not to be a colony in any strict sense. Rather it was intended as a centre for young English emigrants of suitable background and education who, after a period of training in agriculture or divinity, would take up land in the vicinity or be ordained to serve as clergy. The idea was that those who wished to farm would learn something about prairie agriculture, while those who aspired to ordination but had been denied the opportunity in England through lack of funds or preparation would receive appropriate preparation. In this way communities would be established, populated with settlers who shared common interests and convictions. During the initial preparatory period, all would live communally as a Brotherhood of Labour[17] thereby cementing the bond of fellowship between them.

To this end Bishop Anson collected funds in England, purchased a section of land near Qu'Appelle on the main line of the Canadian Pacific Railway (C.P.R.), put up the necessary buildings and installed the Rev. F.W. Pelly as warden of the proposed college and W.S. Redpath as manager of the farm. The house was opened on October 28, 1885, and the Brotherhood of Labour formally inaugurated with the admission of three probationers on November 21st. It was a noble dream but short-lived and unsuccessful. For its failure there are probably several reasons. Anson himself, with his other responsibilities, was unable to enter fully into the scheme. He was unable to find others who shared his vision and who could provide inspiration and leadership. In addition, he wanted to do things too quickly. No sooner had he opened the college than he opened a boys' boarding school in the largely unsettled area. Nor could he attract a sufficient number of eligible emigrants. Anson was of aristocratic background, a brother of the Earl of Lichfield, he had visions of a steady flow of younger sons of gentlemen or yeoman farmers, young men whose families might be relatively impoverished but who themselves were well educated and "to the manor born". The project was almost stillborn and collapsed completely when Anson lost interest, resigned the see, and returned to the seclusion of an English cathedral close.

The story of the Barr colony is both colourful and controversial.[18] Isaac Montgomery Barr, after a somewhat chequered ministerial career, appeared in London in the early 1900s. In September 1902, he issued a pamphlet entitled, "British Settlement in North Western Canada on Free Grant Lands— Canada for the British!" In this pamphlet he held forth the alluring possibility of exchanging poverty in Britain for a landed estate in Canada and the chance of planting an exclusively British colony on the empty prairies. He invited applications from those interested in taking part in such a scheme and was deluged with replies. It has generally been conceded that organization was not Barr's strong point and, at this stage, George Exton Lloyd entered the picture. Lloyd offered his services and persuaded the C. & C.C.S. to appoint him as chaplain to the proposed colony for a period of three years. So successful was the promotion of the scheme that on March 31,

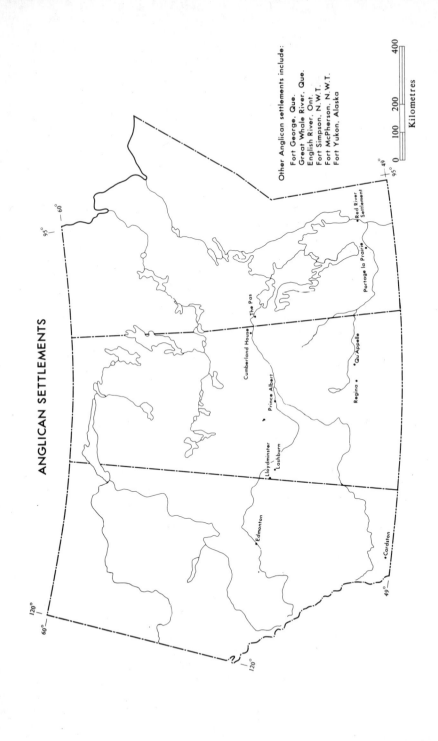

ANGLICAN SETTLEMENTS

Other Anglican settlements include:

Fort George, Que.
Great Whale River, Que.
English River, Ont.
Fort Simpson, N.W.T.
Fort McPherson, N.W.T.
Fort Yukon, Alaska

Kilometres

0   100   200   400

Red River Settlement
Portage la Prairie
The Pas
Cumberland House
Qu'Appelle
Regina
Prince Albert
Lloydminster
Lashburn
Edmonton
Cardston

Barr Colonists at Saskatoon, 1903. Bishop Lloyd in group.

The C. & C.C.S. (Colonial and Continental Church Society) saw its primary responsibility as being directed to Anglo-Saxon settlers. George Exton Lloyd of Barr colony fame and later, Bishop of Saskatchewan exemplified the point of view of those who saw themselves as extending an already established Christian society, the British Empire and the Church of England into new areas.

1903, a party of more than two thousand men, women and children sailed from Liverpool on board the S.S. *Lake Manitoba.* The story of the voyage has been told by Harry Pick, one of the colonists, in his book, *Next Year.*

The problems of meeting the needs of such large numbers were incredibly complex and seemed to be beyond the capacity of the organizer. Moreover, Barr and Lloyd who both accompanied the party on its Atlantic crossing were different in almost every respect. While it is probably true that Barr was incompetent, it seems equally true that Lloyd ruthlessly thrust him aside and took control. The accounts of the trek from Saskatoon to Lloydminster and the vicissitudes connected with it has often been told at length. Eventually the destination was reached and the colony was established. By that time Lloyd was firmly in control. Hence, when the Britannia colony became a reality, its central town was named Lloydminster.

As events turned out, the colony did not develop as the neat, compact settlement which had originally been intended. For a number of reasons, settlement was distributed over twenty or more townships and the intimacy of near neighbours was lost. Other settlers, not always of Anglo-Saxon origin, arrived over the years and took up intervening homesteads. Thus the hopes of a closely integrated community were shattered and the desire of a tightly-knit British Anglican settlement was never realized.

Official Anglicanism saw itself taking advantage of an established society in Canada, as the title of Vernon's book suggests: *The Old Church in the New Dominion.* For both the church leaders and the rank and file of church members, the idea of *continuity* was an important feature of the Anglican ethos. The underlying principle of British policy, certainly during the nineteenth century, was to carry the life and tradition of older communities into the far places of the earth. The monthly magazine of the C. & C.C.S. was significantly named *The Greater Britain Messenger.* The prairies were dotted with wooden Gothic churches with battlemented towers. At the height of the gold rush a missionary in Dawson City could write of his Easter services that they were "fully choral, alms and all. In the evening we had one of Stainer's anthems . . ." emphasizing the similarity to the church from which he had come in Montreal. The concept of a continuing tradition was profoundly important. Anglicans, to the extent that they thought about it at all, did not come to build the New Jerusalem—they brought it with them. But, lest that sound arrogant, they were sadly aware that the Church of God is a "school for sinners" rather than a "museum for saints."

If, however, Anglicanism stood for a continuing tradition, it also stood for flexibility and accomodation to changing times and places. In Anglicanism, the twin ideas of continuity and flexibility are paramount. The officers of the C.M.S. never tired of speaking of the *euthanasia* of their missions. By this they meant that they looked forward to the day when the missions they had established would blossom into indigenous native churches. It is true that the Parent Committee of the Society did not always realize the implications of what they were saying and, not surprisingly, the local missionaries were slower in loosening the controls than they might have been.

Slowly, perhaps too slowly, the Anglican Church of Canada (it did not assume the title until 1955) began to assume a distinctive Canadian identity within the wider Anglican tradition. The church was electing its own bishops as early as 1857. The first western bishop to be so elected was William Day Reeve in 1891. Since that time, all but one of the bishops in the ecclesiastical province of Rupert's Land, have been elected by provincial or diocesan synods. At the same time, until the Second World War, most of the parochial clergy were recruited from the British Isles. Whether this was good or bad, whether the Church could have been staffed otherwise, is now academic. What is certain is that the clergy, different in accent if not in temperament, left an impression that this was the "English Church" interested only in those of British origin.

Anglicanism on the prairies may be seen as the continuation and expansion of the Catholic Faith as received by the Church of England. In spite of some dramatic exceptions, its greatest fault may have been its failure to respond with sufficient speed to the adjustments and accommodations made necessary by the exigencies of a new land.

What has all this to do with the building of the New Jerusalem on the prairies? The editor of this volume has invited us to consider two principles in this connection: first, that the vision of the New Jerusalem is the gift of God, and second, that the vision was given to a pilgrim people. While no Christian would deny these principles in general terms, it seems unlikely that Anglican settlers, as distinct from clergy and ministers, saw them as the motivating force for their migration. There were other and more pressing considerations.

But this does not mean that the vision of the New Jerusalem, or as St. Augustine called it, the "City of God", was absent from the minds of the Anglican settlers. Rather, they thought of it in another way. The Puritan, and indeed any member of a "gathered church", tended to see the congregation as a sort of realized New Jerusalem. In their better moments at least, the Anglicans were sadly aware of the shortcomings of their tradition and realized that the New Jerusalem, desirable as it undoubtedly was, would probably not be achieved on this side of the grave.

And what of the idea of pilgrimage? That, too, was seen by the Anglicans but in a much longer perspective. Certainly they were engaged in a pilgrimage. It was, however, not one which had begun when they first stepped on prairie soil but rather it had begun in the distant past. It was not a pilgrimage which they had initiated but one which they had inherited and into which they had entered. This can be seen in many hymns, such as the two following:

We are travelling home to God
In the way our parents trod;
They are happy now, and we
Soon their happiness shall see.

A noble army—men and boys,
    The matron and the maid;
Around the Saviour's throne rejoice,
    In robes of light arrayed.
They climbed the steep ascent of heaven,
    Through peril, toil, and pain:
O God, to us may grace be given
    To follow in their train.

In short, Anglicans were well aware of the precious gift of the vision of the New Jerusalem; they were aware of their vocation as being on a pilgrimage but they also saw themselves as part of a long procession of history and tradition transcending locality and time. It has been part of the Anglican ethos to carry this vision and sense of tradition into the new world and to share it with all who would accept it.

VI Protestants
Prairie visionaries of the New Jerusalem: The United and Lutheran Churches in western Canada

B. G. Smillie

N. J. Threinen

A chapter on Canadian prairie Protestants presents several challenges. The first challenge is to distinguish the main theological doctrines which constituted the Protestant theology of building the New Jerusalem, using the United church and the Lutheran churches as representative of these beliefs. The reason why these two denominations have been selected is not because they possess the doctrinal patents on Protestant theology, but because the United and Lutheran churches numerically represent nearly forty per cent of the religious affiliations on the prairie (see graph p. 74.) However, it must be recognized that the continuing Presbyterian Church in Canada, the Baptists and other smaller Protestant groups had a similar outlook on the doctrinal positions that characterized the United and Lutheran churches. A second challenge in this chapter is to provide a sympathetic portrayal of how the theological outlook of these churches shaped the religious outlook of the settlers at the beginning of this century. The final challenge is to examine with critical honesty the beliefs of Protestants. This last task is especially important because many prairie Protestants have come from the wealthiest and best educated class of settlers. Yet oftentimes they have seen their own origins as humble and thus have not recognized their power to shape ideas. It is imperative therefore, to contemplate the significance of what Karl Marx, a social political analyst from a different culture, said:

> The ideas of the ruling class are in every age the ruling ideas: i.e.
> the class which is the dominant material force in society is at the

same time its dominant intellectual force. The class which has the means of material production at its disposal has at the same time control over the means of mental production, so that in consequence the ideas of those who lack the means of mental production are in general subject to it![1]

Although this observation was made by Marx in 1845-46 from within the European stage of history, the interdependent material/intellectual force he indentified is still with us in the hands of the powerful. The influence of this force becomes apparent through analysis not only of a society's culture, economics, and politics, but also of its theology.

Especially is this influence manifest in the formulating of three major Christian doctrines which shaped Protestantism on the prairies and its outlook on how to live in the world: the doctrine of election which divided the "sheep from the goats"; the doctrine of moral perfection, given impetus in the vision of a New Jerusalem as an earthly kingdom of righteousness; and the doctrine of two kingdoms, the heavenly (or celestial) and the earthly (or terrestrial) which gave Christians a heavenly goal while living as "pilgrims and strangers on earth."

The doctrine of election was emphasized by Presbyterians in the United Church and also supported by other churches including the continuing Presbyterian Church in Canada, the Congregationalists in the United Church, and the Baptists. The doctrine gave great tenacity to the missionary endeavours of the first pioneers. Unfortunately, it too often became perverted into an Anglophone elitism with racist overtones. The doctrine of moral perfection (rooted in Methodism and the United Church but also given wide support in the "holiness" tradition in other churches) was easily blended into the theology of Baptists, Pentecostals and various fundamentalist sects. This strong moral emphasis, while providing an important moral conscience for society, particularly in setting high goals for the settlers, became reduced to an individualistic moralism and a strong temptation to turn the church into a moral policeman for society. The doctrine of the two kingdoms was given its clearest emphasis by the Lutheran churches in Canada.

Lutheranism, largely prevented by language from exerting the same degree of influence on the culture, economics, and politics of the prairie society, suffered a similar distortion of the major Christian doctrine which shaped its identity—the doctrine of the two kingdoms. Under the prominent influence of eighteenth century European pietism, Luther's teaching of the two-fold governance of God (spiritual and temporal) became the separation of the church and the world. While the doctrine of the two kingdoms, as this development was called, allowed Lutherans as individuals to function in both the spiritual and the temporal realms, it was felt improper for the church to become involved with business and government. As well, Luther's comments on the question of civil disobedience and its limitations, interpreted through seventeenth century Lutheran orthodoxy and eighteenth century pietism, resulted in most Lutherans as individuals being pietistically patriotic or simply uninvolved.

While the problem of non-involvement had a tendency to make Protestant groups with this outlook support the status quo, this emphasis on the separation of the two kingdoms provided an important political dimension in the growth of Protestant sects in the West. Their spirit of non-conformity where emphasis is on a celestial city is particularly represented in the rise of Social Credit and its biblical fundamentalism with the sectarian appeal of William Aberhart and Ernest Manning. But on the whole the contribution of the heavenly-bound theology of the sect members was very political in an unconscious way. As S. D. Clark explains,

> The indifference of the religious sect to politics provided a healthy corrective to tendencies within the church to become greatly occupied with political matters and so entrenched in the political interests of the state. It was in the teachings of religious sectarianism that the threat to liberal principles through the alliance of church and state was most effectively met.[2]

In expanding the three main doctrines outlined above, it is possible to see how they have taken shape in the history of the United Church of Canada and the Lutheran Churches in Western Canada.

The doctrine of election and the western immigrant

Contemporary Canadian society takes pride in not being fanatical and insists on the importance of being flexible and pragmatic. Hence, the idea that peoples of a nation, a race, or a church consider themselves "elect", appears to be the height of arrogance, as indicated in the following parody on election:

> We are the choice elected few,
> Let all the rest be damned.
> There is room enough in hell for you
> We won't have heaven crammed.[3]

In its intention, the doctrine of election is not for the elite but for those who serve. Originating in the Old Testament and first formulated in its Protestant version by John Calvin (1509-1564), this doctrine puts primary emphasis on the sovereignty of God. To believe in God's sovereignty is to emphasize the primacy of God's love. This emphasis is poetically presented by the Scottish Psalter:

> The Lord our God is good
> His mercy is forever sure,
> His truth at all times firmly stood
> And shall from age to age endure.[4]

It is this assurance that gave the Protestant missionary confidence to work and to endure the prairie hardships because everything was in God's hands. The missionaries understood that God's sovereign love expresses itself in the servanthood of the disciple.

Initially, this "servanthood" understanding of "sovereignty" appears to be in reverse to general usage. But Jesus clarifies the reversal, saying: "He who would be greatest amongst you must be servant of all (Matt. 23:11)." The powerful sense of God's calling among the prairie missionaries was evident in their endurance of isolation for prolonged periods of time on meagre salaries so that they might be servants of the Word of God amongst the people. But if the missionaries did sense that they were chosen by God, and if they were confident that all human situations were under God's control, what prevented them from sitting back and leaving it all to God? John Calvin's exposition of the doctrine of election sheds light on the missionaries' conviction: "If the end of election is holiness of life it ought to arouse us and stimulate us strenuously to aspire to it instead of serving as a pretext for sloth."[5]

But the stumbling block in the doctrine of election is its implication that some people are chosen by God and others are damned. Because of this implication, this hard doctrine has often been called predestination. It has also been frequently used by some Presbyterians as a test of orthodoxy. This orthodoxy test is exemplified in the amusing apocryphal story about a theologically liberal student who stood before a conservative ordination committee of the Presbyterian church in the United States. As his orthodoxy was being tested prior to ordination, he was asked, "Do you believe in original sin?" "Yes," was his response. "Do you believe that some are elected to salvation and others to damnation?" "Yes," was the more hesitant answer. Then came the toughest

The Evangelical Lutheran Church of Canada

Jon Judt, a Lutheran pastor, in front of his parsonage, Morse, Saskatchewan, 1913.

The powerful sense of God's calling (election) among the Prairie missionaries was evident in their endurance in isolation for prolonged periods of time on meagre salaries so that they might be servants of the Word of God amongst the people.

question, "Would you be willing to be damned to the glory of God?" To this his reply was prompt, "I would go further; I would be willing to see this whole committee damned to the glory of God!"

The theological profundity in the student's response is not immediately apparent. Paul, the apostle to the Gentiles, in the ninth chapter of the Epistle to the Romans discusses why the Jews have rejected Jesus. He explains that God has hardened the hearts of the Jews and has made the Gentiles the chosen people. In the eleventh chapter of Romans he asks, can the Gentiles now boast that they are privileged? Definitely not, says Paul, as he reminds the Roman church that all have fallen short of God's intention for them. But, adds Paul, "God has consigned all to disobedience that he may have mercy upon all (Rom. 11:32)." As anticipated by the student in his reply, we are damned and saved together. This, then, is important for understanding the Protestant missionaries' view of work among those they often called "the heathen" and those whose brand of Christianity they considered to be "inferior" (for example, Roman Catholics were referred to as the papists). Phrases such as these

RELIGIOUS AFFILIATION ON THE PRAIRIES

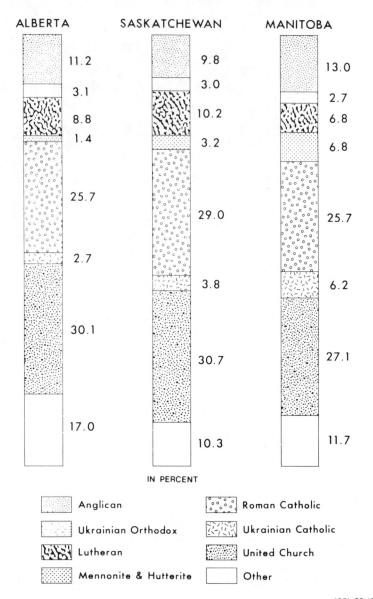

ALBERTA

11.2
3.1
8.8
1.4
25.7
2.7
30.1
17.0

SASKATCHEWAN

9.8
3.0
10.2
3.2
29.0
3.8
30.7
10.3

MANITOBA

13.0
2.7
6.8
6.8
25.7
6.2
27.1
11.7

IN PERCENT

Anglican   Roman Catholic

Ukrainian Orthodox   Ukrainian Catholic

Lutheran   United Church

Mennonite & Hutterite   Other

1971 CENSUS

simultaneously admit and reveal denigration and kinship, damnation and salvation.

But almost imperceptibly, the doctrine of election became perverted to a secular doctrine of Social Darwinism espoused by both church and non-church people. The American historian, Richard Hoftsadter, points out that in the last three decades of the nineteenth century it became clear that "England gave Darwin to the world, but the United States gave Darwinism an unusually quick and sympathetic reception."[6] Darwinism fitted into the economic philosophy of *laissez-faire* capitalism and sanctified the success stories of the industrial tycoons. Herbert Spencer, an English sociologist, cushioned the pessimism of those who were not successful in climbing the economic ladder by assuring them that regardless of immediate hardships for the majority of humanity, evolution meant progress. Hence, whether or not individuals "made it" themselves, the assumption was that they were on the winning team.

However, it was Josiah Strong, a prodigious writer for the American Home Mission Board of a United States mainline church, who gave Social Darwinism a theological base. Strong emphasized that in the struggle of the races, the race that would come to the top would be the Anglo-Saxon. "There is to be no reasonable doubt," he said, "that North America is to be the great home of the Anglo-Saxon, the principal seat of his power, the centre of his life and influence." Strong affirmed that the Anglo-Saxon race would rapidly decay except for the "salt of Christianity." Appealingly seductive to the frontier Canadian was Strong's emphasis on western geography and the cold climate. In the past, claimed Strong, the weak nations had been overcome by wars and, as a consequence, those who constituted the poorer human specimens had been eliminated.[7] The only difference between Strong's United States version of Social Darwinism and the Canadian brand which flourished during the same period was that while Strong predicted that the United States would hold "the principal seat of power," the Canadian view held that the future lay in the rugged North West.

But pervading these Darwinistic doctrines was an underlying racism. In Canada, it took many forms. In *The Christian Guardian*, James Woodsworth (J.S. Woodsworth's father) approvingly quoted an unknown writer who said: "Thirty below weather is relieving Canada of the Negro problem and is keeping out the lazy and improvident white."[8] Robert Haliburton, a member of the "Canada First" movement, spoke lyrically in a rhetorical way when he said: "May not our snow and frost give us what is more value than gold or silver, a healthy hardy dominant race."[9]   It is interesting to note that Haliburton's lecture had to be given in the summer because ill health forced him to spend his winters in warmer climates! Presbyterian Rev. A. J. McLeod, in his report on Indian work at the Regina Industrial School in 1892, emphasized the same Anglophone racism by making English the language of civilization. He said, "There never was a period in our history as a school when so little Indian was spoken. I have not heard an Indian word for days."[10] And in recounting the work of James Sutherland (a Presbyterian elder in the Red River Area in 1811), Edmund Oliver says his arrival was seen as "the sunrise of Christianity in this benighted land."[11] Other examples of racism pertained to the arrival of immigrants who were defined as "a swelling tide of Empire in righteousness and truth."[12]   Doukhobors were considered to be "flouting Canadian ideals. . . . Their children will rise up and call us blessed if they become Anglicized."[13]   Ruthenians were described as "poor dirty ignorant Slavs."[14]

   With such insulting denigrations based on Social Darwin Anglo-Saxon superiority, is it surprising that Indians, Metis and minority ethnic groups have reacted with bitterness? The Protestant mind set, which equated being British with being "civilized" and "godly", constituted a serious form of condescending oppression.

   However, there were also missionaries who, while they possessed this Anglophone mentality, nevertheless exemplified dedication and service as apostles of God's call. One such was Rev. James Evans, a Britisher who introduced Methodism to western Canada on his arrival in 1840.   He established a church and a school at Norway House in northern Manitoba, the centre of converging canoe routes on the western frontier. His greatest achievement was to make "birch bark talk."[15] By reducing Cree to an alphabet of eight consonants and four vowels (nine characters in four positions), he invented a simple but complete syllabic system for the Cree language.[16]

   Another Methodist missionary was R. T. Rundle (Mount Rundle in the western Rockies was named after him). His sense of election and mission is best seen through his own writings which were collated by Rev. Gerald Hutchinson into *The Rundle Journal*. Rundle worked in Canada for eight years. In 1846 (six years after he had begun travelling the western missionary circuit, most of the time in Alberta) Rundle wrote from Carlton House to the Methodist Missionary Society in London:

> I have abundant reason to bless God for his gracious dealings
> toward me since I have landed in the far distant Saskatchewan.

He has shielded me, unworthy as I am, in the hour of danger, both from the strife of tongues and amid the perils of the wilderness. May He ever guide me by his counsel and after death receive me to glory![17]

In another section of his journal, Rundle's letter to "Uncle Benjamin" gives poetic insight as he describes his harmonizing of the missionary zeal of the Christian faith with the natural habitat of the native people:

We bend our course again toward the West and to the Rocky Mountains before us like stern monuments of a world that once was. How majestically their towering peaks shout into the midnight heavens . . . look however into their recesses. There you behold the sons of the forest . . . amid their vast solitudes. Gaze again and enliven the scene. On many of the children have been fixed the sacramental seals of baptism and in many a tent is raised an altar to the God of Israel. The power of the cross has attracted them and like the prophet in the wilderness they have turned aside to see what the great sight meant.[18]

The Presbyterian missionaries' sense of God's election was similar to that of the Methodists. Oliver's *History of Saskatchewan* outlines Presbyterian exploits. Rev. J. Black, the First Presbyterian ordained minister, arrived at Selkirk in Manitoba around 1851, some forty years after the original request for a minister for this area. At his induction service September 28, 1851, at Kildonan, Manitoba, a letter was read to him from Dr. Robert Burns, minister at Knox Church, Toronto. The letter has the authority of a minister giving God's instruction to a fellow worker:

You are called at an early period of life to a most important duty, and on the manner in which you shall discharge it will depend, under God, the position which we as a Church may be called upon to occupy in regard to the progress of Christ's Kingdom in these western regions.[19]

Black worked amongst the Red River settlers for over thirty years.
The Protestant doctrine of election provides some insights into the motivation of Protestant missionaries who possessed a strict sense of being agents of God's call to serve people who they believed needed to be brought from darkness to light. Closely tied to this call was the common purpose most Protestants shared in establishing the Kingdom of God. It produced both heroism and bigotry. The

judgement of history is still to bring in its verdict on how well they performed.

The New Jerusalem takes shape in moral perfectionism

> It is the hour of highest privilege and duty. We are laying the foundations of empire in righteousness and truth. The heralds of the Cross must follow the adventurous pioneer to the remotest settlement of the Saskatchewan, the Qu'Appelle and the Peace River and the vast regions beyond.[20]

These words, from the 1883 report of General Conference of the Methodist Church of Canada, convey not only a strong sense of election but also of commitment, and reflect why Methodism had a powerful impact on the West. Emphasizing good behaviour rather than complicated doctrine, a theology based on moral perfection stressed a religion of good works, something that the smallest child or the most sophisticated business man could identify clearly. John Wesley, under whose Reform ideas British Methodism was founded, endorsed a practical religion easily understood in the everyday events of life. In his sermon based on Isaiah 5:4 and entitled, "On God's Vineyard," Rev. John Wesley attacked those who "bring forth wild grapes"—those who live in "the pride of life" wearing fancy clothes and living for the "pleasures of the imagination." He castigated the rich for their greed. "Do you put a knife to your throat when you sit down to meat, is not your belly your god?" He saw the danger of a life of carousing, engaging in "drinking and other pleasures of the senses."[21]

In this tradition of establishing a kingdom of moral righteousness, Saskatoon was founded in 1882 under the auspices of the Temperance Colonization Society. In the same year that it was incorporated an ambitious settlement programme was initiated, where "alcoholic beverages should not be manufactured or sold."[22] The Temperance Colony idea sought to found an oasis of moral purity. It had originated among clergy and members of the Methodist Church in Ontario. The Colonization Society was incorporated with a capital stock of $2,000,000 made up of $100 shares.[23] The Western historian, Lewis H. Thomas, describes how John Lake, a former Methodist minister who had moved into the real estate business in Toronto, set out in 1882 with a party to survey the land for the Colony and establish a townsite. "While camping along the east bank of the river between Clark's crossing and the Sioux reserve," Lake noted, "We camped on the hill over the river thinking that it was a fine spot for a town. [This site was probably in the vicinity of the present Nutana Collegiate.] At the bend of the river on the south and east side the bank gradually rises to a hill or plateau."[24] Lake saw the even heights on either side of the river as a good location for a railway bridge in the near future. The sight of saskatoon berries growing close by inspired John Lake and his party to name the new Temperance Colony "Saskatoon." In 1883, to attract newcomers, the colonists placed an advertisement in the June 21st edition of the *Regina Leader* which said "Homes for all where they will be forever free from the accursed influence of the liquor traffic."[25] By 1885 the Colony was incorporated in the city of Saskatoon. The short life of the Colony is explained by Thomas:

> In 1884 a dispute arose between the government and the Society regarding the latter's attempt to enforce their temperance policy on applicants for homestead lands within their tract.[26]

Sir David MacPherson, the acting Minister of the Interior, in 1881 had given the organizers of the Temperance Colony the impression that they would receive a solid block of land where alcoholic liquor would be banned. The Colony's publicity had reflected this outlook. "This led to charges of fraud against the organizers when it became known that the government would not permit the company to enforce temperance principles on homesteaders."[27] The temperance scheme was abandoned by 1886. But the incentive to found a kingdom of righteousness built on the pure moral life continued to take many forms in the temperance movement, long after the demise of the Temperance Colony.

The general intent of building a kingdom of righteousness found its theological source in the Social Gospel, a theology that reacted against the political quietism of Protestant orthodoxy. This theological position (spurred on in the United States by the worst excesses of the Industrial Revolution) emphasized that God would immediately respond when called on and would not be limited to inscrutable undisclosed plans. The emphasis was on "humanity first" instead of on the transcendence of God, hence, God became the projection of the highest ethical ideals. As well, social perfection was stressed in the hope that everyone could help to change society from secular to sacred by acts of moral goodness. A reason why this movement had impact was that it combined its theological idealism with a strong social-political analysis of the conditions under which people lived.

It is interesting to observe what the eschatological vision in which theological emphasis is on building the kingdom of heaven meant to the Protestant missionaries as the churches became established. James Woodsworth, as superintendent of Methodist missions in western Manitoba and the North West Conference with a responsibility for establishing Methodist churches from the Lakehead to Vancouver Island, was reassured in his mission as he saw Methodists grow in number from 5,038 in 1886 to 9,895 in 1890.[28] His writing reveals a cosmic optimism. On the completion of the Canadian Pacific Railway in 1885, he described a church service called to celebrate the driving of the Last Spike. The service was held amongst the rocky peaks in the canyon. As the words from the hymn "All hail the power of Jesus' Name" echoed back from the mountains "Crown him, Crown him", Woodsworth said (quoting a member of the congregation), "It seemed to me the angels were calling on us to take this land for Christ."[29] In the midst of this theological idealism, there was also a strong practicality in these church leaders. James Robertson (who was Superintendent of Missions in the Presbyterian Church at the same time as Woodsworth was working for the Methodists) said that when he was recruiting ministers in Britain for arduous work on the frontier, the criterion he used for assessing qualifications was expressed in the words, "I would rather have a man know less Latin and more horse."[30]

The next generation of writers, commenting again out of the practical experience of the missionary frontiers, interpreted eschatology in more immanental terms—they grounded the Christian hope in the practical world of social analysis and politics without losing sight of a New Jerusalem vision of a better world.[31] This eschatological trend was illustrated by two leaders, one a Methodist, J. S. Woodsworth, the other a Presbyterian, Edmund Oliver. J. S. Woodsworth, considered to be the founder of the Cooperative Commonwealth Federation party, was well known as the "Bishop to the Immigrants," particularly during his life in Winnipeg. From 1907 to 1913, he was Superintendent of the All Peoples Mission and later, he served as Director of the Bureau for Social Research for the three prairie provinces. However, he was dismissed in 1916 from this latter post for criticizing the "National Service Registration Scheme."[32] Woodsworth saw this scheme as a clandestine design to lead Canada into a policy of conscription. Aware that many immigrants had come to Canada to escape "militarism," Woodsworth prepared an article with charts (published by the Bureau of Social Research) which showed that the population increase in Canada between 1901 and 1914 was

2,906,022. This figure was particularly impressive alongside the total population of Canada which in 1901 was 5,371,315.[33] In this setting, it is not surprising that he was alarmed at a registration drive which would turn immigrants into potential "canon fodder" when conscription came.

Some historians have interpreted Woodsworth as having an Anglo-Saxon bigoted attitude toward these immigrants. This interpretation lacks archival research on the development of Woodsworth's outlook on the immigrant.[34] That he was a champion against their exploitation is apparent in his words:

> We have talked long enough about assimilating the immigrants. To what are we to assimilate them? After what likeness are we to fashion them? Our own? Heaven forbid. We are not good enough, or attractive enough. These immigrant peoples have a great contribution to make to Canadian life. They may help us to create a higher type, which will embody the best elements of all . . . 'God has many best' is the way in which a wise teacher once put it . . . We Canadians need a catholicity of spirit, and still more, perhaps imagination, and, above all, a great and worthy ideal.[35]

Another characteristic of the Social Gospel that had a strong influence on building the hope of prairie people was the emphasis on local control and the spirit of cooperation. This emphasis on local and regional control was strong in the United Church of Canada which was formed in 1925 by the union of the Methodist, Presbyterian, Congregational and Local Union Churches. But the spirit of cooperation, particularly stressed by Edmund Oliver, derived much impetus through the Social Gospel and appealed to the general spirit of sharing on the prairie. Edmund Oliver, in his history entitled "The New Spirit, Cooperation and Radicalism," surveyed community cooperation on the international and prairie scenes. Writing in the middle of the Depression, he said:

> One of the most remarkable and hopeful features of western life is the extraordinary development of the community spirit. In the freer air of the far reaching prairies . . . It meant much for a place to get a good start. The phenomenon known as "boosting" was after all, a kind of place or regional loyalty, an attempt to give a character or identity to place or village or community that it might be distinguished as progressive, and its interests and growth fostered and developed. Economic conditions fostered a disposition to get together to solve

common problems. Old time political ties and denominational loyalties were greatly loosened in the West. Farmers were neither Liberal or Conservative but Grain Growers. Denominational sectarianism was a reproach. In place of all this came a community spirit, a desire to organize and integrate local forces, to develop a provincial consciousness to work out a method of united action.[36]

An important observation made by Oliver was that the spirit of cooperation was all-embracing. There were cooperatives for creameries, elevators, and hail insurance, cooperative purchasing (binder twine, fences, flour, feed) and marketing (live stock), and cooperatives in large school units in rural municipalities. And the apex of cooperation was the union movement in the churches which culminated in the formation of the United Church of Canada.

While Oliver outlined the spirit of cooperation as a progressive movement, those who have lived on the prairie know that it has also been a reactionary movement. Because it accepted the ideology of control by local opinion, this movement was slow to initiate change. For example, the Homestead for Women Movement of 1901 arose in reaction against the discriminating limitations of the Dominion Lands Act of 1872 which stipulated that "every person who is the sole head of the family or any male eighteen years of age or over is eligible to 160 acres of free homestead land in the surveyed portion of the West."[37] But for a woman to be eligible, she had to be "head of the family"—widowed, separated, divorced, or deserted with dependent children under eighteen years of age.

Spearheaded by Isabel Beaton Graham (Women's Editor of the Grain Grower's Guide) and Lillian Laurie (Women's Editor of the Manitoba Free Press), the Homestead for Women Movement increased public awareness, but it did not succeed in winning homestead rights of ownership for women.[38] The situation in Alberta and Saskatchewan improved in two stages. In 1910, the Alberta legislature passed a Married Women's Relief Act which authorized a judge to overrule a man's will if he left his wife an inadequate (less than one-third) inheritance. The Saskatchewan Devolution Estates Act of 1919 made the same provision. Stage two came in the Saskatchewan Homestead Act and the Alberta Married Women's Home Protection Act, both passed in 1919. Under this legislation, a husband was forbidden to sell, mortgage, transfer or bequest the family home or the land on which it stood without his wife's written consent. In Manitoba, these two provisions became law under the Dower Act of 1918.

However, one piece of progressive action relating to the professional self-consciousness of women did originate in the United Church of Canada. This was the ordination of women. In Protestant churches, although the largest number of members attending church are women, denominations have been tardy in supporting their ordination to the ministry of Word and Sacrament. The traditional arguments that continue to oppose female ordination are that Jesus had twelve male disciples, and that apostolic succession of church leadership has historically been male. Underlying this patriarchal domination has been the assumption that there is a certain order of creation which puts men above women. Several Pauline texts have been used to reinforce this subjugation, for example, "Let a woman learn in silence with all submissiveness. I permit no woman to teach or have authority over men, she is to keep silent (I Tim. 1:12-13)." Against these scriptural passages supporting the suppression of women in the church, Edmund Oliver waged a successful campaign to have Lydia Gruchy ordained in 1936. Using Paul's words (Gal. 3: 27-28) as his central text, Oliver gave an address in 1935 in which he said:

Some will claim that there is no demand for the ordination of women. There *is* the demand of simple justice, for women carry the burden of the church work no less than do men. . . . the church that sprang out of the teaching of the New Testament believed that in 'Christ Jesus there is neither male or female.' There is the demand made by the neglect of the great opportunity of service in unsupplied fields waiting cultivation that in some cases women could best give. Why should a church refuse ordination to a Lydia Gruchy? She attended St. Andrew's College. She stood head of her class each year. She has served on difficult fields now for eleven years doing all the work of the ministry. Is it fair to expect a male candidate for the ministry to serve twelve months on a field, and to ask Miss Gruchy to put in an apprenticeship of fourteen years? She has had some of the most difficult fields in the church. She preaches at seven different points and does everything that a man does except that when she has prepared a class of young boys and girls for communion she has to say, 'I am a woman. You must receive the Bread and Wine on Sunday next from a stranger.' Lydia E. Gruchy will doubtless be the first ordained woman in the United Church of Canada—a worthy contribution to the Saskatchewan Conference she has so long served and so ardently loved.[39]

In 1935, Edmund Oliver died at the age of 53; in 1936, Lydia Gruchy was ordained to the ministry of the United Church of Canada.

In summary, the United Church of Canada, a major Protestant denomination on the prairies, had a doctrine of election based on a high commitment to serve the frontier people of western Canada. God's hand was seen in the bleakest settings of missionary endeavour. But while espousing Anglo-Saxon cultural values of "teaching everyone English" and extolling the British way of life, the missionaries failed to recognize that they were simultaneously expounding an elitist social Darwinism because they looked upon themselves as common folk of the frontier. Since their hope for building the kingdom of Christ was closely tied with their hope of building a "kingdom of righteousness" in Canada, their idealism was always anchored in the practical issues of survival in a harsh environment. And although they believed they were champions of minority groups, they often appeared as racist proselytizers. As for the ordination of Lydia Gruchy, perhaps this was a token response to the liberation of women, but when viewed alongside the position of some churches on this issue today, it did indicate that the United Church was fifty years ahead of most other Protestant denominations.

The doctrine of the two kingdoms and the Lutheran immigrant

The Lutheran immigrants who flowed into the Canadian prairies were a diverse group coming from many different countries and speaking about eight different languages. Many of them came directly from Europe—the Icelandic and the German-speaking settlers were predominantly in this category, although most of the latter came not from Germany but from scattered German colonies in eastern Europe and Russia. Many others came from the United States. Most of these, among whom the Scandinavian settlers predominated, were however, only a generation removed from their European origins. All of them came with one goal in mind—to acquire land which would enable them to pursue their earthly calling and to provide more adequately for their families.

The influx of Lutheran immigrants to the prairies in turn prompted home missionaries to be sent by Lutheran bodies which had developed in the United States. Although sometimes there was bitter rivalry among these home missionaries due to the fractured state of Lutheranism at the time even within the same language groups, they all had a single purpose—to serve the spiritual needs of the Lutheran immigrants by gathering them into local congregations and by ministering to them with Word and Sacrament. The dedication with which these home missionaries attended to their task can be seen in a report by a Winnipeg-based pastor, Hermann Buegel, dating from the year 1892. His report echoes the experience of many others:

> In one month I travelled 900 miles by train and 130 miles partly by wagon and partly on foot. In eight months I travelled a total of 7,000 miles. Last month I was home only three days.[40]

The object of Lutheran missionary activity was, by intent, narrowly confined to people who spoke the same language. The report comments:

> In Manitoba . . . there are not many Germans. Most of the inhabitants are English, Scandinavian or Indian. Scouring the area, I was able finally to establish six preaching stations of two, four or six (German) families. . . .[41]

Nonetheless these missionaries had a vision of a Lutheran Church flowering on the prairies. In line with the historic Lutheran Confessions which defined the church as the assembly of believers "among whom the Gospel is preached in its purity and the Holy Sacraments are administered according to the Gospel,"[42] the focus was on gathering the Lutheran immigrants into congregations. Yet the church, through its individual members, did not need to remain aloof from its society. Nor was this always the case. In the Lutheran doctrine of the two kingdoms, God was thought to work through the Christian's activity within society as surely as within the church. While the church was distinguished from society it was not to be separated from it; it was the other side of the coin.

Although the doctrine of the two kingdoms is attributed to Luther, one must recognize that he did not originate it. It must be seen as evolving against the backdrop of the apocalyptic New Testament tradition as transmitted through Augustine. In this tradition God's power in history is seen to be engaged in a relentless struggle with the kingdom of the devil until the end of time. God fights against this power of evil in every dimension of creaturely existence, with the ultimate intent of establishing his kingdom. To wage battle against the devil and to establish his kingdom, God works through the preaching of the Gospel to create faith by the power of the Holy Spirit and through works of love in which

Christians deal positively with others and with the world in which they live. For his two-fold governance (spiritual and temporal), God makes use of institutions set up by human "reason." (In the classic theological and philosophical sense reason is participating in what is good and true, promotes sharing in the good of all, and gives stability.) These institutions in Luther's time were the church, the state, and the economic institutions.[43]

The doctrine of the two kingdoms was for Luther yet another outgrowth of his emphasis on justification by grace through faith. Church and state have different functions. While the real purpose of the church is to proclaim the good news of God's grace in Christ, the state's is to ensure that people behave themselves. However, both the church and the state are contexts within which the Christian who has been justified by grace, not by works, responds to God's love by caring for the neighbour.[44] As Luther said in his advice to the Christian nobility:

> Just as those who are now called 'spiritual' . . . are neither different from other Christians nor superior to them, except that they are charged with the administration of the Word of God and the sacraments which is their work and office, so it is with the temporal authorities. They bear the sword and rod in their hand to punish the wicked and protect the good.[45]

Under the influence of the eighteenth century pietism, Lutherans stressed salvation for the individual and restricted Christianity largely to the personal inner sphere, with other spheres of life dualistically viewed as secular. The two spheres of God's activity through the Christian, which under Luther had been unified and complementary, were thereby effectively separated. In the United States' experience, through which most of the pastors and many of the Lutheran immigrants in western Canada passed, Luther's distinction between the spiritual and the temporal distorted by this subsequent individualistic-pietistic thinking, was easily identified with the American separation of church and state. A letter to Walter Rauschenbusch from a U.S. Lutheran church president, part of whose constituency was in western Canada, is illustrative:

> We believe in a vigorous and thorough treatment of social questions by Christians in the state, but we believe that this work should be done by them as citizens, and not as Christians. . . . We believe in the old-fashioned doctrine, which is good also for America, of the complete separation of the functions of church and state. . . .[46]

To be sure, there were some who felt that the church should not be restricted to preaching Gospel. At the very least, Lutherans building the kingdom of God on the prairies should also be involved in establishing Christian schools and charitable institutions. To do this it was important to consolidate the struggling and overlapping congregations which had developed as the different Lutheran bodies had each tried to reach the immigrants. Such a plan of consolidation was put forth as a proposal by Herbert Stuermer, a printer of a German newspaper in Regina in 1922.[47] While the proposal appears to echo the sentiments of the discussion under way in the merging United Church of Canada, its basis was more one of practical economics than of the Social Gospel. Yet it did call for a transcending of doctrinal differences among the churches and union under the general Lutheran banner. What finally halted the agitation for union of the German Lutherans in western Canada was the opposition of the church leaders. Under the doctrine of the two kingdoms, God provided for order in society and in the church. In the church the pastors had been placed in authority and bore the responsibility of ruling. Because the Stuermer proposal called for the authority of pastors to be bypassed, church leaders saw it as a proposal for anarchy, and Stuermer's own church president branded it "spiritual Bolshevism."[48]

Even those who opposed Stuermer's union proposal saw the need for the church to be active in matters touching on society, particularly that part of society which involved Lutheran people. One of the German Lutheran bodies in western Canada, the Missouri Synod, had a particularly great concern for schools. Wherever the missionaries of this body went they invariably taught school among the scattered immigrant communities. As the governments of the prairie provinces attempted to extend and upgrade their public school system, many of the church schools were closed by the public school inspectors who found them inadequate. Consequently a 1914 pastoral conference in Winnipeg held a lengthy debate about how the principle of the separation of church and state affects parochial schools. (The U.S. influence is apparent even in the way the problem was expressed.) A statement which was ultimately adopted was:

> When a Christian congregation calls a teacher candidate to teach in a public school then one has a mixing of church and state because thereby the congregation is imparting Christian instruction at the expense not of the church but of the state.[49]

The sharp separation of church and state in the matter of schools did not, however, prevent the same body from later requesting that its school board become a clearing house for matching up Lutheran teachers with public school districts in which the constituency was made up of Lutheran settlers.[50]

The ability of Lutheran churches to relate to matters touching society without technically mixing church and state is seen more clearly in the immigration societies of the 1920s. As early as 1914 representatives of the Canadian Pacific Railway had approached the Lutheran bodies with a plan for settling new immigrants in areas where their co-religionists had already established communities. The plan was appealing to the churches because the immigrants could be served spiritually without pastors continuing the pattern of seeking out scattered small communities. To tie in to the railway's plan the Lutheran Immigration Board of Canada (LIB) was formed by mission leaders of the three German Lutheran bodies in 1923. To avoid direct church involvement with the transportation companies and the government, however, the LIB was established as an organization of individual Lutheran pastors. While their strategic positions in the churches made the distinction almost academic, they could thereby be viewed as functioning individuals rather than as church representatives. The LIB ceased functioning when the Great Depression of the 1930s dried up the flow of immigrants. While it had come under severe criticism (from the church constituency which was not directly involved) for the way it functioned, and while it had become entangled in the railway rivalry of the times, the LIB did in fact enable the churches to be involved in the vital work of immigration.

Following World War II a similar challenge faced the Lutheran churches as a result of the 1945 Potsdam Conference which endorsed the decision of Soviet and east European authorities to expel the German-speaking minorities within their territories. The eviction of some ten million ethnic Germans along with those officially recognized as displaced persons confronted the western world with a refugee problem of even greater proportion. This time the Lutheran churches formally took action to establish an agency, Canadian Lutheran World Relief (CLWR), to work hand in hand with the government to address the refugee problem through material aid and by providing assistance to refugees to emigrate to Canada. Although the majority of the refugees were German-speaking, Lutheran bodies of every ethnic background became involved in the mammoth undertaking. CLWR worked in concert with other Christian groups to influence government policy on the refugees and otherwise to facilitate their immigration through the Canadian Christian Council

Lutheran Council in Canada

Immigrant group having coffee and cookies.

*The Lutheran churches formally took action to establish an agency, Canadian
Lutheran World Relief (CLWR), to work hand in hand with the government to
address the refugee problem through material aid and by providing assistance
to refugees to emigrate to Canada.*

for Resettlement of Refugees. In its international contracts CLWR
plugged into Lutheran World Service through which its efforts were
coordinated with similar agencies in other countries.

In spite of its intimate relationships with the Canadian
government and with the transportation companies, the activities of
CLWR were not restricted by the Lutheran two-kingdoms doctrine.
This is partly because of the overwhelming human need which
overrode all other considerations. Also Lutherans had begun to
emerge out of the isolationism caused by language and pietism.
Their greater openness to participation in the Christian ministry in
nonchurch contexts, both furthered and illustrated by their earlier
involvement in the Canadian chaplaincy program during World War
II made it possible for Lutherans to enter into involvements such as
those called for by CLWR's activities, albeit not directly through the
church but through a church agency.[51]

In reviewing the history of western Canadian Lutherans, the
feature most notable is their skill in setting up secular organizations
for immigration which simultaneously retained strong Lutheran
connections. Lutherans did not join the Social Gospelers in

criticizing the railways for their enormous land grants and profits. Neither did they take the side of the farm movements in the agrarian protest. The strong conviction to obey the authorities as agents of God's good order made Lutherans partners in the railway's immigration plans. However, they provided little help for other immigrants like the Chinese, the Japanese and the many ethnic groups who belonged to other religious affiliations. Even today, Lutherans have a tendency to favour their own confessional and ethnic groups as they determine who they will support. To obtain Lutheran sponsorship a Danish, Norwegian, Icelandic or German Lutheran background is helpful.

On the other hand, Lutherans did bring hope to many dispossessed people, particularly Germans uprooted after two world wars. Their support is remarkable in that it covers every facet of these people's lives, which includes providing opportunities for gainful employment. Like the descendants of United Church immigration, their communion membership is largely drawn from the upper middle class. And it is interesting to note that many environmental issues, for example, the movement against uranium mining and refining spearheaded by the Roman Catholic and United Churches, are receiving strong Lutheran support today. In addition, the Lutheran tendency to support only their own kind is changing. This can be seen in the support given to native groups in Canada and to measures being taken to alert people to injustices in Third World countries.

What has happened to the Protestant vision of the New Jerusalem? Is the naive liberal doctrine of progress still prevalent today? This vision is perhaps less optimistic than it has been, but today a tenacious vision of people (Protestant and other) for a better tomorrow is being upheld.

Always, there exists the danger of falling either into immobilizing cynicism which paralyzes action, or into rosy optimism that refused to look at reality. The American theologian, Reinhold Niebuhr, (noted for his political realism rather than for his optimism) provided an important insight into Christian hope. Writing in the middle of the Depression, he said:

> The inertia of society is so stubborn that no one will move against it if he cannot believe it to be more easily overcome than is actually the case. And no one will suffer the perils and pains involved in the process of radical social change, if he cannot believe in the possibility of a purer and fairer society than will ever be established.[52]

VII New Jerusalem on the prairies: Welcoming the Jews

Abraham Arnold

Jerusalem is indelibly inscribed in the past, the present, and the future of the Jewish people and may be traced back to the words of Isaiah: "For out of Zion shall go forth the law, And the word of the Lord from Jerusalem."[1] There was also the Psalmist who declared during the first captivity of the Jews in Babylon:

> If I forget thee, O Jerusalem,
> Let my right hand forget her cunning.
> Let my tongue cleave to the roof of my mouth,
> If I remember thee not. . . .[2]

And at every Passover Seder, Jews recite the words: "Next year in Jerusalem." Later Jewish interpreters have also proclaimed: "Jerusalem is destined to become a lantern to the nations . . . the metropolis of the world . . . [and] All nations, without exception, must go up towards Jerusalem . . ."[3]

Jewish tradition speaks only of returning to Jerusalem and of extending Jerusalem to the world. The concept of building a New Jerusalem finds its origin in the New Testament which is not part of Jewish tradition. The belief that immigrants came to western Canada to build a "New Jerusalem" on the prairie must therefore be seen primarily as a Christian concept.

In the light of the invertible proverb: "As the Christian, so the Jew," it may be suggested that the Jews who settled in western Canada—on the prairies—sometimes accepted too easily the Christian idea of "New Jerusalem" as synonymous with the Jewish memory of an eternal hope for Jerusalem. There are, however, revealing differences in the Jerusalem of the Jewish scriptures and the "New Jerusalem" of the New Testament. Isaiah said after the first captivity: "Jerusalem: She shall be built."[4] And, in the book of Tobit from the Apocrypha, it is proclaimed: "Jerusalem shall be built again as His house unto all the ages."[5] But it is the New Testament that speaks of "the holy city, New Jerusalem, coming down from God out of heaven . . ."[6] The first New Testament reference to New Jerusalem, which appears in Revelation, can hardly give comfort to the Jews since it follows by a mere three verses, these lines: "Behold, I will make them of the synagogue of Satan, which say they are Jews, and are not . . ."[7] While many Christians have indeed been willing to share the Jerusalem ideal with the Jews, there are others who have misused the deplorable "synagogue of Satan" concept. Thus the question to be considered as Jews settled in the west is: how well were they accepted by their Christian neighbours?

The first initiative for Jewish settlement in western Canada followed the intensification of anti-Jewish persecution in Russia in 1881. A meeting to protest the Russian persecution took place at the Mansion House, the Lord Mayor's residence in London, early in 1882. It was attended by the Archbishop of Canterbury and Cardinal Manning; by political leaders like the Earl of Shaftesbury and Alexander Galt, Canada's first High Commissioner to London; by members of the Rothschild family and other Jewish leaders.[8] This meeting led to the establishment of the Mansion House Committee to assist emigrants from Russia; Galt suggested that some of them might be sent to the west.

There was a clear religious motivation expressed in opposition to Russia's anti-Jewish laws. This is apparent, for example, in Cardinal Manning's words:

> . . . there are laws larger than any Russian legislation. . . . the laws of humanity, of nature and of God—which are the foundation of all other laws; and, if in any legislation these are violated, all nations of Christian Europe, the whole commonwealth of civilized and Christian men, would instantly acquire a right to speak out loud.

With what seems now like a prophetic vision, the Cardinal also referred to the "anti-Semitic movement in Germany" of the previous twelve months which he looked upon:

> . . . with abhorrence as tending to disintegrate the foundation of

social life, and secondly, with great fear lest it may tend to light
up an animosity which has already taken fire in Russia and may
spread elsewhere.[9]

Alexander Galt advised Sir John A. Macdonald that he had
written to one of the Rothschilds about settling some of the
"agricultural Jews" in Canada. He called them "a superior class of
people, partly farmers, but generally trade people."[10]

Support for a Jewish settlement project also came from John
Taylor who was the Icelandic agent at St. Andrews, Manitoba, and a
lay missionary with the British Canadian Bible Society. In a letter to
the Governor General, Lord Lorne, Taylor urged the same
consideration for the Jews as had been granted to the Icelanders. He
asked that a bloc of land be set aside:

> . . . to carry out the benevolent design of providing new homes
> (for the Jews) far removed from the cruelties and atrocities so
> shamefully perpetrated on this people in the name of religion.[11]

Taylor's letter was forwarded to the Prime Minister but if any
religious motivation affected Macdonald in his attitude to the Jews,
it came from a different source. First, he advised the Governor
General that Galt "has been attending to the Jews" and he added:
"We are quite ready to assign the Jews lands."[12]

In his reply to Galt, however, Macdonald referred to the Jews as
"The Old Clo' move," and said: "They would at once go in for
peddling and politics and be of as much use . . . as Cheap Jacks and
Chapmen."[13] Macdonald's attitude became even more revealing in a
second message to Galt in which he said:

> After years of ill-concealed hostility of the Rothschilds against
> Canada, you have made a great strike by taking up the old clo'
> cry, and going in for a Jew immigration into the Northwest. By
> following up this subject, and establishing a Jew colony here,
> whether ultimately successful or not, a link—a missing link—
> will be established between Canada and Sidonia.[14]

The comment about the Rothschilds probably referred to failed
efforts to obtain financial support from them toward construction of
the Canadian Pacific Railway. The reference to Sidonia recalls the
ancient Phoenician seaport of Sidon whose traders were denounced
for their practices by the Old Testament prophets.[15] It appears,
therefore, that whether he placed them in the contemporary role of
"Cheap Jacks" or in the biblical setting of "Sidonia", Macdonald

took a deprecating view of the prospective Jewish immigrants.

In the spring of 1882, when Winnipeg was being proclaimed the "Chicago of the Northwest," the first Russian Jews reached the city and thought they had arrived in a new "Mitzrayim"—a new land of Egyptian bondage. One of the new arrivals, S. F. Rodin, wrote back to a Jewish publication in Russia:

> They have sent us to a desolate place to become servants and maids to work for nothing for the local inhabitants (who) will build for themselves houses, palaces and fortresses and we will make the bricks. We will tread mud into clay with our feet which are bruised and fatigued from the wandering and tribulations we have endured.

A few months later Rodin began to change his mind. He reported that his first letter may have been a little exaggerated and wrote:

> Thank God, the situation has improved somewhat. We have gradually accustomed ourselves to the hard work . . . even the cultivated and well-bred among us have had to discard our starched shirts and shined shoes and have gotten down to work.

Rodin also described how the newcomers observed Rosh Hashanah, the Jewish New Year, "fully and completely" in a tent at a railway station forty miles from Winnipeg. They had taken up a collection among themselves and raised one hundred dollars with which they ordered "a fine Sefer Torah and a Shofar" (ram's horn) from New York City.

> On the New Year days we ceased from our labors and we gathered in a large tent. . . . We prayed and read out of the Sefer Torah. The local residents looked on with wonder and admiration, commenting: 'Look! though far removed from their homes and their people, they nevertheless make every effort to worship in the manner known to them'.[16]

It is in the sense of being free to conduct their own religious observances that Jews carry with them the belief in Jerusalem. But freedom of religion itself was not enough to turn a place into a Jewish "New Jerusalem." Jewish education for children was considered vital and as early as 1882 there were complaints about the lack of such facilities in Winnipeg. Over the years Winnipeg did develop its own Jewish schools. These were entirely religious schools at the outset but soon there were also schools that emphasized the Yiddish language and its literary and cultural heritage, a secular approach, and social justice. In this all-encompassing sense of Jewish religion and culture, Winnipeg eventually became known in some quarters as the "Jerusalem of North America" or at least the "Jerusalem of the West," since some other Jewish communities in North America probably claimed a similar title.

The "Jerusalem of . . ." title ascribed to a Jewish community in western Canada arose from remembrance of the East European Jewish heritage where the city of Vilna had become known as the Jerusalem of Lithuania because of its once flourishing Jewish culture.

The real test of Jewish acceptance into the New Jerusalem on the prairies must be related to land settlement because for decades, only those immigrants who were prepared to become farmers were encouraged to settle in the west. And many Jews did go west to take up land as did most other immigrants, but soon the view developed that they were not suited to land settlement and this view may have been one reason why more Jews did not take up farming.

Contrary to the belief that Jews had no farming background, in Europe there had been a Jewish back-to-the-land movement in the nineteenth century and for about sixty years (1805-1865) some Russian Jews were permitted to take up farming. Then, as anti-Jewish regulations and anti-Semitic repression came into play, land privileges were cancelled. As late as 1899, however, some 100,000 Jews were still farming in Russia.[17]

Jewish emigration from Russia was accelerated following the massacres of 1881 when an idealistic Jewish youth group founded the *Am Olam* back-to-the-land movement. *Am Olam*, Hebrew for "eternal people," implied that no people could be eternal without ties to the land.[18] Perhaps there was some *Am Olam* influence among the more than 300 Russian Jews who arrived in Winnipeg in the spring of 1882. However, in spite of promises made by government representatives, no land was available for them. Only through the further intervention of Sir Alexander Galt with the government in Ottawa was some land opened up in the spring of 1884.[19] But the dream for a better life on the land could not endure a two-year wait. Thus, by the time a site was assigned at Moosomin, most of the Jews had found other pursuits or had departed elsewhere. Only twenty-seven Jewish families were left to begin the land experiment which became known as "New Jerusalem."[20]

This "New Jerusalem" soon failed and within a few years the Jews who attempted to settle at Moosomin all turned to peddling, an occupation rejected by *Am Olam* as contrary to its ideal. But the

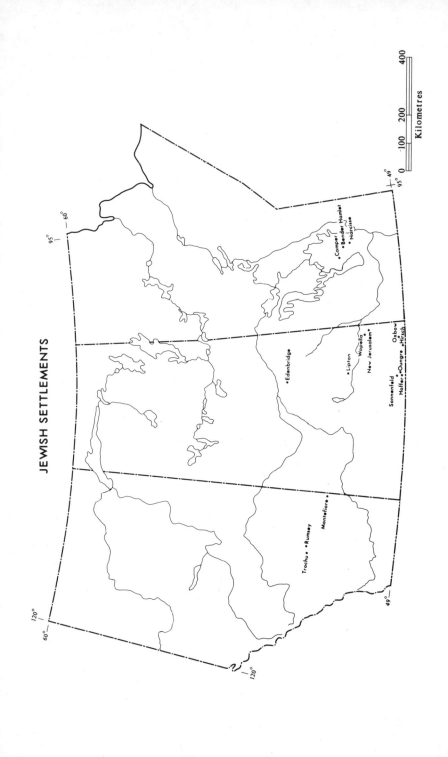

JEWISH SETTLEMENTS

Campers
Bender Hamlet
Narcisse

Edembridge
Lipton
Wapella
New Jerusalem

Sonnenfeld
Hoffer
Oungre
Oxbow
Hirsch

Montefiore
Trochu
Rumsey

Kilometres

0   100   200   400

Jewish Historical Society of Western Canada

Abraham Klenman at Wapella, reading a paper, 1890.

Within a few years of the failed experiment at Moosomin, another group of Jews began farming at Wapella. It was there, in the 1880's, that the ideal of returning to the land to become regenerated as a people became evident among religiously motivated Jewish homesteaders.

Jewish farmers at Moosomin did not fail just because they turned to peddling—they were pushed into peddling by three immediate and consecutive bad crop years.

Within a few years of the failed experiment at Moosomin, another group of Jews began farming at Wapella. It was there, in the late 1880s, that the ideal of returning to the land to become regenerated as a people became evident among religiously motivated Jewish homesteaders.

In 1886, a group of eight young Russian Jews took homesteads at Wapella with the help of Herman Landau, a London Jewish Financier, who obtained certain concessions from the CPR. Landau claimed that his proteges were "an entirely different class" of people from the earlier settlers at Moosomin who had acquired an unfavourable reputation.[21] Nevertheless, when John Heppner and the others in the Landau group arrived at Wapella, they were not favourably received. On the contrary, the Liberal-Conservative Association of Wapella adopted a resolution of protest, claiming injury by the government over the reservation of land for the Jews who were described as "a most undesirable class of settler."[22]

In immediate response to this resolution, a homestead inspector was sent to investigate the Jewish settlers even as they were getting started. A. M. Burgess, the Deputy Minister of the Interior in Ottawa ordered that no action be taken on the demand in the resolution that the land reserved for the Jews be thrown open to more "desirable" settlers. But, H. H. Smith, the land commissioner at Winnipeg, acted on his own initiative before receiving the Ottawa directive and cancelled the land reserved for the Jews.

The homestead inspector, R. S. Park, reporting in mid-July, spoke strongly in favour of the Jewish settlers and stated: "The English settlers speak highly of these Jews and don't desire better neighbours." Since numerous English names were on the petition against the Jews, this may seem surprising, but by this time, the main demand of the petitioners (cancellation of the land reserve) had been met.[24]

The "more desirable" settlers did not rush to Wapella, and more Jews were able to take homesteads. Among them were Abraham Klenman and his son-in-law, Solomon Barish, who may have been the first to act clearly in accordance with the religious motivation of the Jewish back-to-the-land movement. Fortunately, their idealism was combined with practical experience. Klenman (at fifty-seven years of age) had been overseer of an agricultural estate in Bessarabia; Barish had farmed in the Russian Jewish farm colony of Dombroveni.

Arriving in Montreal in the spring of 1888, Klenman and another Jewish immigrant travelled west that fall to pick a settlement site. After visiting several places, they came to John Heppner and his friends at Wapella where they were impressed with the fertile black soil, the wooded area and the opportunity to settle on adjacent homesteads (a CPR concession) among Jewish neighbours.

Abraham Klenman took a homestead immediately and began to build a house while his companion returned to Montreal to report to other farmers-in-waiting. Winter came before Klenman could do more than dig a cellar and thus he spent his first prairie winter below ground. Undeterred, he finished his house in the spring, and his wife and family came to join him.

Solomon Barish remained in Montreal to earn additional money for farming needs. He tried peddling on foot with a backpack in a French district, but speaking neither English nor French, he quit after one day. Still short of funds, he worked in a cigar factory for a while. Then he went to Chicago to train as a *shochet* (ritual slaughterer) for fowl. In the spring of 1892, with one hundred dollars in savings, Barish reached Winnipeg where he bought a team of oxen, a wagon and a plough before going on to Wapella. At the homestead, some wild prairie chickens had been trapped for him to slaughter according to Jewish dietary ritual.[25]

The arrival at Wapella of the Klenmans and several other new Jewish families brought the same response from non-Jewish neighbours in 1888 as the arrival of the Heppner group two years earlier. The Liberal-Conservative Association again protested that the reservation of land for the Jews was "detrimental to the interests and welfare of the district."[26]

Nevertheless, about twenty-five Jewish families did prove themselves as farmers at Wapella during the 1890s. It was a period of increased efforts by the organized Jewish community to place more Jews on the land. But the failure of the "New Jerusalem" project at Moosomin overshadowed the success at Wapella in the effort to start a larger farm settlement.

In 1891, the Young Men's Hebrew Benevolent Society in Montreal began to seek help for a New Jewish farm settlement in the West. Because of the Moosomin experience, Jewish leaders in London rebuffed their appeal. But a promise of help came from Baron Maurice de Hirsch, the leading Jewish philanthropist in continental Europe who was beginning to establish the Jewish Colonization Association to aid Jewish emigrants from Russia to become farmers.

The Montreal leaders met with Prime Minister John Abbott and Minister of Agriculture Sir John Carling to seek land for a Jewish colony of 2,000 families (10,000 persons) in "contiguous" sections to form "a whole and undivided colony." The government did not object to the proposed numbers but rejected the idea of a contiguous land grant.[27] These developments, however, did lead (in the spring of 1892) to the establishment of the Hirsch settlement some twenty miles from Oxbow where a few independent Jews had settled earlier.

The Hirsch settlement was the first Jewish farm colony established under Jewish community auspices (by the Montreal Young Men's Hebrew Benevolent Society which established the Baron de Hirsch Institute after becoming his beneficiary). Direct community sponsorship proved a mixed blessing since the colonists were often treated like charity cases and the Montreal leadership frequently displayed an unenlightened approach. In addition, the response of government authorities and non-Jewish settlers towards the Jewish farmers was mixed—some were friendly, others were ambivalent, and some were clearly hostile.

A delegation sent to locate a site for the Hirsch colony, carried a government letter of introduction asking land agents to do all in their power to assist the object of the Jewish settlement. At the same time, a government handbill seeking to attract new immigrants from the German agricultural population of Russia announced: "No Jews will be brought out under this scheme." On the other hand, a German notary public, D. W. Riedle of Winnipeg (who had assisted in establishing some Mennonite colonies), wrote to the Jewish society in Montreal offering advice and help with the Jewish settlement.[28]

Additional Jewish farm settlements were established at Lipton and Cupar in the Qu'Appelle Valley in 1901; the Edenbridge colony along the Carrot River about twenty-five miles northeast of Melfort in 1906; the Sonnenfeld colony near the United States border about fifty miles west of Estevan in 1907; the Bender Hamlet colony in the Manitoba Interlake about 1902; and at Rumsey, Alberta in 1910. There were Jewish farmers at other locations in Manitoba, Saskatchewan, and Alberta but all together the number of Jewish farm families never reached the hoped-for total of 1,000.

On the farms and in the towns and cities, the Jews invariably carried with them their religious ideals. At Wapella, where they never had a synagogue, whoever had a two-room house would lend one of his rooms for religious services. At Hirsch, at Lipton-Cupar and at Sonnenfeld, schoolhouses also served as synagogues.

The early Jewish settlers were often qualified to conduct services and fulfill other religious functions even if they were not rabbis. They followed the Jewish tradition that wherever there was a *minyan*, a religious quorum of ten men, they constituted a congregation from which they could elect a rabbi. However, a man usually had to be specially qualified before he was regarded as a rabbi. There were three such men among the early Jewish settlers at Wapella in 1889. Brotman conducted services and performed marriage ceremonies, including one outdoor wedding ceremony—in the ultra-orthodox Jewish tradition—on December 25, 1898, with the temperature reportedly fifty below zero.[29]

Another farmer-rabbi was Jacob Wasserman who also spent some time at Wapella. He was devout and observant and fully qualified in all religious functions including that of ritual slaughterer (*shochet*). Preferring to farm, he took land at Oxbow in 1896. From his farm he travelled to other communities to conduct religious services from time to time and, in the early 1900s, he served as the first Jewish religious functionary in Regina.

In 1899, Marcus Berner became the farmer-rabbi at Hirsch. A Hebrew teacher, Berner was appointed a Jewish minister by the

Chief Rabbi of Britain where he served before coming to Canada. He farmed and served as the rabbi at Hirsch until 1931. He was also a municipal councillor and chairman of the Hirsch Public School Board. When his farming efforts faltered, he accepted the pulpit of the synagogue at Victoria, British Columbia where he served until his death.[30]

The most unique prairie Jewish farm settlement was Edenbridge, in northern Saskatchewan, settled by two different elements of Jews from Lithuania. The first group migrated to South Africa where they became storekeepers before making a second migration after hearing about the Canadian offer of a quarter-section of land for ten dollars. The second group began as factory workers in London, became imbued with socialist beliefs, and decided to try to realize their ideals on the land in western Canada.

Officially Edenbridge was only a rural post office but the Jews who lived there (never more than fifty families) became more than farmers. They built and maintained, for a time, the varied cultural institutions that became the hallmark of larger urban Jewish communities in Winnipeg, Saskatoon, and Calgary. At Edenbridge, there was a community of religious Jews and a community of "free-thinkers." The religious element built a synagogue in 1908 which continued to serve as a house of worship until 1964. It is now an historic site recognized by the Saskatchewan government. The free-thinkers opted for a community hall where they conducted meetings and discussions on the great topics of the day, sponsored a theatre group, conducted classes in Yiddish for the children, and published a Yiddish newspaper. The religious element conducted classes in Hebrew and religion. There were also two public schools.

In Edenbridge, as in larger centres, there was a great interest in politics among the Jews. Edenbridge Jews served on the school board and the township council and several, notably from the Vicker family, served as reeves of the rural municipality.[31] Everywhere in the West, Jews became active in each of the major political parties. Eventually, the old ideological differences became weakened and there was some crossing of lines. This was an evolutionary-like process, for example, Norman Vicker was born in Edenbridge and was a member of the cabinet in Saskatchewan's New Democratic Party's government. Vicker's family arrived at Edenbridge via South Africa. They were builders of the synagogue and their entrepreneurial interests led them to the world of business and merchandising when they moved away from the farms. Yet Norman Vicker, a staunch free-enterpriser, was part of the moderate socialist N.D.P. government that was defeated in Saskatchewan in 1982.

Liberty Temple activists, Jewish Cultural Centre, Sholem Aleichem School.

The foundation of western Canadian Jewish idealism was laid many decades ago in North Winnipeg... known as a Jewish Jerusalem: it incorporated both the religious and the secular, including socialist and cultural ideals.

Canada's social democratic movement, spawned in the West with the founding of the Co-operative Commonwealth Federation (CCF), was built in large part by people who were imbued with the idealistic universal vision of New Jerusalem embodying Jewish as well as Christian ideals. Jews were among the builders of the CCF-NDP movement from the very beginning. Many had given up formal religious ties, but nevertheless carried with them humanitarian ideals usually acquired from their Judaic background.

The foundation of western Canadian Jewish idealism was laid many decades ago in North Winnipeg—that polyglot community which was the first urban home to so many religious and ethnic groups who sought to build a new life on the prairies. Winnipeg North became known as a Jewish Jerusalem: it incorporated both the religious and the secular, including socialist and cultural ideals. And, to the extent that all the ethnic communities learned to live together in Winnipeg North, it may be considered a New Jerusalem for a multitude of groups.

Although reality seldom lives up to ideals, it was from the Winnipeg North bastion of social democracy that the various ethnocultural communities of Manitoba joined together to assert their political power with the election to government of the New Democratic Party under Edward Schreyer, now Canada's Governor General. The Schreyer government had three Jewish members, all from Winnipeg North, serving along with Ukrainians, Poles, Icelanders, and Mennonites.

When ethno-religious groups like the Mennonites, Hutterites and Doukhobors migrated to the prairies, they were firmly resolved to achieve cultural autonomy. Each group wanted to build its own New Jerusalem. The Jews had a similar desire, but they pursued it with less ethnocentric exclusiveness.

Some Jews did seek the goal of territorial and cultural autonomy, however, and this desire fathered the belief that it could happen. An oft-quoted statement attributed to Sir Wilfred Laurier contributed to this belief. While attending Queen Victoria's diamond jubilee in London in 1897, Laurier, responding to a request for support of a new Jewish agricultural project in western Canada, was reported to have said:

> If you will take up this question seriously and select any part of Manitoba, the Dominion will grant the Jews such a measure of self-government as will enable them to make their own by-laws, substituting Saturday for Sunday.[32]

Four years later, however, there was a negative conclusion to negotiations between the Jewish Colonization Association and the Canadian government for the establishment of a new colony of Romanian Jews in the West. Laurier accepted the recommendation of Sir Clifford Sifton, his Minister of the Interior, opposing such a colony and forwarded a memorandum on this decision to the High Commissioner in London. This memorandum reached London after the first group of Romanian Jews were enroute to Canada. They were not turned back and they became the founders of the Lipton-Cupar Jewish farm settlement in the Qu'Appelle Valley.[33]

But Laurier's statement continued to be repeated after it was made public in a lecture given by Herman Landau in London in 1906. Landau claimed the Canadian Prime Minister had made the statement to him, and his disclosure came while the Canadian Parliament was debating the Lord's Day Act. This Act aroused the concern of the Jews because it provided for compulsory observance of Sunday as a day of rest. In those years, many Jews were strict Sabbath observers. Thus the Laurier "promise" of a colony where Saturday might be legally substituted for Sunday attracted great interest.

Another reason for this interest was a *pogrom* against the Jews of Kishinev in 1905, which led to a renewed effort to bring Russian Jews to Canada. Laurier appeared at a Jewish meeting in Ottawa to protest the Russian persecution and promised "a hearty welcome" to Jews coming to Canada. In 1907, however, Laurier was interviewed by the *London Jewish Chronicle* and denied any promise to assist the establishment of a new Jewish farm settlement, large or small.[34]

Ten years earlier, the World Zionist Organization had been established to work for a Jewish homeland in Palestine. Not all Jews supported the idea of a Palestine homeland, however, and some of them established the Jewish Territorialist Organization to seek a Jewish autonomous territory in any part of the world where Jews would be welcome. The territorialist movement was led by Israel Zangwill, the Anglo-Jewish author who had also heard of Laurier's "promise." In the summer of 1907, Zangwill sent a special emissary to Canada, Dr. Nachman Syrkin, to attempt to negotiate an autonomous territory for the Jews, but the mission ended in failure.[35]

Nevertheless, the major growth of the Jewish population of Canada and of the prairies occurred during the Laurier years and up to the outbreak of the First World War. After the war, Canada's increasingly restrictive immigration laws made it more difficult for Jews to enter the country than for any other emigrants from Europe. Moreover, as the threat of Nazism in Europe developed in the mid 1930s, Canada's doors were virtually shut to Jews seeking escape from the worst anti-Semitism and racism the world has ever known. It is now acknowledged that anti-Semitic attitudes in high places brought about the closed-door policy toward the Jews at the time of their greatest need.[36]

In the years between the two world wars, the people on the prairies firmly established their reputation as the creators of populist movements of dissent and reform on the right as well as the left. While Jews were able to find a place in each of the old established parties (the Conservatives and the Liberals), when it came to populism, there was no room for Jews on the right.

Jews were active in the Independent Labor Party which, in 1926, elected A. A. Heaps from Winnipeg North. Heaps was the first Jew from the prairies to win a seat in the House of Commons. Jews were involved in the One Big Union and later, in the CCF and the NDP.

But western populism also spawned the Social Credit after the demise of the United Farmers in Alberta. Jews never found a place in the Social Credit party partly because of the fundamentalist groups that helped to establish it. Among them were the British Israelites whose view of New Jerusalem encompassed the "Synagogue of

Satan" attitude to the Jews. The west also saw the development of a Ku Klux Klan movement in the 1930s and a western branch of the Canadian Nationalist Party which openly spread Nazi propaganda in the years before the war.

Generally, however, the attitude of the prairie population towards the Jews was probably more friendly and receptive than that encountered in the east. An example of this attitude is found in the 1934 group libel amendment (to the provincial libel law) adopted by the Manitoba legislature to stop publication of anti-Semitic propaganda by the western Nazi paper, *The Nationalist*. The amendment had been introduced by Marcus Hyman, a Jewish MLA who represented the Independent Labor Party and sat with the Opposition.[37] In Ontario and Quebec, during the same period, each legislature had a Jewish member sitting on the government side, yet their efforts to introduce similar group libel provisions failed.

Today, in spite of changing ideology and in spite of denominational changes in the Jewish religion, the synagogue continues to be a focal point of Jewish life in every city with a viable Jewish community. Winnipeg has at least ten active congregations serving a population of approximately 18,000 Jews. Calgary and Edmonton each have three congregations for their respective populations of 3,500 and 3,000. Regina and Saskatoon are active one-synagogue towns, each with a Jewish population of under 1,000. In many smaller centres across the prairies, the once-active synagogues are now closed due to the removal of the Jewish population to larger centres. Only Prince Albert in Saskatchewan and Lethbridge in Alberta still have active congregations outside the larger centres. For religious Jews, the synagogue is a constant reminder of Jerusalem and at every service, the entire congregation is called upon to rise and face eastward in ritual reminder of the Holy City.

The established Christian denominations on the prairies have usually looked with favour on the flourishing of the synagogue in their midst. For example, in 1887, before the first synagogue was built in Winnipeg, the *Manitoba Free Press* did a survey of churches and found "three congregations of the Hebrew faith" but no synagogue. The Free Press writer said of Winnipeg's Jews:

> . . . outsiders are apt to underestimate the work accomplished . . . owing to the divisions which exist . . . United the Hebrews would form a Congregation of very respectable numbers and they would soon possess a building creditable alike to themselves and the city.[38]

Two years later, the Jewish community of Winnipeg did build the first synagogue on the prairies. It was called Shaarey Zedek ("gates of Justice") and a principal participant in the cornerstone ceremony in September 1889 was the grandmaster of the local Masonic Lodge, the Reverend Cannon James Dallas O'Meara. This unusual participation in the founding ceremony of the synagogue was due to the Masonic association of some of the earliest Jewish settlers in Manitoba, who had preceded the Russian Jews. They came from England and western Europe where Jews had been associated with the Masonic Order as far back as the seventeenth and eighteenth centuries. This was the second time in western Canada that Masonic leaders were invited to participate in the founding ceremony of a synagogue. (The first occasion was in 1863 at the cornerstone ceremony of the Victoria synagogue, today the oldest synagogue existing in Canada.)

From their early association with the Masonic Order in various prairie centres (the first Jewish services in Calgary were held in a Masonic hall in 1894), Jewish involvement in all community endeavours is noteworthy. In the post-World War II period, this involvement has ranged from helping to build the United Way in every major centre to the founding of theatre and ballet companies and assistance in the building of symphony orchestras, art galleries, and museums.

In the century since the Jews of Eastern Europe first began to settle on the prairies in significant numbers, manifestations of Jewish religion and culture have undergone important changes. The loss of Yiddish as a spoken language, the modest development of modern Hebrew in emulation of the Hebrew revival in Israel, the rise of beautiful synagogue edifaces in Winnipeg, Calgary and Edmonton, the development in Winnipeg of the Chai Folk Ensemble (a Jewish performing arts group), and the Jewish Historical Society are all a reflection of the changing times.

While some Jews cling to tradition, beliefs are reinterpreted to suit the times. Hence today, Jewish religious groupings range from Chassidism (Jewish mysticism) through traditional Orthodoxy, Reform and Conservative movements, to Jews who believe in religion without supernaturalism (Reconstructionist) and to secular Jews who still consider themselves free-thinkers. Religious Jews, however, do not reject the secular and Jewish secularists do not always turn their back on religious belief and tradition.

In Jewish tradition, life and death are considered merely different aspects of the same reality. Moreover, according to **Rabbinical** Sages, the "World-to-Come" is described as *Gan Eden,*[39] literally the Garden of Eden or Paradise, to be achieved not through divine intervention but as a result of the upright conduct of people during their lifetime.[40] God would not enter the "Heavenly Jerusalem" before a new "Earthly Jerusalem" (another designation for the kingdom of God) would be established through man's striving for righteousness. This is in keeping with prophetic eschatology which recognizes no distinction between the present world and the world to come.[41]

There is an apocalyptic "Day of Judgement" known to Jewish tradition when Elijah will appear to herald the coming of the Messiah.[42] This is recognized at the Passover Seder when, toward the close of the ritual, a cup of wine is filled for Elijah and the door is opened to see if he is ready to appear. Apart from the apocalyptic, Jews observe a Day of Judgement each year at Rosh Hashana (the Jewish New Year), when mankind's future for the coming year is considered and finally determined on Yom Kippur, the Day of Atonement.[43]

The Rabbinic Sages also taught that the formal observance of Rosh Hashana in the synagogue was, by itself, insufficient for the achievement of true repentance. In addition to prayer and introspection the rabbis emphasized the importance of carrying out acts of loving kindness towards other people.[44] We may see this as a call to action for social justice in our times and at this point enlightened Jews and enlightened Christians should be able to join in pursuit of a common New Jerusalem ideal, whether on the Canadian prairies or elsewhere. If, however, Jews or Christians are unduly affected by the reality of Jerusalem today in the continuing Arab-Israel controversy it is well to recall the words of the rabbis of long ago who said: "Jerusalem will be rebuilt only through peace" and redeemed "only through righteousness."[45]

VIII Mennonites and the New Jerusalem in western Canada

T.D. Regehr

On July 1, 1873, a seemingly insignificant but alarming incident occurred at White Horse Plains in Manitoba. A Dominion immigration agent had brought out a four-member delegation to look over various tracts of land in Manitoba. If suitable land could be located, an immigration of up to 10,000 new agricultural settlers was in prospect.

Indians and Metis had hunted the buffalo on these plains for countless generations. The French Metis had established their own semi-nomadic society at White Horse Plains—a society based on the buffalo hunt but supplemented by freighting, carting, and marginal trading and farming operations. They were justifiably concerned that a major influx of new agricultural settlers would seriously disrupt and probably destroy their traditional way of life. The legal guarantees, recently obtained by the Metis under the Manitoba Act, had already proved inadequate and disappointing and the Indian camps and Metis settlements were restless.

Word of the land seekers aroused the Metis to action. They intercepted and harassed the new arrivals with verbal threats, much whooping and yelling, and an ostentatious display of firearms. Much alarmed, the land seekers sought refuge in House's Hotel (a crude local hostelry) while their agent stood guard at the door with a loaded shotgun. An urgent message was dispatched to the Lieutenant-Governor who promptly ordered the local military forces to the trouble spot. Fearing a repetition of the Riel-led Red River resistance of 1869-70, members of the local governing council also arrived at White Horse Plains. The troops quickly dispersed the

Metis and arrested several of their leaders.[1]

This was the inauspicious beginning of Mennonite agricultural settlement in western Canada. The society, or the kingdom the Mennonites wished to establish on the Canadian prairies, was to be very different from that of the Metis or of the Indians or of other agriculturalists who lived in Manitoba.

Many western Canadians, particularly those who came from Ontario or the British Isles and who were very often the political and social leaders in the West, hoped to build a "British" society—British parliamentary institutions, British laws, British imperialism. British social and cultural values were to be established and fostered in the new land, but without the blemishes wrought by industrialization, urbanization and a rigid class structure.

The Mennonites wanted to establish their own utopia, separate and somewhat different from these British ideals. They found the militarism of the imperialists and the prejudices of those who insisted on the use of the English language in the schools and in society generally very hard to accept. They seriously distrusted the democratic principles on which British parliamentary government is based, recognizing that the Canadian government had granted them important concessions but that these concessions could be removed by any hostile parliamentary majority.

The men looking for land on that Dominion Day of 1873 were delegates of their co-religionists in Russia who had become dissatisfied with the Russification programs and reforms instituted by their government. Their search was for a new land where they would be free of unwanted government intervention in the affairs of their communities and schools. Although the White Horse Plains incident was frightening, the local government was supportive and the federal government, eager to attract more agricultural settlers to the West, granted the Mennonites all the political and religious concessions they asked for. To guarantee that no future reformist or democratic agitation would deprive them of their special concessions, the Mennonites travelled to England to obtain the support of Queen Victoria for their Canadian venture.

The first group of Mennonite settlers arrived in Fort Garry on the riverboat, the *International,* on July 31, 1874. Initially, their arrival aroused suspicion and hostility among many of the local Winnipeg people. Their garb, their language, their religion, and above all, their proposed settlement patterns were at sharp variance from those of the Canadians. Could such people ever become useful citizens of the young and growing Dominion? Were they the right kind of people to build a new and better society in the West?

Some of these questions were answered for the local Winnipeg merchants soon after the first group of Mennonites arrived. They had substantial sums of money and were aware that the purposes of Divine Providence can be expedited by the power of economics and self-interest. Consequently, resisting the blandishments of merchants they encountered enroute, they held on to their money until their arrival in Manitoba where they purchased the supplies, equipment, and livestock necessary to begin their new agricultural settlement. Within three days of their arrival, more than $20,000 of Mennonite money changed hands in Winnipeg—for some of the local merchants this was more business than they had done during an entire year! People bringing such important benefits to the community could be forgiven other peculiarities so hope quickly grew that more Mennonites would find their way to Manitoba—and to shops and warehouses of the merchants.[2]

The exchange of economic services for special religious and political concessions is a dominant theme in the history of Mennonite agricultural settlers.[3] It reflects the unusual views Mennonites held about secular governments and religious ideals. Appropriately, Mennonites have been described as a people of two kingdoms—a people who are citizens of secular kingdoms but who claim a higher allegiance to a religious or spiritual kingdom.[4]

Perhaps in reaction against the abuses and failings of the old Holy Roman Empire and against attempts by the Roman Catholic Church to build a holistic Christian state on earth, Mennonite leaders developed a pessimistic view of human nature and of all human societies and governments. They believed that man was a "fallen" creature and that all human endeavours would inevitably fail. Futhermore, since virtue could not and should not be legislated, a truly Christian society could not be established unless each member of that society was personally committed to follow the teachings of Jesus.[5] Since most members of society have never made such a commitment, the best any secular government can do is to set rules and limits for the essentially evil and selfish impulses of its members. Therefore, governments are merely charged with management and control of actual or potential evildoers.[6]

Although Mennonites voluntarily committed themselves to the rigorous discipleship required to meet the standards of conduct taught by Jesus, they were still members of secular kingdoms. Hence, it was their duty to obey, respect, and support secular authorities who conducted the essentially negative duties of limiting and controlling evil. But secular authorities must be obeyed only if they made demands which were not contrary to the teachings of

Jesus. Of course, Jesus' teachings were not considered binding or even relevant to many of the secular obligations. Within their mandate secular authorities could not "turn the other cheek" to evildoers. In dealing with some of the evils, they often demanded police action or military service as the only practical solution, although the Sermon on the Mount pointed to a different and better way of dealing with the problems of evil.[7] This, however, required individual commitment and dedication lacking in most members of secular societies. For the Mennonites, a new ethic of love superseded the normal human responses to evil.[8]

During the early years of Mennonite history, severe persecution convinced many that the real kingdom of God was only to be achieved in heaven. Many, however, believed that they also had some responsibility on earth. But what was this responsibility and how was it to be discharged? One answer was to try to persuade more people to commit themselves voluntarily to the ideals of the Sermon on the Mount.

Another alternative was presented when several European rulers gave fugitive Mennonites sanctuary in their realms. William of Orange, one of the first rulers to recognize the economic value of the Mennonites, was willing to grant them important religious concessions.[9] As other monarchs followed his example, Mennonites were able to establish themselves and to build their own communities in many countries.

Although many of the original Mennonites had been urban intellectuals and artisans, because of severe persecution and because the areas available as sancturaries often lay on the eastern European or western American agricultural frontiers, Mennonites gradually became an agricultural people. Living in self-contained and isolated frontier communities, they voluntarily committed themselves to Jesus' ideals and teachings and thus attempted to build the Kingdom of God on earth.[10]

In this endeavour, they saw some success in Prussia under the rule of Frederick the Great.[11] But after his death, Mennonite privileges and autonomy were sharply reduced and consequently, many of the Mennonites migrated from Prussia to Russia where a virtually autonomous Mennonite commonwealth came to be established. Particularly in the two large colonies of Chortitza and Molotschna, Mennonites sought to build the Kingdom of God on earth, protected but unmolested by the Russian secular authorities.[12]

Catherine the Great and Alexander I were particularly supportive. Alexander's successors, however, were more intent on reform and Russification. The emancipation of the serfs in 1861 was

L. Klippenstein, Mennonite Heritage Centre
Winnipeg, Manitoba

An Altbergthal farmyard in the West Reserve — 1½ mile west & ½ mile south of Altona, Manitoba.

Although many of the original Mennonites had been urban intellectuals and artisans, because of severe persecution and because the areas available as sanctuaries often lay on the eastern European or western American agricultural frontiers, Mennonites gradually became an agricultural people. Living in self-contained and isolated frontier communities, they voluntarily committed themselves to Jesus' ideals and teachings and thus attempted to build the kingdom of God on earth.

followed by a series of measures which gradually restricted the extensive privileges enjoyed by the Mennonites and other groups. Nevertheless, the Russian experience provided a model which Mennonites who emigrated from the country in the 1870s tried to re-create in the new world.

It was the hope of the Mennonites arriving in Manitoba in 1874 to establish their own communities which would be isolated from the surrounding host society.[13] They demanded and received a large tract of land reserved exclusively for their use, complete exemption from military service, control over their own schools, complete religious freedom, and a substantial degree of local autonomy. Here they hoped to build their own Utopia—a society in which the ideals and principles of the New Testament would be put into practice. A second reserve was later established in Manitoba and two Mennonite reserves were established in the 1890s in Saskatchewan near

Saskatoon and Swift Current.[14]

The attempt to establish Mennonite Utopias separate from the mainstream of Canadian society met with only partial success. Serious rifts developed early within the Mennonite community. Disagreements over the proper relationship of the Mennonite community with the larger surrounding Canadian society (particularly the use of the English language, participation in municipal governments, and the acceptance of government financial support for schools) became troublesome.[15] The primary language of instruction in the schools, or worship in the Church, and of communication within the community was German, but those who had business or other contacts with the outside world also had to learn some English. But how much? And where should it be learned? Making matters worse was the fact that the educational concessions obtained by the Mennonites from the federal government proved largely ineffective because the Canadian constitution assigned responsibility for education to the provinces which exerted pressure or offered inducements for more English instruction.[16]

Some Mennonites saw no harm in accepting government assistance to finance and improve their schools and to teach more English in these schools, provided that they retained control over the curriculum and the hiring of teachers. Others found any government involvement and any deviations from the school curriculum, as they had known it in Russia, unacceptable. Even a new cover picture on the new edition of their old and familiar German primer which was otherwise almost unchanged was too much for some of the most conservative elders and some primers with the old covers had to be printed for the Canadian Mennonite market.

There were also serious difficulties in determining Mennonite relations with local rural municipal governments.[17] Municipal boundaries, unfortunately, did not coincide with the boundaries of the Mennonite reserves, although Mennonites constituted an overwhelming majority in several municipalities and could therefore control the local government if they chose to participate. If they refused, a small and probably hostile minority, would dominate the local government. Most Mennonites, therefore, decided to participate but the question then arose whether these local governments would reflect or act upon the values and practices of the secular or of the spiritual kingdoms to which the Mennonites claimed allegiance.

The difficulty was in part due to the lack of experience of the Mennonites with democratic forms of government. Traditionally, they had been governed by autocrats who rarely asked their advice and gave them no opportunity to determine affairs of state. In Holland, Prussia, Poland, and Russia, popular and democratic elements had generally been hostile to the Mennonites and their special privileges. Mennonites who had emigrated a century earlier from Switzerland to Pennsylvania and later to Ontario, had achieved a limited accommodation to democratic forms of government, but there was comparatively little contact between these Mennonites and the new Manitoba settlers.[18]

Mennonites still believed that they were a people of two kingdoms but the boundaries between the two kingdoms were becoming blurred. Where clear advantages could be gained from participation in local municipal governments which the Mennonites could control, they became involved. Local governments, hostile to their interests or beyond their ability to control, were avoided or, if necessary, petitioned in the same manner Mennonites had generally petitioned ruling autocrats.

The isolated Utopias were failing, as the earlier Israelite theocracy of the Old Testament had failed. That failure was accentuated by the arrival in the 1920s of over 20,000 more Mennonites from Russia. Uprooted by the disasters of revolution, civil war, and constant harassment, thousands of Russian Mennonites who had accepted the limited Russification programs of the 1870s found they could not retain the essentials of their faith in the land of the Soviets. Canada was their preferred destination, even though they knew that there were no longer large vacant tracts of land, and that no additional Mennonite reserves would be established.These newly arriving Mennonites had to settle in accordance with established Canadian homestead laws and procedures.[19]

As the physical and geographical boundaries of the Mennonite Utopia became more indistinct, some resorted to the historic response of the Mennonites to intrusion of worldly or secular influences. They packed their goods and removed themselves to new and more isolated frontiers, first in Saskatchewan and Northern Alberta and British Columbia, and later in Mexico, Paraguay, and British Honduras.[20]

Others began to redefine the nature and characteristics of the Kingdom of God they were trying to build in Canada. Perhaps the Kingdom of God could be defined vertically rather than spatially. Mennonites are occupants of both a lower physical or secular kingdom and of a superior spirtitual or godly kingdom. Together with non-Mennonites, they inhabit the same physical world and are citizens of the same secular kingdom, but they have also voluntarily committed themselves to live on a higher plane and to follow

MENNONITE SETTLEMENTS

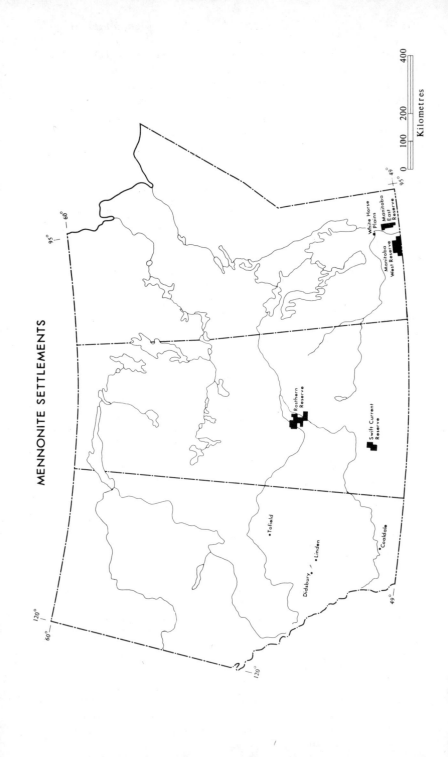

White Horse Plains

Manitoba East Reserve

Manitoba West Reserve

Rosthern Reserve

Swift Current Reserve

•Tofield

Didsbury •Linden

•Coaldale

60°

95°

49°

95°

120°

60°

120°

49°

0 100 200 400

Kilometres

superior teachings and ideals. They are, in the words of the scriptures, "in the world but not of the world".[21]

Mennonites had to redefine their concept of the Kingdom of God at a time when many other Christians, very strongly influenced by the Social Gospel, also rethought their positions. The Social Gospel, however, had very little influence on Mennonite thinking. What little influence there was, was almost entirely negative. The Social Gospel in Canada was essentially a gospel of English-speaking and Protestant reformers who tended to see the Mennonites and other non-Anglo-Saxon Canadians as people in need of some measure of reform and Anglicization. J.S. Woodsworth, for example, regarded the Mennonites as honest, hard-working, and virtuous people but regretted their isolationist attitude and urged that stern measures be taken to hasten, if necessary through compulsion, their Canadianization.[22] Other reformers such as J.T.M. Anderson, later the Premier of Saskatchewan, were more outspoken and said:

> The voices of these [Mennonite] children who are caged up in these private schools, whose minds are being warped by incomplete development, who are being reared in an environment of mental darkness are calling out to us over these free Canadian prairies. Born on our liberty-loving soil, new Canadians in the truest sense of the term, they are to all intents and purposes still on some dark European plain.[23]

Dr. E. H. Oliver, the principal of the Presbyterian Theological College in Saskatoon (St. Andrew's College, after 1923) and a leading advocate of the merger of reform-minded Protestant denominations into the United Church of Canada, was severely and at times very unfairly critical of the Mennonites. He condemned their reluctance to become Canadianized and denounced their educational concessions on the basis of limited knowledge of the situation.[24] In Alberta, Norman Priestley, a United Church minister and prominent leader in the farm and co-operative movement, noisily and belligerently opposed all Mennonite immigration in the 1920s.[25]

As long as Mennonites were treated as a needy mission field rather than as partners in a common endeavour, there was little prospect that they would associate themselves with the Social Gospel in the building of a New Jerusalem in Western Canada. Theologically, Mennonites had very serious doubts about the practicality of building the New Jerusalem with fallen unregenerates, and practically, they found the Social Gospel hostile to their distinctive culture, language, and social practices.[26]

Some Social Gospel ideas, nevertheless, appealed to the Mennonites. Historically, reform-minded democratic movements had almost always been very dangerous for the Mennonites, particularly when they had grown prosperous or when there were acute military pressures. But there were different ways in which secular governments could discharge their essentially negative functions. Some were certainly to be preferred to others and, in a democracy, each voter had some influence in determining the composition of his government and its policies. Politics might well remain simply the art of the possible. It could not replace religion in the pursuit of the ideal. But the scope for good or ill within the bounds of what was politically possible was still very great. What obstacle was there to using the influence of the ballot box or even the influence of capable individuals in the councils of the nation to achieve the best that was possible in an evil and fallen society?[27] In this respect, Mennonite attitudes toward participation in democratic governments were akin to the attitudes of many dedicated socialists toward progressive labour reforms. On the one hand, they believed the entire system was bad and should be overthrown and that reform simply postponed the coming of revolution. But reforms do ameliorate real suffering, and so the debate between reformers and revolutionaries rages on.[28] Mennonites are as pessimistic about secular governments as socialists are of capitalist societies. Reforms, without individual regeneration or commitment, will certainly not usher in the New Jerusalem, but they can make contemporary society better. Many Mennonites became convinced that they could and should associate themselves with such reforms. Historically, their contributions were economic but there has been a considerable broadening of the Mennonite vision in this respect. Active participation in politics, in social reform, and in the improvement of everyday life in a secular society has come to be regarded as laudable, although not a substitute for the higher ideals of life within the congregation of believers.[29]

Further major developments in Mennonite attitudes toward social, economic, and political problems took place in the 1920s. Those Mennonites who had remained in Russia found themselves in a desperate situation after the overthrow of the Tsarist government. In their desperation these Russian Mennonites appealed to their North American co-religionists for help. That help was generously given and took two forms—assistance to facilitate the emigration of approximately 20,000 Mennonites from Russia to Canada, and material aid to overcome famine and pestilence and to promote the economic reconstruction of the Russian Mennonite colonies. A special arrangement whereby the Ford Tractor Company shipped over one hundred small tractors and plow units to the colonies proved particularly effective. It was in part subsidized by the American government with the balance being paid by North American Mennonites.

Before the 1920s the various Mennonite groups had little contact with one another. The relief efforts of the 1920s, however, required more co-ordination and a special all-Mennonite relief agency—the Mennonite Central Committee—was created. This committee was so successful that its work was altered and expanded when, in 1929, Canadian immigration restrictions and Stalinist economic policies made it impossible to provide further aid to the Russian Mennonites. The practical and obviously useful work of providing material aid to those in need was simply broadened and expanded to encompass compassionate responses to needy people who were not Mennonites. World War II and the subsequent Mennonite refugee problems again led to a preoccupation with Mennonite needs, but after these refugees were looked after, and particularly during the Korean and Vietnam wars the Mennonite Central Committee became involved in the assistance to the victims of those unfortunate conflicts. This led, particularly in the 1960s, to a much greater emphasis on active rather than passive ways of making peace.

Before 1923 Mennonites had been active in various mission programs, but missionaries had emphasized the need to save the heathen from their sinful life and to introduce them to the higher standards of life outlined in the scriptures. The Mennonite Central Committee added a new practical emphasis. The mission programs are still run separately by the various Mennonite conferences, but in practical relief programs there is very successful inter-Mennonite co-operation and co-ordination. The two-world view of the Mennonite persists, but increasingly they are seeking to make a contribution in both.

The Mennonites who first began coming to Canada in 1874 participated in the relegation of the Metis to the periphery of western Canadian society. They rendered significant economic services in the establishment of western agricultural communities. Initially, they hoped to build an isolated community or kingdom within whose narrow and restricted boundaries the principles and teachings of Jesus could be implemented. The isolation on the Manitoba and Saskatchewan reserves was never complete and contact with other people seeking to build other kingdoms was inevitable. As the prospect of a spatially separate society faded, many sought a

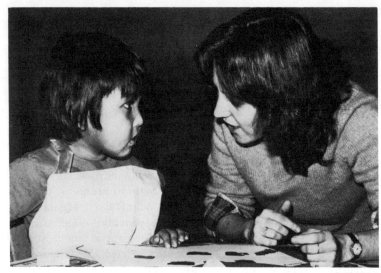

Robb Nickel
Mennonite Central Committee

Elaine Peters, a Mennonite Central Committee voluntary service worker instructing a child in finger painting at Port Hardy Reserve School, B.C.

As the prospect of a spatially separate society faded, many sought a redefinition of the Kingdom of God in spiritual and non-spatial terms. In time they also came to see the possibilities of doing something to improve not only the economic but also the social, intellectual and political aspects of Canadian society.

redefinition of the Kingdom of God in spiritual and nonspatial terms. In time, they also came to see the possibilities of doing something to improve not only the economic but also the social, intellectual, and political aspects of Canadian society. Today, many have become active participants in the effort to make our Canadian society and the world better while at the same time striving, within the smaller congregation of believers, toward the higher standards and teachings of Jesus.

IX The western settlement of Canadian Doukhobors

Koozma J. Tarasoff

Often in my youth and my teens I drove with my parents to Russian language school, to my Doukhobor relatives across western Canada, and to demonstrations for peace. During World War II, I remember my father being one of the registrars for Doukhobor conscientious objectors in the Langham-Saskatoon region of Saskatchewan. Since that time I have attended numerous *sobranies* or meetings, was editor-publisher of the first English language publication of the group, attended youth festivals, wrote several books on the movement, and participated in a history tour of the Doukhobor areas in the Soviet Union.

"Who are these remarkable people—the Doukhobors?" was one of the first questons that I had to answer in one of my university essays. Through encyclopedias I learned that they were known as a religious group or a sect that arose in Tsarist Russia over 250 years ago and after having a conflict with the state and church, some of the Doukhobors migrated to Western Canada in early 1899.

As I searched through dozens of volumes, interviewed hundreds of people, pored over thousands of clippings and documents, talked to other people and observed them, I learned things about these people that at times defy logic and are not even known to themselves. While the group reflects a religious spirit, it is not a religion nor a sect. It arose originally out of the cataclysmic ferment of the religious dissent in Tsarist Russia, but quickly transformed itself into a social movement (based on spiritual beliefs), challenging the legitimacy of both church and state.

Like Lev Tolstoy, the mentor who assisted their migration to

Canada, the Doukhobors had little use for the formal trappings of
the church, the priests, parts of the Bible, in fact the entire institution
itself. The spirit of conscience within, as with the Quakers, who also
assisted the Doukhobors' passage to Canada, was their guide. The
sound of bells was inimical to their senses. As an alternative they
used their voices, *a cappella*, to sing the hymns, psalms, and songs
that echoed the past, reinforced ethical values, and passed on their
history and teachings from generation to generation by word of
mouth. They opposed the state church and called their place of
worship, a "Community Home" or a "Prayer Home." Until lately,
theirs was an oral tradition that served exceedingly well in the old
times especially when schools were unavailable to the masses and
when book-learning was the purview of the ecclesiastical and state
elite whose intent appeared to be more to control than to educate.

The early Russian Doukhobors were largely illiterate. Isolated
from the urban centres where educational facilities were still few in
number they contributed to the illiteracy rate in the country where it
approached 95 percent. Because the available schools were often
operated or influenced by the clergy, this fact alone made the early
Doukhobors suspicious of formal education.

In Canada, Doukhobor parents were hesitant to send their
children to school because they objected to having their children
salute the flag, pledge allegiance to the crown, participate in exercise
drills, etc. Doukhobors believed that they could not serve God and
mammon at the same time. Their allegiance was to God and not to
the militaristic regimes of government.

A more compelling reason for the early distrust of official
authorities was the Doukhobors' unequivocal opposition to military
service linked to their questioning of the legitimacy of the state to
wage wars. This was an area in which there could be no compromise
and which remains to this day a firm deep-rooted value of Canadian
Doukhobors.

The Russian soil nurtured older ideas and life support systems.
The *mir* or commune—an ancient system of land ownership and
organization, permeated much of old Russia wherein all adults were
equal partners in the community and each had a democratic say in its
operations. The land was considered as a public commodity to be
used by those residing on it; it was not to be bought or sold.
Doukhobors believed all people are equal in the eyes of God and this
should be reflected in their way of living—equal distribution of work,
wealth, and property. The first Doukhobors who settled in the Milky
Waters district of the Crimea adopted the *mir* system for survival,
and while they didn't use it consistently, the inherent values of

cooperation stuck with them. The "we" took precedence over the "I". And it was this gestalt principle that was later transferred to Canadian soil where it clashed with the individualistic ethic of private ownership.

The prosperity of the Doukhobors in the Milky Waters lasted barely forty years before the church and state forced orthodoxy and state conformity on them, resulting in their exile to the Transcaucasian region of the isthmus between the Caspian and Black Seas. Here in the midst of the crucible of marauding tribes of Kurds, Turks, and others, the government and religious leaders expected these people—who were in the 1800s considered to be among "the most pernicious" in Tsarist Russia—to be ground down to model citizens. However the Doukhobors resisted assimilation into their hostile neighbourhood. Rather, they extended the tenet that "God is love" and thus established a peaceful co-existence with their neighbours.

But the Doukhobors continued to assert their own minds. When the Tsar introduced military conscription and demanded all to take the oath of allegiance to the crown, these people refused to listen. Secretly, they gathered together their firearms and knives in three separate districts, set fire to them in a public demonstration proclaiming that the institution of militarism should end once and for all, and in its place be established a peaceable community based on the commandment, "Thou shalt not kill." That day, June 29, 1895, was an indelible learning experience for these Russian peasants that consolidated their ranks and reaffirmed their strivings for peace and universal brotherhood. With the Hebrew prophet Isaiah, they envisaged the time when the nations of the world would "beat their swords into plowshares, their spears into pruning hooks, [nor would] they learn war anymore" (Isaiah 2:4). Doukhobors were ready for this now. Not so the government officials who felt their authority threatened and, in response, commanded the Cossacks and the military to whip them, broke up their settlements, and exiled the leaders and those of military age who refused to take up the gun.

Even in those days of limited communications, the plight of these isolated people could not be kept secret from the world. Tolstoy and his friends soon learned about the Doukhobors whom they considered to be the seeds of Christ that had been germinating for generations and now had come to fruition. With the help of Quakers and other humanitarians, money was collected to assist these persecuted peasants. At the same time, an organizing committee in London (composed of Tolstoyans and Quakers) met and began to seek a new haven for these people

Almost by accident, Canada was chosen as the most appropriate place for their settlement. Peter Kropotkin, the celebrated anarchist prince, had just recently visited the prairies and was impressed by the Mennonites who settled in Manitoba and were living an exemplary life. The pacifist Mennonites had been the Doukhobors' neighbours in the Milky Waters and a number of them moved to Canada in the 1880s to avoid the military and the oath of allegiance question. Here they settled in villages under the Hamlet Clause of the Homestead Act; they were exempted from military service under a Canadian Order-in-Council which earlier permitted the Quakers and Tunkers similar exemption. Moreover, the Canadian government, spearheaded by Clifford Sifton as the energetic Minister of the Interior, was anxious to settle the West with people having agricultural skills, strong backs, and sound work habits. The Doukhobors matched these requirements well.

Migration began in early 1899. They came on four cargo cattle boats from Batum on the Black Sea, one arriving in Halifax, another in St. John, New Brunswick, and one in Quebec City, then by the Canadian Pacific Railway to their destination—the Canadian prairies. When the last ship landed in June of that year, 7,500 Doukhobors (out of a total settlement of 30,000 in Russia) had arrived in Canada. Up until this time, this was the largest single migration of a group to Canada.

Clifford Sifton and his colleagues in the Laurier administration were impressed by the robust physical specimens they met. They prided themselves in being able to provide at least some of the manpower needed to build railway lines on the prairies, to build roads, and to cultivate the soil and construct the houses and villages so urgently needed on the open prairies. With a work force comprised of these and other immigrants, it would be possible to prevent the attraction of immigrants to the southern neighbour and therefore ultimately prevent the annexation of Western Canada by the United States. The settlement of the west for Canada was assured.

In their turn, the Doukhobors were impressed by the attention given to them at the ship docks, in the quarantine quarters, during the train trip across eastern and central Canada, and at the immigration sheds in Winnipeg, Selkirk, and Brandon. Although most were penniless, they were in good spirits and looked to the time they could settle on productive land and rebuild their lives in the spirit of a universal brotherhood free from the pressures of the church as well as free from the constraints of militarism and the oath. So they thought.

The first year of settlement was especially trying. Advance teams of workers went by train and then by horse teams and on foot to select sites for villages on three blocks of land in what is now Saskatchewan: the North Colony in the Pelly area bordering the Manitoba border; the South Colony stretching from Kamsack on the west to Buchanan on the east; and the Duck Lake or Saskatchewan Colony in the Blaine Lake-Langham district between Saskatoon and Prince Albert. They homesteaded over 773,400 acreas in all. The settlers moved to these sites and began constructing sixty-one villages. Because the able-bodied men had to be away on railway contracts earning the much-needed money for the community, the women, children, and old men had the task of constructing the villages. Because horses and oxen were few (barely enough to haul supplies from Yorkton on the Canadian Pacific Railway line, some forty to eighty miles from the North-South colonies), the group had to rely on human power to break the soil for planting their first garden. This meant that there were occasions when women hitched themselves to the plow in a heroic pioneering effort to cultivate the soil for the first crop of potatoes and vegetables. Thanks to government aid in providing seeds, building supplies, and food; and to the Quakers of Philadelphia who gave spinning wheels, livestock, and more food; to the women's organizations in Ontario, who donated wool, box stoves, and carving tools; and to friends in California who sent four carloads of dried fruit; the Doukhobors barely survived what turned out to be an especially severe winter during the first year on the Canadian prairies. At this time the Doukhobors were without the support of their main leader, Peter V. Veregin, who was serving time in Siberian exile and was not expected in Canada until late 1902; this meant that decisions about collective actions were either deferred or made only after agonizing discussion and arguments.

The main issue concerned the style of ownership and social organization. While communal experiments were previously attempted as an ideal form, the Doukhobors now faced a different opportunity—that of private ownership. At the first convention of the Doukhobors in July of the first year of their settlement the delegates (after long deliberation) decided to continue the communal ideal. Survival seemed to dictate this for the time being, expecially since gifts of food and supplies came to a central fund. By 1903, the Doukhobor Trading Company was formed under a communal umbrella which encompassed common agricultural work, and several brick factories and flour mills. And with the coming of the railroad, the administrative centre in 1905 moved from the village of

Doukhobor Community, Veregin, Saskatchewan, 1908—communal flour mill
in background.

*By 1903, the Doukhobor Trading Company was formed under a communal
umbrella which encompassed common agricultural work, and several brick
factories and flour mills. And with the coming of the railroad, the
administrative centre in 1905 moved from the village of Otradnoe to the new
village of Veregin, located between Kamsack and Canora in Saskatchewan. By
this time, the Doukhobors had established the largest experiment in pure
communism in North America.*

Otradnoe to the new village of Veregin, located between Kamsack
and Canora in Saskatchewan. By this time, the Doukhobors had
established the largest experiment in pure communism in North
America. For them communal living was strongly based on spiritual
beliefs, promulgated in their *sobranie* meetings, the focal point of
every village.

The combination of being pacifist, of Slavic origin, speaking
Russian, and leading a style of life which competed with the
dominant mode of private enterprise did not sit well with many
Canadians of British stock who still lived under the fading shadow of
colonialism. These British Canadians were already at odds with the
Chinese workers who, after completing railway contracts in British
Columbia, decided to stay in Canada and survive as best they could
by washing the dirty linen and serving food at cheap prices. The
British Canadian model was that of the crucible of assimilation in
which all of the impurities in its domain would be crushed leaving the

pure British stock, who would remain as the administrative, ruling class. This was the social policy long before the multi-cultural trend arose in the 1970s following a reappraisal of Canada's new social reality.

This view was reflected by the opposition party politicians who criticized not only the Doukhobors but all eastern European settlers as well as the "yellow peril" who did not conform to the Anglo-Saxon mold. Sifton was wrong, they proclaimed, to have allowed entry of these "men in sheepskin coats." Others called them "garlic-smelling" Slavs, "as stubborn as cattle," "un-Christian," not fit to be Canadian citizens. This view was found among ranchers who were hostile to all settlers because of a selfish wish to have unhindered access to the prairie lands. As well, this view was found among some businessmen who criticized the cooperative structures for being unfair to the free enterprise system of the country. "Unfair competition," they cried. And as more settlers came (the population of Saskatchewan rose five-fold from 1899 to 1905), pressure arose for more free homestead land. The Doukhobors had three reserves which included some of the best land in the country. "Why should they be so privileged?" neighbours asked. Finally, there were the militarists who, determined to recruit more people for cannon fodder, said: "If these people refuse to take up the gun, they are not fit to be citizens and should be deported." And so, the arguments mounted against these Russian peasants from the Caucasus who simply envisaged a different kind of society—a universal brotherhood where cooperation instead of conflict would be the norm and where discussion and honest work would replace the old institution of militarism. The new clashed with the old.

As long as their old friends such as Clifford Sifton were around to support them, the Doukhobors and the government were able to come up with some compromise. When Sifton was replaced in 1905 by Frank Oliver, who was hostile to all Slavs, the tide turned against these people. When the renowned Methodist minister, John McDougall, headed a land commission and recommended to Oliver that the communal structure of land ownership be abolished, the government acquiesced. An ultimatum was issued which required Doukhobors to become naturalized and swear the oath of allegiance to the Crown before they would be eligible for the free homestead land. The result was drastic: seventy-five percent of the improved land (258,000 acres or two-thirds of the improved land) reverted to the Crown and was sold in public auction in what turned out to be the largest land rush for many years. The loss to the Doukhobors was around eleven million dollars.

DOUKHOBOR SETTLEMENTS IN WESTERN CANADA

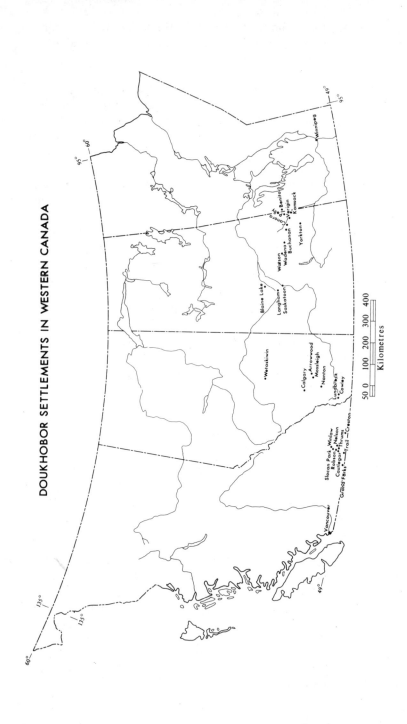

Doukhobors travelling from the village in the Yorkton area to Broadview, Saskatchewan, the embarkation point to British Columbia, 1909.

When the renowned Methodist minister, John McDougall, headed a land commission and recommended to Oliver that the communal structure of land ownership be abolished, the government acquiesced... The result was drastic: 75% of the improved land... reverted to the Crown and was sold in public auction... Five thousand members were led by Veregin to a new settlement in the southern interior of British Columbia.

James Mavor of the University of Toronto, who earlier assisted the Doukhobors in negotiations with the government, called this "a breach of faith." Under the Homestead Act, naturalization involved the taking of an oath "to defend the king"—a "technicality" that the Doukhobors knew nothing about (and would have objected to if they had known about it) before coming to Canada. Most of the Doukhobors thought that such an oath would lead to a negation of exemption from military service, an exemption they had secured under a government Order-in-Council.

The loss was a major blow to the Doukhobor community, and immediately caused a split into three camps. Those in conscience who would affirm rather than take the oath (the affirmation was not made known to most Doukhobors, in contrast to the Mennonites who had such a clause written into their immigration arrangements) were able to maintain their homesteads and remain in Saskatchewan. Known as Independent Doukhobors they were also of an independent mind and were suspicious of a hereditary type of leadership which had recently emerged under the Veregin name.

Many of their number, while remaining Doukhobors, soon became prosperous farmers. Their sons and daughters, over several generations, adopted the ways of the dominant society, aspired to higher education, and achieved many of the prestigious occupations of the larger society. This resulted in a gradual erosion of Doukhobor prayer services, cultural traditions, and the Russian language. Many became assimilated and joined other churches, while others do not attend any church except on special occasions.

The large party, known as the Community Doukhobors (and later as the Orthodox Doukhobors) was the one that initially suffered a major land loss. Its members were headed by a charismatic leader, Peter V. Veregin. Five thousand members were led by Veregin to a new settlement in the southern interior of British Columbia in the former mining town centres of Brilliant, Castlegar, Slocan Valley, and Grand Forks. Instead of the single street village with single storey houses (as in Saskatchewan), the Community Doukhobors opted for seventy-two double houses built as village units but organized as one commune in which individual incomes were turned into a central office. No oath of allegiance was required since this was a private purchase. Later, this large group bought more land in the Cowley district of southern Alberta and in the Kylemore district of Saskatchewan where settlements were also founded. The headquarters was at Veregin, and, since 1931, at Brilliant where a major jam factory operated under the company name of the Christian Community of Universal Brotherhood (CCUB).

The third group comprised less than ten percent of the Doukhobor population in Canada. Representing those who did not fit into the other two groups, it was the least organized. As deviants, this group was initially known as the seekers of freedom, then as pilgrims, later as the Sons of Freedom, and today, it can best be described as the zealots. Beginning originally as a handful of sincere seekers of "the free way" who questioned the rapid modernization of the Doukhobor community, they sought what they considered to be "the straight path of Christ." In protest, several of them burned the canvas on the binder used to cut the grain. Others, protesting government pressure to change the communal structure towards individualism, initiated 1,700 members to trek across the prairies in October, 1902. Although the land issue was the main cause of the protest, some spoke of a Rousseau-type of "back to nature" movement; others wished to find a warmer climate; still others spoke of meeting Christ. For some, "meeting Christ" meant seeing Veregin released from Siberian exile, as he was soon after. Their inspiration came from anarchists like Alexander Bodyansky, who lived with them for several months; from Veregin's letters, which were inadvertently published by the Tolstoyans and released early in 1900; and from Lev Tolstoy. Tolstoy had praised the Doukhobors for remaining aloof from governments, refusing to take the oath, and for condemning private property. He also praised them for their abstinence from meat, tobacco and intoxicants, and proclaimed: "The Christian teaching cannot be taken piecemeal: it is all or nothing."

When the original trek no longer appealed to the masses, a handful of zealots stripped naked, personifying themselves as pilgrims helping to put the main group back on track. When the public reacted with horror to nudity, the "technique" stuck, and over the next seven decades, was used spontaneously by psychologically unstable individuals or deviants who imagined themselves as martyrs for a cause, but who at times were seeking to "do their thing" or get attention. And attention they got from the mass media, usually at the expense of other Doukhobors. These deviants were often rejected from membership in other groups, and often were an embarrassment to the whole Doukhobor population. Naked bodies on the cover of a magazine article or newpaper sold copies, but did nothing to enhance the image of the Doukhobors.

The burnings and bombings that rocked the Kootenays of British Columbia for some seventy years and the limited destruction in Saskatchewan and Alberta were more problematic and of a different character. Some of the earlier burnings were "protest" fires; for example, the 1916 burning of Otradnoe Community Home was in protest to the lavishness of Peter Veregin's lifestyle. In protest burnings, the culprits remained at the scene of the crime. However, the majority of burnings were "secret" in nature and in these cases, the culprit or culprits were usually not found. Some $100 million damage to date (to schools, community centres, businesses, railway tracks and power lines, jam factories and grain elevators) has caused much anguish both within and outside the Doukhobor community. A still unsolved Canadian Pacific Railway explosion took the life of Peter V. Veregin and eight other passengers in 1924. Many point their fingers to the zealots, but the authorities have seldom found anyone who is specifically responsible. The public blames all the Doukhobors who are incensed by this wholesale condemnation and at times feel that this is a conspiracy to undermine the whole movement.

With the passage of time, these new immigrants again showed their creativity as they virtually built a garden of Eden in the untamed wilderness. Productive orchards arose where previously only tall firs and cedars stood. Sawmills transformed these evergreen giants into manageable lumber for community dwellings, grain elevators, and flour mills, schools, *banias* (saunas), and offices. Extra lumber was exported.   Brick factories arose on the prairies and in British Columbia. Their products were used for export and for construction of more permanent dwellings—community centres, jam factories, blacksmiths shops, and public schools. Strawberries, raspberries, apricots, and other fruits were preserved as top-quality jams made only from pure ingredients. Flax was converted into durable linen; wool was changed into socks, mittens and scarves; seasoned wood was shaped into ladles (used to eat borshch—a special vegetarian soup with a potato, cabbage, dill and tomato base).   The Doukhobors constructed a bridge across the Kootenay River, carved out roads from rocky terrain, and established water and irrigation systems for their domestic use. And they found time to sing (which they were very good at) and to discuss and share their inner thoughts at *sobranie* meetings.

Their *sobranies* were multipurpose. In the religious part, men stood on the left (as you entered the meeting from the back), and women on the right.   The symbol of equal and trustworthy humanity—bread, salt and water—stood at the front separating the sexes. Russian continued to be the language used in these gatherings. There was no Bible reading, for Doukhobors considered it only as an ordinary book.   Nor were musical instruments permitted. Instead, the people (standing) sang *Otche*, which is the Lord's Prayer. Included as well were several psalms and hymns. These were either Christian in origin, borrowings from inspired leaders, or creations of their own depicting their history and the values of hard work, morality, and pacifism based on their spiritual beliefs.

The second type of *sobranie* was separate and often followed the Sunday religious part; it dealt with business—both social and specific other interests of the local community were shared, discussed, and decisions made. In both cases, the *sobranie* was (and still is today) an adaptation of the decision-mechanism used in the old Russian *mir* or village system, where all adults had a "democratic" vote in the affairs of the village community.

Sobranie meetings and visits between the colonies of western Canada immersed the Doukhobor pioneers in the life of their community.   All senses seemed to come alive as they realized the physical fruits of their labour, heard the sound of hammers above the *a cappella* voices of the people, tasted the fragrant sweetness of their K-C jams, breathed the clean prairie air, and felt the surge of energy that permeated their communal experiment. The Independents who were not part of the Community, also experienced some of these sensations as they constructed their individual holdings, while overcoming the pioneering hardships that taxed every muscle, nerve and one's cerebral cortex. In or out of the Community, they spoke Russian and learned English, and all shared the common values of pacifism, equality, and love. And annually, they participated in the peace day gatherings in June. In and out of season, young and old shared both hardships and the fruits of a common culture.

To the outsiders, the Doukhobors appeared as remarkable people, yet peculiar in their ways. Their hard work, industriousness, and cleanliness were above reproach. Yet their isolation from other institutions (like the church and social clubs), their use of a foreign language, and their unequivocal stand against militarism were in question.

Government officials were displeased by Doukhobor behaviour—some refused to register their births, marriages, and deaths for fear that these official proclamations in a "police register" would invalidate their stand against wars. There were also those who opposed public schools on the ground that schools glorify wars, downplay the cooperative ethic, and wean children away from physical labour, respect for parents and for rural living. Hence, many Doukhobors had no schooling in either English or in Russian.

The land crisis of 1907 provided one opportunity for the government to break up the Doukhobor community; the war years and the economic Depression provided further opportunities for stamping out a "pernicious" movement. These interventions took several forms provincially and federally. The British Columbia Government in 1914 passed an emergency Anti-Doukhobor Community Regulation Act which put the onus on the Community to register births, deaths, weddings, and insure regular attendance in schools. The Community was to be punished for the delinquent actions of individuals. Later, when fines were imposed and the Community refused to pay, the authorities seized a large Community truck and other assets on distress warrants; a few days later, schools were mysteriously destroyed by arson—causing anger on both sides. It took another three decades before the education issue was smoothed over.

Following World War I and the anti-pacifist mood of the country, the British Columbia government temporarily barred Doukhobors and other conscientious objectors from voting. And later that year, a Canadian Order-in-Council prohibited the landing in Canada of any immigrant of Doukhobor, Hutterite, or Mennonite origin (this was repealed for Hutterites and Mennonites in 1921, for the Doukhobors in 1926). Again, in 1931, all Doukhobors in British Columbia were barred from voting, while in 1934 the Federal Government barred Doukhobors in British Columbia from voting federally. Originally, the intent of R. B. Bennett, Prime Minister of Canada, was to bar all Doukhobors, but he failed to get the support of Parliament. It was only in 1956 that the British Columbia and Federal Governments lifted the ban. Voting resumed the following year, thus erasing from the law books a long-standing discriminatory act against a group of Canadian citizens.

In 1933 the Federal Government, in cooperation with the Government of Saskatchewan, made an abortive attempt to deport Peter P. Veregin, Community Doukhobor leader. An independent Doukhobor lawyer, Peter G. Makaroff of Saskatoon, frustrated R. B. Bennett's gestapo-like tactics, and the case was successfully fought in a Halifax court just in time to prevent the deportation.

During the height of the Hungry Thirties in 1937 when the Community Doukhobor organization (the CCUB) was unable to meet its commitments to finance companies, the Community went into bankruptcy. To prevent eviction and also avoid unpleasantness during the upcoming visit to Canada of King George VI and Princess Elizabeth, the British Columbia Government intervened and took over Community property worth six million dollars for less than $300,000. The Doukhobor Community could have kept it if the Canadian Government had intervened and used existing legislation to preserve this group as it had other cooperatives. It didn't. It was only in 1961 that the British Columbia Government began to sell back the land to the Doukhobors. The rapport between the Doukhobors and the government had again been broken. Together with the earlier land loss, it was clear that governments were not to be trusted.

The destruction in the 1970s of two Doukhobor landmarks in British Columbia and the failure of the authorities to find the culprits have been unsettling to the Doukhobor community. Both incidents took place in Grand Forks, British Columbia, in the centre of the Community Doukhobor headquarters called the Union of Spiritual Communities of Christ (USCC). The first was the destruction of its organizational centre, a bi-weekly publishing house, a rare Russian language library, and a Co-op Store. The second, in 1977, involved a large Community Centre which handled the needs of the Doukhobors and wider public. Both have been rebuilt, but the increased insurance together with twenty-four hour surveillance has placed a large economic and psychological burden on the

Community Doukhobors, with the gnawing question always in mind, "When will it all end?" Most people can't wait for that most welcome day. But the indications are to the contrary; the authorities appear helpless in finding the culprit, or as some think, they are not trying hard enough.

For over eighty years, the Doukhobors have survived in Canada. They number over 30,000; most are located in Saskatchewan and British Columbia; some are in Alberta. Several hundred reside in California and Oregon and 20,000 live in the southern USSR. Among them, there are many farmers, doctors, lawyers, teachers, mechanics, engineers, artists, and others. Yet with increased mobility, industrialization and urbanization, and with inter-marriages, it is not surprising that active membership in Doukhobor organizations in Canada has dwindled drastically during the past two decades. Assistance from the Canadian Government in the form of grants for museums, the writings of histories, and the opening of historic sites have been useful, but not sufficient. In an effort to avert this cultural erosion and at the same time to revive their thrust in the historic peacemaking role, the Doukhobors have turned to the Soviet Union for assistance. For many Doukhobors the country of their origin is a rich storehouse of resource materials in language, literature, art, music, and the sciences.

With the assistance of Society Rodina (the cultural society of the USSR) the Doukhobor youth have developed an educational exchange program in which Canadian students spend several months or years in language and/or in a general arts program in the Soviet Union. In exchange, the Soviets have sent to Canada published works, magazines, periodicals, and films, as well as cultural performing artists such as the mini-Bolshoi dance group.

Increasing the links between the East and the West is one way to reduce the causes of fear and suspicion that threatens survival. Coming from Russian and Canadian backgrounds, the Doukhobors have continually sought to extend these links. Paradoxically, these increased ties have threatened some Canadians who consider the connection to be foreign to the purist isolationist view of the former colonial elite. Fortunately, multicultural arguments have diluted this stance and there is a growing realization that links across cultural and ideological boundaries are important if we are to survive as a human civilization. In this light, the Doukhobors' bridge-building role is sufficient justification for their existence, their enthusiasm, and their maverick ways. But inherent in this role is their idealistic attempt to set things right; to create a world where reason instead of guns dictates its welfare; to bring back love, respect, equality, and beauty into human relationships. In brief, to become civilized again. Hail to those remarkable pioneers on the Canadian prairies who are helping to build the New Jerusalem on planet earth!

To stem and hopefully reverse the tide of attrition, in recent years some Doukhobors began to translate prayers, hymns and songs from Russian into English. As a result of their efforts, "The Book of Life" has been translated as well as several hymns and songs.

In 1981, the Women's Auxiliary of the Doukhobor society of Saskatoon decided to participate in Saskatoon's Folk Fest by setting up a Doukhobor pavillion. The popularity of this pavillion stimulated the Society to appoint a committee to develop the future direction for Doukhobors and to restore the consciousness of their predecessors who considered themselves to be the "corner stone" upon which to build a happier and peaceful society.

X Building the New Jerusalem on the prairies: The Ukrainian experience

Stella Hryniuk
Roman Yereniuk

In a period so evidently saturated with secular humanism, writing about the experiences of religious denominations which were little known and even less well understood in Canada at the turn of the century is like writing about the first wheeled transportation in an age of space shuttles. The force of time has performed its task of eroding the intensity of the ritual expressions of the Ukrainian people of Canada, no less than it has eroded their allegiance to their ancestral Churches—the Ukrainian Orthodox and Ukrainian Catholic.

Their homeland, the Ukraine, once a powerful unitary and independent Christian state, became divided after the fifteenth century into two unequal territorial conglomerates—one on the east bank of the Dnieper River, the other on the western bank stretching to the Carpathian mountains. Common religious sentiments which bound the two together in Christ were derived from the Ukraine's acceptance of Christianity from Byzantium. The outward manifestations of these sentiments harmonized effectively with the exuberant and liberating force which was the eastern Christian rite.

In the sixteenth century, most of the eparchies of the Ukrainian Church accepted union with the Catholic Church (Union of Brest, 1596), yet maintained their eastern Christian orientation. This event greatly altered the religious history of the Ukrainians, divided them into two factions with major doctrinal differences but common eastern Christian heritage and rite.[1] Through successive political protectorates (Polish, Lithuanian, Rumanian, Hungarian, Russian) the Ukrainian peasantry maintained an almost undiminished strength of association to their traditional religion.[2] Immigration to the New World in the robust nineteenth century was just another test of the strength of that association.

In the social history of Canada, a theme (not frequently nor extensively investigated) has been the relationship in the religious sphere between the Ukrainians and their host society. The influx of approximately 150,000 Ukrainians, between 1896 and 1914,[3] altered not only the religious expression of the Ukrainians but also the collective and lasting nature of Canadian society.

Who were these people? What was their ancestral faith? What gave them the energy to build rudimentary churches before there were priests to serve in them? And what motivated them to resist invitations from more established Canadian religious denominations and to maintain (even to the present) a distinctly separate religious experience? The Ukrainian immigrants in Canada were the product of a massive population transfer from Europe to the New World which had begun in the middle of the nineteenth century. Canadian immigration statistics show that from 1896, a steadily increasing number of Ukrainians arrived annually and settled in the three western provinces. The majority came from Galicia and Bukovina, the eastern provinces of Austro-Hungary. By occupation, they were small agriculturalists or unskilled labourers mainly drawn from the more ambitious, adventurous, economically and intellectually advanced strata of the peasant class and psychologically receptive to influences other than those found in their villages. The Austrian state religion was Catholicism, and the 1900 census showed that ninety percent of the population declared themselves members of the Roman, Ukrainian, or Armenian Catholic jurisdictions.[4]   In Bukovina, the population was predominantly Orthodox, sharing the same faith with the Moldavians but ethnically separate from them.   In both these provinces, the monolithic nature of their churches precluded any cognizance of Protestant denominations.

The Ukrainian peasant was not overly concerned with church administration or structure, nor was he well grounded in the intricacies and subtleties of eastern Christian theology. He did not question the Church's teachings and could not discourse on its content. For him, religion was an integral part of his way of life and of day-to-day living. Christianity was internalized and expressed in various ways during the course of his day, week, month and year. For example, his work cycle revolved around the liturgical year, the feasts and the lenten period of the Church.[5] The state calendar as such had little influence on them. The Ukrainian peasants were

Ukrainian Museum of Canada

Graveside prayers following a family memorial service in a country church.
Seen are the priest, family and the cantor. The memorial "kolachi" or round
loaves of bread denote everlasting life and are customarily used in memorial
services in several regions of Ukraine. Circa: 1940

Eastern Christianity is sometimes criticized by the Protestant west as being too
concerned with otherworldliness or with the life here-after. However this
emphasis on eschatology has allowed the Ukrainian Church and other eastern
Churches to persevere in the most trying and difficult periods of their history,
including the period of settlement in Canada.

concerned primarily with the manner of expressing their beliefs in the
religious heritage of the Ukrainian peoples. Thus, it is
understandable that upon their arrival in Canada, the pioneers began
to establish their religious life as a carbon copy of the life of the
villages.

Eastern Christianity is sometimes criticized by the Protestant
west as being too concerned with other-worldliness or with the
life here-after. However, this emphasis on eschatology has allowed
the Ukrainian Church and other eastern Churches to persevere in the
most trying and difficult periods of their history, including the period
of settlement in Canada.

The Church and its liturgical life in eastern Christianity derives
its uniqueness from its teaching of New Jerusalem, the new Sion—
the initiated Kingdom of God. Nowhere is this better expressed than
in the celebration of Christ's resurrection, the feast of feasts in the
Ukrainian Church. Christ's Church has replaced the Church of the

Old Testament through the risen Saviour and as such, welcomes forth all the believers of this miracle. During the Resurrection Matins, the Church triumphantly proclaims in the Paschal Canon:

> Lift up your eyes, O Sion, and behold:
> Here are thy children streaming forth toward thee
> Like divinely kindled stars,
> From the west, the north, the south and the east,
> As in thee they bless Christ's name forever more.[6]

And in the same celebration, the Church is identified as the New Jerusalem and proclaims:

> Shine forth, shine forth O New Jerusalem,
> The glory of the Lord has risen upon thee!
> Rejoice and exult now, O Sion.[7]

The image of the Church as the New Jerusalem in eastern Christendom includes not only the Church on earth (the Church militant) but also the invisible Church (the Church triumphant). Both participate in the celebration of Christ's resurrection:

> For meet is it that the heavens should rejoice,
> And that the earth should be glad,
> And that the whole universe both visible and invisible
> Should celebrate the Feast![8]

In addition, the Church includes the departed among its numbers. This inclusion is best portrayed in the Resurrection hymn *par excellence* of the eastern Church:

> Christ is risen from the dead,
> Trampling down death by death,
> And bestowing life to those in the grave.[9]

Eastern Christianity emphasizes not only the potential life-giving force granted to all those departed[10] but also the beginning of another life for the living. Thereby the Church, at this feast and continually in its life, lives in the expectation of the second coming of Christ, His final judgement, and the establishment of His Kingdom.

New Jerusalem intimately connects the earthly Church and the heavenly Church as well as the souls of the departed members.[11] This bond fully and totally permeates the life of the Church, its community, and the liturgical celebrations. The eastern liturgy, both that of St. John Chrysostom and St. Basil the Great, is often portrayed as the symbolic representation of the earthly life of Christ. During this celebration symbolism is replaced by realism in the transformation of the bread and wine into the Body and Blood of Christ.[12]   Through participation in the liturgy, the believer experiences a journey or procession that leads him to the final destination—the New Jerusalem. Even as the priest commences the liturgy with the words, "Blessed is the Kingdom of the Father, the Son and the Holy Spirit," the believer is reminded of the New Jerusalem as the final destination.[13]

The faithful, gathered in the church under the leadership of the priest, constitute the *ecclesia*—the Church.   The liturgy is the gathering of those who are to meet the risen Lord and to enter with Him into His Kingdom. For the Ukrainian Orthodox or Catholic believer, the act of the entrance into the church is considered to be the transformation from the temporal and profane world to that of the sacred, eternal.[14]   Therefore, a foretaste of the New Jerusalem is experienced even in this life by the believing Christian. This is well expressed in the hymns of the liturgy—the Trisagion, Sanctus, and particularly the Cherubic Hymn: "We who mystically represent the Cherubim, and who sing the thrice holy hymn of the Life-giving Trinity, let us now put aside all worldly cares." Even as the ranks of the angels, the believers have now entered into the Church's heavenly dimension and ascended into heaven. Subsequently, after the eucharist, the eschatological banquet of the Kingdom, the Church proclaims triumphantly, "we have seen the true light and partaken of the Holy Spirit. . . ." Thus, the believer has experienced eternity, has seen the New Jerusalem, and is sent back into the world as a new person to evangelize and convert others. For the believing Christian, the Church—the New Jerusalem—was realized and is continually realized through the liturgy.

For the eastern Christian, the New Jerusalem was not only consummated in the church building and during the liturgy, but was also enacted in each home which, in popular religious writings, was referred to as the "home church" (*domashnia tserkva*). In the home, a wall or a corner of a room (usually one associated with mealtime and in most cases facing eastward (toward Jerusalem) was reserved for the icons (*obrazy*) of the family. This became the place and direction of the family prayer, which was generally led by the father or the eldest male in the household, who represented the priest in the Church. Many pioneer homes were endowed with the holiness of icons (or framed paper copies) brought from the homeland. The "home church"—the extended family—represented the smallest cell of the Christian community. Often the pioneers had no clergy to look after the spiritual needs of the community. Therefore, one of the homes became both the center of the family's and of the community's religious life. This experience is described by Maria Adamowska in her recollections:

> Our poor settlers consulted among themselves and decided to meet every Sunday and sing at least those parts of the liturgy that were meant to be sung by the cantor. Since our house was large enough, that was where the meetings were held. On Sunday mornings everyone hurried to our house the way one would to church ... And so it was that we were able to gratify, at least partially, the longings of our souls.[15]

Local church buildings in Canada soon replaced these first humble and primitive dwellings, using models of church architecture in the homeland. For the eastern Christian Ukrainian (both Orthodox and Catholic), the church building itself was considered as the center of eternity in microcosm on earth and the believer's entrance into the edifice was presented as a foretaste of the eternal kingdom. This is clearly indicated in one of the most often quoted texts from the *Primary Chronicle* composed in the first half of the twelfth century. According to tradition, when Prince Volodymyr (980 - 1015) sent envoys to investigate the major religions of the world, they reported to him about their visit to a church (probably St. Sophia) in Byzantium in the following words:

> We knew not whether we were in heaven or on earth.
> For on earth there is not such splendor or such
> beauty, and we are at loss to describe it . . .
> for we cannot forget that beauty. Every man,
> After tasting something sweet, is afterwards
> unwilling to accept that which is bitter. . . .

This report had a profound effect on Prince Volodymyr and contributed to his acceptance of Byzantine Christianity for the Kievan State.

The celebration of the liturgy is an experience that truly involves the total person and his or her senses. Illustrative of this involvement in the church are the burning of incense and the use of the censor, the rich decorating of interior walls with icons and the importance of the iconostasis (icon-screen) in dividing the interior into two parts, the richly coloured (especially golds and silvers) church vestments, the polyphonic singing of the community with instrumental accompaniment, and the continual exchange of singing between the priest and the faithful. All this can be referred to in the language of the 1980s as truly "a light and sound manifestation." This was, and is, the heart of eastern Christian piety—an experience of eternity in this world which sustains the believer from one liturgy to the next. All this was possible, however, only with the presence of a priest. At first the churches stood idly by for the lack of clergy, but the religious life of the Ukrainian peasant could not be postponed.

The pioneers with their meager belongings almost always brought with them the necessary and important religious "inventory"—icons, liturgical church books and prayer beads. Due to the importance of the liturgical worship, most of the books were for the ritual and cult. Although the most important book should have been the Bible, the more popular were the books for the liturgy, especially the *Molytovnyk* (Prayer Book) for corporate and private worship, *Apostol* (the readings from the Epistles of the Disciples used for the liturgy) and, to a lesser extent, the *Trebnyk* (Service Book for the Sacraments), *Chasoslov, Oktoikh, Psaltyr* (used for the specific and moveable parts of the liturgical celebration). Another popular book was the *Zhytia Sviatykh* - the *Lives of the Saints* according to the days of the liturgical year.[16] Many of these volumes were published by the Lviv Stauropgia Institute press.[17] Often large crosses, reminiscent of the crosses of freedom in Galicia which commemorated the emancipation of the serfs in 1848, were erected on the new soil as a symbol of gratitude for the safe arrival and beginning of new life in Canada. In addition, this symbol of the faith was believed to be effective in warding off evil and blessing the community with its sacredness.[18] In the construction of their religious and cultural institutions, the Ukrainians always separated the sacred from the profane. The Church was dedicated to the service of God, while another important structure, the *Narodnyi Dim* (National Home) was dedicated to the cultural and national work.[19] Both institutions had their function in the community and there was never any attempt to accomodate religiosity and culture under one roof.

Home church worship and other religious practices of the Ukrainian settlers were adapted to the scarcity in Canada of priests of their own rite. In their homeland, the priest had been regarded as one of the most important sources of spiritual and intellectual knowledge and guidance.[20] In the limited lives of the peasants, often the ecclesiastical authority outweighed the civil authority in the respect and obedience that he generated. But few of the village clergy had been permitted (or had chosen) to emigrate to America with their charges. A Vatican decree of 1894 had forbidden married clergy to come to serve in America.[21] And since the majority of Ukrainian Catholic clergy were married, this decree automatically excluded many priests from emigrating even if they had wanted to. Existing evidence suggests that many priests did not emigrate because they were in a stable situation in Galicia and therefore were not attracted to the new world. Consequently, there was a gap in religious leadership into which many were willing to step. Until 1897, the religious life of the Ukrainian communities was severely neglected. Occasional visits to the colonies by itinerant priests or ministers of various denominations were sad reminders of a lifestyle the Ukrainians had abandoned forever. A poignant example of this was the 1898 visit to western Canada of a Ukrainian Catholic priest, Father Nester Dmytriw. Contemporary accounts indicate that his visit was the occasion for both great joy and great sorrow.[22] Individual communities made some effort to obtain their own priest by writing to their former parishes and to the religious orders in Galicia. An example of such a letter, written in 1899 by a Ukrainian settler in Manitoba, was published in the journal of the Basilian Order in Galicia, *Misionar:*

> Dear Fathers,
>   Life here is very good for our bodies, there is no physical deprivation, but what of that, when there are great deprivations of the soul. There is enough to eat, drink, wear. But our soul is poor, very poor. This is because it has nothing to eat, or drink, nothing from which to live, no roof to stand beneath. It can only shelter itself under strangers' roofs and listen to them, but it does not hear, and does not understand.[23]

The strangers this writer referred to were the visiting missionaries from the Tsarist Russian Orthodox Mission in the United States of America, the Presbyterian and Methodist missionary societies, and the Roman Catholic priests of the Latin rite, all foreign to them. Competition for the souls (or votes) of the unsuspecting immigrants was well under way within months of their arrival in Canada. They had brought with them a deep faith, expecting the freedom to live it out in Canada. What they hadn't expected was the variety of denominations, political parties, and private interests which would exploit this faith.

   The Roman Catholic Church was one of the first and foremost antagonists they encountered. In the west, it was headed by Louis Philippe Adelard Langevin, Archbishop of the Diocese of St.

Stella Hryniuk and Roman Yereniuk

A cartoon by the Ukrainian-Canadian church painter, Hnat Sych, depicting
the strife between the Ukrainian Catholics (centre) and the Ukrainian
Orthodox as well as Presbyterian Mission (right).

*Competition for the souls (or votes) of the unsuspecting immigrants was well
underway within months of their arrival in Canada.*

Boniface (1895 - 1915). Langevin had an idealistic view of a Western
Canadian Catholic empire inhabited by fecund farmers speaking
many languages, all grateful to the French and to him. Meanwhile,
the Ukrainians had a vision of freedom from religious, political and
social restrictions imposed by an alien culture like that of the Poles in
Galicia. These visions were challenged immediately upon the arrival
of the Ukrainian Catholics in Western Canada where a
predominantly Anglo-Saxon Protestant population was living in
precarious harmony with a French Catholic minority. It might seem
that the common denominator Ukrainian and French Catholicism
would have been a source for greater and easier collaboration
between these two groups toward common ends. However, this was
not the case, largely because of Archbishop Langevin's personality
and ideology.

Appeals flowed into Langevin's diocesan office from the
Ukrainians who begged him to obtain priests for them. At first he
tried to accomodate them with Polish Catholic priests and churches.
As the Ukrainian population grew, and with it, the need for priests
for their own rite, Langevin appealed to the Vatican, to the Austrian
Emperor, and to Metropolitan Sheptycky, the head of the Ukrainian
Catholic Church in Galicia.[24] Only a handful of Basilian monks and

nuns arrived by 1902. Parallel to this development, missionary activity was begun among the Ukrainians in Canada by some Belgian members of the Redemptorist Order who had gained a working knowledge of Ukrainian and who were accepted into the Byzantine rite. As well, a few French Canadian secular priests were recruited for this work and transferred to the Byzantine rite. This number of priests was insufficient to care for the religious needs of the constantly increasing Ukrainian population. Furthermore, the Ukrainian population was often suspicious of these ministrations and the Roman Catholic Church organization on which they were founded.

By 1912, there were twenty-one Catholic missionaries serving this area: five Basilian, four Redemptorists, eight secular Ukrainian priests and four French priests. In 1912, thirteen more secular priests and eight nuns of the Sisters of Servants of Mary Immaculate arrived from Galicia. Together with the early missionaries, this was the corp of men and women who dedicated their lives to serving the Ukrainian Catholic population which, by 1914, was about 150,000.

Meanwhile, the Bukovinian Orthodox immigrants (predominantly in southern Manitoba and in the area northeast of Edmonton, Alberta) also faced the problem of lack of clergy. Until 1917, their needs were partially answered by the Tsarist-subsidized Russian Orthodox Mission in the United States.[25]

Interested less in the New Jerusalem and more in building the new Canada, Protestant churches (particularly the Presbyterian) attempted to Canadianize the Ukrainian settlers by evangelizing them into seeing the Kingdom of God taking shape in the streets of the prairie cities. Equally concerned with the effect of Ukrainian settlers upon Canadian society were some English-speaking philanthropists such as A. Hunter and J. S. Woodsworth, who hoped to lead the immigrants (by means of their social and religious agencies) to understanding and adhering to the British-Canadian ideal and to Protestantism.[26] Instead, in their ignorance of the tenacity with which the Ukrainians had informally, individually and collectively decided to retain their separateness of language, religion and culture, these various groups succeeded in further alienating the Ukrainians and in sending them into the waiting hands of a class within the Ukrainian community—the "village intelligentsia." It was this group (rather than any alternative English-speaking figures) that many settlers respected and followed because the intelligentsia established a coherent and meaningful, organized community life for the Ukrainians.

Several young men of this intelligentsia had come to Canada

with the immigrating peasantry and now surfaced as the ideological influences among their people. They were distinguished by their espousal of the tenets of the Radical Party in Galicia, by their loyalty to the peasantry, and by their intense anti-clericalism.[27] Their views were applied in the new world but took on different colouring as the Ukrainians were left without guidance from their traditional churches. These young men believed intensely in the need to build and maintain group solidarity and they actively defended their heritage when it was threatened by the aggressive Canadianizers— the Protestant churches and the public schools.

Among these men were C. Genik, I. Bodrug, I. Negrych, P. Krat, O. Zherebko and P. Svarych who, by 1910, were trained as Canadian school teachers and became the defenders of the Ukrainian national life in Canada.[28] At first, many of these leaders themselves professed adherence to various Canadian Protestant sects or syncretic institutions sponsored by these sects. Later, some of them founded the Ukrainian Orthodox Church in Canada. Understandably, they encouraged similar religious orientation among the immigrant masses.

Believing that the Catholic Church was responsible for much of the social and political backwardness of the Galician Ukrainian, these men resisted Catholicism because they wished to break the hold of this Church over the immigrants in Canada. From the early years after their arrival in Canada, the intelligentsia had been convinced that Protestantism (with ideological objectives similar to those of the Radical Party) was the route by which dependency on the Catholic clergy might be countered in Canada. Some of them saw their own attachment to the Presbyterian Church and its evangelical methodology as an answer to the problem of modernizing the Ukrainians. They tried using hybrid forms of Eastern Christianity. Still others retreated from religion entirely and personally experimented with radical political ideologies. In the dealings with their Ukrainian compatriots, they were fully aware of the intense attachment of Ukrainians to Eastern Christianity. Therefore, they made its ritual the focus in the syncretic religious insitutions they created to influence the Ukrainian pioneers.

The first example of such an institution was the church organized by the pseudo-bishop, Serafym (Stefan Ustvolsky), in 1903. It was known as the All-Russian Patriarchal Orthodox Church or commonly as the "Serafymite Church." This was an abortive atttempt by C. Genik and associates of his to establish a church independent of the Roman Catholic and Russian Orthodox churches. Serafym proceeded to ordain into the priesthood cantors,

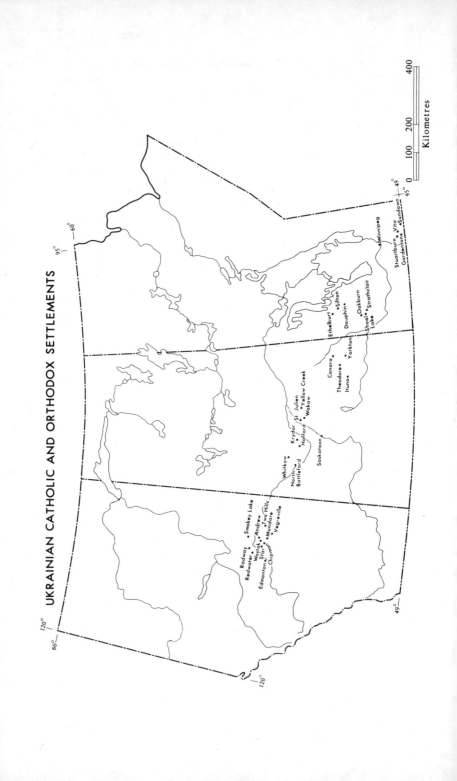

UKRAINIAN CATHOLIC AND ORTHODOX SETTLEMENTS

Radway • Smokey Lake
Redwater •
Wostok •   • Andrew
Edmonton • Star •   • Two Hills
Chipman •   • Mundare
• Vegreville

Whinkow •
North •
Battleford

Krydor •   St. Julian
Hafford •   • Yellow Creek
• Wakaw

Saskatoon •

Canora •
Theodore •
Ituna •   • Yorkton

Ethelburt •
• Sifton
Dauphin •

Oakburn •
Shoal •   • Strathclair
Lake

• Winnipeg

Stuartburn •   • Vita
Gardenton •   • Sundown

Kilometres

0   100   200   400

60°
95°
120°
60°
49°
95°
49°
120°

sacristans and anyone who presented himself (many of these were not well educated and soon lost their credibility in the community). However, failing to legitimize his ecclesiastical authority, Serafym departed from the scene in 1907. After his departure, a Russian Orthodox monk, Makarii Marchenko (Monchalenko), proclaimed himself as archbishop, but due to his eccentric behaviour and leadership, his following waned and he also soon disappeared. Although the Byzantine rite was quite well adhered to, the institution was self-defeating because the Ukrainian settlers soon realized that beyond the veneer of the rite, there was nothing else.

In 1904, Ivan Bodrug organized the Independent Greek Church which received inspiration and financial support from the Presbyterian Church of Canada.[29] Its first leaders, who came from the Serafymite Church called a convention in 1904, accepted a charter and disassociated themselves from Serafym. The Church enjoyed a considerable following for almost a decade. Although it maintained the facade of the Byzantine rite,[30] nevertheless under the Presbyterian influence, changes were gradually introduced to bring it into the mainstream of Protestantism. By 1913, the Independent Greek Church was integrated into the Presbyterian Church and by the end of the decade had lost its credibility in the Ukrainian community. Eventually, a majority of these Ukrainians dropped their affiliation with the Protestants and, along with others who were also disgruntled with Catholicism, established a Ukrainian National Committee in 1918 and then incorporated as a Ukrainian Orthodox Brotherhood. The Brotherhood established Ukrainian Orthodox parishes and came to have a substantial following on the prairies. Some Ukrainian Catholic parishes and most of the Bukovinian parishes that had been in the Russian Orthodox fold before 1918 went over to the new church.[31]

One final matter of importance for the religious experience of the Ukrainians in Canada was the need for a legitimate Ukrainian Church hierarchy. It is noteworthy that because both of the hybrid Churches (the Serafymite and the Independent Greek Church) had insurmountable problems in establishing their legitimacy according to the teachings of Eastern Christianity, they eventually disappeared. Many Ukrainian Catholics did not recognize the authority of the Latin-rite French bishops under whose jurisdiction they found themselves. From the outset they desired their own bishop. After considerable efforts were made towards this end, the Vatican (on the recommendations of the Latin hierarchy of Canada and Metropolitan Sheptycky of Galicia) appointed Bishop Nykyta Budka in 1912. He and his successors formed the Ukrainian Catholic ecclesiastical province of Canada which exists to the present day as the largest church of the Ukrainians in Canada.[32]

The Ukrainian Orthodox Church also attempted to legitimize itself in 1918. The founders—the Ukrainian Orthodox Brotherhood—sought and eventually received the ecclesiastical communion of Bishop Germanos, exarch of the patriarch of Antioch. Several years later, this church established ties with the Ukrainian Autocephalous Orthodox Church in the Ukraine and came under the obedience of Bishop (and later Metropolitan) Ivan Teodorovych, resident in the United States since 1922. After the Second World War, this jurisdiction accepted as their hierarch, Metropolitan Ilarion Ohienko, previously a bishop in the Autocephalous Orthodox Church of Poland (which, in the interwar period, had been composed mainly of Ukrainians). Today this church constitutes the second largest Ukrainian following in Canada.[33]

Despite the many hardships associated with the settlement period, the two traditional Ukrainian churches were formally re-established by 1918. The pioneer era (1891-1918) was filled with intense rivalry between the two churches—often over nationalistic and not strictly religious matters. This rivalry carried over into the interwar and the postwar periods and still emerges from time to time in a greatly attenuated form even today.

While stressing and maintaining the common Eastern Christian heritage, the churches continued to grow in membership and strength along distinct and separate administrative patterns. By 1931 (see table opposite) the membership in the two bodies constituted eighty-three percent of the Ukrainian population in Canada. The second and third waves of Ukrainian immigration (the second between the World Wars and the third after World War II) introduced not only a further 100,000 Ukrainians to Canada but also many new national and political dimensions into Ukrainian Canadian society. By 1971, however, the two traditional churches claimed only fifty-two percent of the Ukrainians in Canada, with a marked shift of allegiance from the churches of the eastern rite to the Roman Catholic and Protestant denominations (especially to the United Church, see table). Although this shift from membership in the traditional churches is dramatic, the lives of the remaining adherents continue to be affected by their association with the traditional churches. Over the years since 1918, the churches performed an important function as the hub of religious life and as focal centres for the maintenance of a separate Ukrainian identity in a multicultural Canada.

Year	Ukrainian Catholic	Ukrainian Orthodox	Roman Catholic	United Church	Anglican	Lutheran	Other	Total
1971	32% (186,460)	20% (116,700)	15% (88,835)	14% (80,785)	5% (26,950)	2% (10,175)	12% 70,750	100% (580,660)
1961	33% (157,559)	25% (119,219)	17% (79,638)	13% (59,825)	4% (19,140)	1% (6,590)	7% 31,366	100% (473,337)
1951	42% (164,765)	28% (111,045)	14% (56,650)	7% (28,190)	3% (10,082)	1% (3,435)	5% 20,876	100% (395,043)
1941	50% (152,907)	29% (88,874)	12% (37,577)	3% (9,241)	1% (3,131)	1% (1,686)	4% 12,513	100% (305,929)
1931	58% (130,534)	25% (55,386)	11% (25,781)	2% (3,667)	1% (755)	1% (1,180)	3% 7,810	100% (225,113)
Change	-26%	-5%	+4%	+12%	+4%	+1%	+9%	

Ukrainian Population in Canada by Religious Denominations, 1931-71

Today, this function persists but to a lesser degree. The churches have become increasingly accepted as truly Canadian religious institutions and, like them, have suffered a decline in numbers of members and prominence. Therefore, the dissociation of Ukrainians from their traditional churches is not solely a function of their being Ukrainian institutions. It would be safe to say that this dissociation is a function of wider trends which have afflicted Canada in the 1970s—materialism, secular humanism, hedonism.

Can the New Jerusalem continue to survive and be revitalized in the 1980s? This is the challenge for the two traditional eastern churches of the Ukrainians in Canada.

XI St. Peter's: A German-American marriage of monastery and colony

Bede Hubbard

Roman Catholic and Eastern Orthodox monks have traditionally sought to recapture in this world the joy, the harmony, and the simplicity associated with the biblical vision of the Garden of Eden. The ideal expressed in such imagery is no attempt to live in the past, but is a radical expression of the Christian belief that it is both possible and necessary to begin living on earth the justice and fellowship which are the promise of the Kingdom of God, the "New Jerusalem" or, as St. Augustine called it, "the city of God."

"New Jerusalem" was the unspoken dream and the underlying hope of every monk as he went out into the deserts of Egypt, into the forests and swamps of Europe and, eventually, onto the prairies of Canada. The Benedictine monks at Muenster, Saskatchewan, inherited that same Christian and monastic vision and attempted to adapt it to a German-American colony. Their dream may today appear as a paradox, attempting to unite a contemplative heritage with prairie settlement, yet the tensions and contradictions involved were already at work in the monastic movement centuries ago.

The history of German Catholics in Saskatchewan, which includes German, German-American and German-Russian immigrants, is as varied as the geography of their settlements. In the western part of the province, in the area of Tramping Lake, is the former St. Joseph's Colony (a settlement involving the parochial ministry of German-speaking Oblates of Mary Immaculate); in central Saskatchewan surrounding Humboldt is St. Peter's Colony; in the south are a number of smaller settlements (including Balgonie, Sedley, Grayson and Claybank); and in the cities of Regina and

Saskatoon are sizable German communities.[1] St. Peter's Colony, encompassing 1,800 square miles of land around Muenster and Humboldt, includes the villages of Peterson in the southwest corner, Cudworth and St. Benedict in the northwest, Lake Lenore in the northeast, and Watson and Leroy in the southeast.

It is unique because of its size, its German-American background and its association with a Catholic monastery, the Benedictine community of St. Peter's Abbey at Muenster. In the United States it was not uncommon for Benedictine monasteries to be situated among settlements of German immigrants, but in Canada only one of the nation's three abbeys followed that pattern. Unlike both the American and Canadian monasteries, however, St. Peter's is responsible for its own ecclesiastical territory, a kind of diocese, of which the abbot of the monastery is the presiding elder or, in Catholic canonical terms, the "ordinary." Only one other North American abbey has shared this same distinction of being an abbey-nullius (an abbey outside of a diocese.)

The monastic movement

The monastic heritage goes back to a fourth-century reform and rebellion in the Christian church, traditionally situated in Egypt. Characteristics of this desert reform were withdrawal from society, celibacy, poverty, obedience to a spiritual elder, simplicity of life and reflective prayer. By the fifth century the movement had spread to Western Europe as well as Asia Minor and Greece. Benedictines trace their rule and spirit to St. Benedict of Nursia, a sixth-century Italian who composed his rule for monasteries by drawing on the main monastic traditions of his time. Benedict, whose 1,500th anniversary of birth was celebrated in 1980, included in his rule the observances characteristic of Egyptian monasticism but tempered them with an emphasis on community living, moderation and discretion. The rule of Benedict, which assumed the monastery would be located in a rural setting, insisted on a harmony of prayer, work, and study.

Scholarship, which became an essential part of medieval Benedictine life, together with a second later tradition, that of combining monastic life with ministry in the church (already seen, for example, in Augustine of Hippo) gave Benedictinism a practicality that was to be put to use in the ninth century by Charlemagne and his fellow Frankish rulers. Monasteries became the outposts of Carolingian civilization, educating the civil servants needed for the new empire and serving as centres from which law and order could be administered. Charlemagne's grandfather, Charles Martel, founded Reichenau Abbey on Lake Constance in 724, which in turn founded Metten Abbey in the diocese of Regensburg, Bavaria, in 766. Metten, designated as a "royal cloister" by Charlemagne, eleven hundred years later founded the first North American Benedictine foundation, which was the ancestor of Canada's first Benedictine monastery in Muenster.

Ludwig I, King of Bavaria, having allowed Metten to reopen its doors after the wake of the Enlightenment, encouraged new members to join the diminished ranks of the monks. Among the first to do so in 1833 was Boniface Wimmer, a recently ordained member of the diocesan clergy who soon decided that his monastic and priestly vocation was to serve the German-Catholic immigrants of the United States. Wimmer, realizing the importance of clergy who spoke the language of the people they were serving, also believed that the Benedictines, with their tradition of stability and of agriculture, would be well suited to assisting German settlers in America. In 1846, with a handful of novices, he founded St. Vincent's Abbey in Latrobe, Pennsylvania, which within twenty years founded eleven other monasteries, each providing German-speaking clergy as well as high school and college educational opportunities.

The ministerial and educational involvements of the monks, however, was not without its critics, among them some of Wimmer's own men, who complained that the degree and type of involvement expected in Latrobe's foundations, by disrupting the traditional balance of prayer, work and study, diminished opportunities for contemplative prayer and withdrawal from society. One of these critics was Oswald Moosmueller, a talented and, for most of his life, heavily involved administrator who in 1882 received permission to found a contemplative monastic community.

Moosmueller's priory, established in southern Illinois and named Cluny, in honour of the famous tenth-century French abbey, had great hopes; with the biggest barn in Illinois, complete with hand-hewn walnut beams, the monastery was built to house fifty monks. Surrounded by swamps, snakes, malaria, and Protestants, however, the experiment did not succeed. By 1902 Moosmueller had died and its eight monks were appealing to Rome for a new prior. The founder's successor was Alfred Mayer, a member of St. John's Abbey in Collegeville, Minnesota, which had been founded by St. Vincent's in 1856. A pastor at Duluth, he soon concluded that Cluny needed a more promising site with better opportunities for pastoral and educational work.

Beginnings of the colony

About this same time German-speaking Catholics in Minnesota, who were looking for homestead land, were also expressing concern over losing their language and religion through assimilation. Because of their interest in new farmland and their expressed desire for German-speaking clergy, St. John's Abbey in 1902 sent Father Bruno Doerfler, then principal of the abbey's university in Collegeville, together with three lay men—Moritz and Henry Hoeschen and J.H. Haskamp—on a long and arduous journey by train and wagon from Minnesota through Winnipeg and Calgary, up to Wetaskiwin and over to Battleford, finally ending in what today is the Cudworth area and what was soon to become the gateway to St. Peter's Colony. That same year thirty-one homesteads were filed in the new settlement. By 1903 Cluny priory had accepted an invitation from St. John's Abbey to join the Canadian venture while another thousand German-Americans filed for homesteads. By 1906 the population of the colony was 6,000; by 1920, 9,000. Today approximately 12,000 Roman Catholics live in the area, mostly descendants of the German-American settlers; it is also estimated that about another 20,000 have moved from St. Peter's Colony to other parts of Westen Canada.

Most of the colonists spoke German and English, having been raised and educated in the United States. They seem also to have been prepared to make accommodation for French-Canadian interests; at least the German-American monks were not hesitant to join forces with the French-speaking clergy and bishop of Prince Albert, while festive days at Muenster were celebrated with sermons in English, German and French. Within a year the monks at the new monastery had established what was then Canada's only German-language weekly newpaper, *St. Peter's Bote*, which, although meant for and especially supported by the German-Americans of the colony, over the years gathered readers from beyond the area.

Transitions

As World War I was coming to an end, suspicion and fear about German-speaking elements in Canada were growing. *St. Peter's Bote* had to publish in English for one year and, as with other German-language papers published by the Mennonites, its articles had first to be filed with government censors in Ottawa. Annoying as the enforced use of English must have been, it may have provided the extra stimulus needed for the monastery to begin within a few years an English-language weekly. Called at first *The St. Peter's Messenger*, simply a translation of the title of its sister German weekly, the new periodical addressed itself to the "young people" of the colony, a sign that another generation was growing up which felt more at home with the English language. Within a few years *The St. Peter's Messenger* became *The Prairie Messenger,* while *St. Peter's Bote* continued under its own editor until 1947.

German continued to be taught in the homes and schools of the colony. Even until as late as 1958, the Grade Eleven class at St. Peter's College had about as many students studying German as were studying French. Three years later, however, there was only one student studying German at the college and he was Ukrainian. During the 1950s and 1960s German continued to be used in anecdotes and jokes, but twenty years later only elderly people conversed in German, while few middle-aged people were fluent in the language and no one under thirty was at all familiar with it. Today in the area there is no more interest in German than in any other foreign tongue and little consciousness of the language as a cultural heritage. Similarly there is no longer popular awareness of the area having been a German-American colony. While in 1958 references were still made to "the colony," in the 1980s it is unfamiliar history to the young and only an historical fact considered with some curiosity and little nostalgia by the middle-aged.

There is no doubt that a sense of religious heritage was much more important to the colonists than was their concern for language and culture. In the discussions that were to arise about education, for example, both clerical and lay leaders were open to discussion and compromise over the question of language even in their parochial schools, but the Catholic faith was not open to such questioning.

Settlers in the colony built large, imposing churches, furnished with altars, paintings and statuary often imported from the United States and Eastern Canada. Nor did church construction end with the first generation, for right into the 1940s new rural churches were being built, while the number of rural churches remaining open for services even today is unique in Saskatchewan, although some have closed over the years. As the 1980s begin, however, there is growing awareness that the few remaining rural churches as well as those in the smaller villages may soon be closed, not only because of diminishing congregations but because of fewer clergy. Catholics from the urban areas of the province express amazement at what they consider the high proportion of people in the former colony regularly attending church, yet local clergy and lay people insist that, with some families no longer going to church plus the not uncommon problem of getting young people to Sunday services, church attendance is not what it used to be.

In 1908, St. Peter's Colony was the site of Canada's first Katholikentag ("Catholic Convention"), a festive gathering to foster a sense of community and heritage. Becoming an annual event over the next decade, gatherings were held not only in the Muenster-Humboldt colony but in St. Joseph's Colony, Regina, and Winnipeg. By 1909 the Volksverein, a Catholic social and cultural movement, which originated in Germany but ended under the Nazis, had been founded for the German Catholics of Canada by Bruno Doerfler, the Abbot of Muenster at that time, who became one of the main leaders. The last Katholikentag in the colony was held in 1933; two years later western Canada's final Katholikentag met in Regina, after which the Volksverein declined, until in 1952 its financial accounts were closed. A high school student at St. Peter's College could ask in 1958 what a Protestant was: being from the predominantly Catholic area of the former colony, he had never met anyone who was not Catholic. Within six years, however, it became a major issue in the boarding school to enforce the traditionally compulsory chapel attendance. In 1972 the high school closed; among the least represented in its dwindling student body were students from the local area.

By the time the former colony celebrated its diamond jubilee in 1978, there was little distinctive culture left to celebrate. Although visitors returned from California, Minnesota, British Columbia, and Alberta for the two-week homecoming, at the civic rally entertainment was supplied by the Dumptrucks from Saskatoon, and the Yevshan Ukrainian dancers provided the ethnic memories. Despite a fine band program in the neighbouring schools, the colony's great-grandchildren did not want a diamond jubilee of their settlement to interfere with their summer holidays, so the Saskatoon Lions Band was also imported—a strange contrast to pioneer celebrations when many of the local villages had their own parish bands.

Parting of ways

Monastic love for the land is basically an expression of stewardship and harmony. Whether on the mountains or in the plains, monasteries offer a practical expression (through gardens, well-tended fields and productive herds) of the monastic desire to live in harmony with God, neighbour and nature. When St. Peter's Colony began, the area was heavily bushed with aspen groves. Today, although the abbey has preserved an area of the original bush and in

Prairie Messenger, St. Peter's Abbey
Muenster, Saskatchewan

View of the Abbey from nearby grainfields.

Whether on the mountains or in the plains, monasteries offer a practical expression (through gardens, well tended fields and productive herds) of the monastic desire to live in harmony with God, neighbour and nature.

addition has planted hundreds of trees for shelter belts and beauty, not many neighbours in the colony are so inclined. Every year more bush is destroyed and the shelter belts of former homesteads bulldozed. During the 1930s the farm at St. Peter's was used for demonstration purposes by the University of Saskatchewan and the federal and provincial Departments of Agriculture. By the late 1950s, however, farms in the area were already more sophisticated in farming practices and more dependent on mechanization than was the abbey which continued stooking grain and employing manual labour. As the 1980s begin, farming is big business in the former colony, known as the "sure crop district"; its farmers are wealthy, its farms growing larger.

The expense and limited opportunities for young farmers getting into agriculture today has influenced two distinct movements in the area. A number of small manufacturing industries are successfully operating in the Humboldt-Muenster area, an endeavour both economically successful as well as helpful in stablizing the population of one of Saskatchewan's most heavily populated rural areas. Within the abbey itself and on some local farms there is also a movement toward organic and intensive farming and gardening, accompanied with differing opinions by those in the monastery who would like to recapture and adapt the values and techniques of subsistence farming and those who, either wholeheartedly or resignedly, have accepted the contemporary faith in mechanization with its inevitable aggrandizement of farm holdings.

Benedictine monasteries almost always had schools associated with them, though not so much for educating the people of the area as for teaching the monks themselves. The study of Scripture and of the writings of the fathers of the church was considered indispensable for monastic prayer and meditation, and the literature of pagan Greece and Rome was preserved as a vehicle for literary education during the Middle Ages.

Schools were important in St. Peter's Colony. Research by Dr. Clinton White of Campion College, Regina, has shown that the teachers and schools of the colony, even in the earliest years, were easily as good as and often better than schools and teachers elsewhere in the province. The schools were multilingual, despite editorial warnings in the Regina newspapers that German Catholics, insisting on their own school system, were overemphasizing German. One school inspector reported that the Catholic schools in the colony had marvellous English-speaking students, better than in the public schools. Elizabethan Sisters who came to the colony from Germany in 1911, founded a nursing school and hospitals in Humboldt and Cudworth. Ursuline nuns who arrived from Germany two years later, established a girls' academy in Bruno and staffed many of the area's separate and public schools. In 1921 the Benedictine monks opened St. Peter's College, a boarding school for high school students which five years later also became a junior college of the University of Saskatchewan.

Years later, in 1973, Carlton Trail Community College was established in the Humboldt area, one of the first of four pilot projects for community colleges in Saskatchewan. At Muenster the junior college still continues, with facilities being provided for a one-year office education program from the Saskatchewan Technical Institute in Moose Jaw and also for a special education centre operated by the Humboldt Rural School Division. Adult education is alive and well in the area, with credit and non-credit courses being offered through the community college and through St. Peter's. In the local area there is also provision for elementary special education as well as a sheltered workshop and a classroom for the mentally retarded in Humboldt.

Thus it might seem that the tradition of scholarship and learning continues to thrive in the colony, except that local school authorities and parents complain about educational disagreements and lack of facilities. The school libraries are below standard and there are few opportunities for courses like home economics, industrial arts and other high school options. Having chosen to maintain local schools and not to consolidate or centralize, the former colony has at the same time failed to encourage schools to co-operate, so that, for example, up-to-date science, home economics, and industrial facilities at Humboldt are not available to students attending Muenster high school only seven miles away.

The settlers and their descendants over the years were known for their generous support for church concerns. In the 1930s they gave generously for relief to the drought-stricken areas of southern Saskatchewan; after World War II they sent donations to Germany; and today they have a reputation for being among the most generous of Catholics not only in the province but in Canada. Despite that, there has been a shift in religious involvement. The monks at St. Peter's have not had a monk from the area make final profession of vows since 1967; the Elizabethan Sisters have not had a candidate remain since the early 1960s, the Ursulines since the early 1970s.

Gathering from the 1978 jubilee celebrations of the colony's settlement, there is no doubt that local people do have a sense of being a distinct community, part of which comes from having a common past and partly because they are a special church community. But apart from the abbacy, there are few symbols left to keep any cultural distinctiveness alive in the former colony. The sons and daughters of the colonists learned well the lessons of assimilation, with World Wars I and II taking their toll as did also the ethnic and religious prejudice which shook Saskatchewan in the 1920s. When the area celebrates its centenary, few probably will be aware of their local history, judging by the lack of interest among local students and teachers. When the provincial department of education and the local superintendent of schools recently gave permission for a chapter on the history of the colony to be included in a social studies program, Humboldt town schools were enthusiastic but the rural schools discovered most of the teachers were not only disinterested but also convinced that their students would not be interested either.

While it appears that the former colony is becoming completely assimilated within the general blend of prairie culture, in the monastery there are signs of a new insistence on distinctiveness. The traditional monastic habit, over the last decade often discarded in favour of an ordinary suit, appears to be gaining new respect and more wearers. Associated with the monastery today are five hermits

GERMAN CATHOLIC SETTLEMENTS

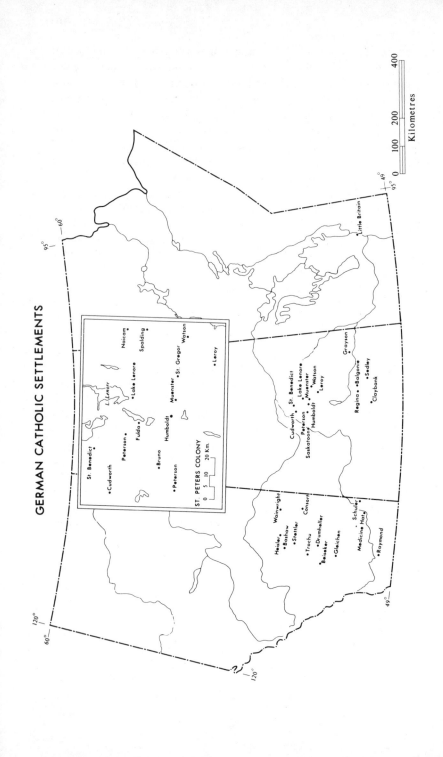

ST. PETERS COLONY

0   5 10   20 Km.

Cudworth
St. Benedict
Peterson
Fulda
Bruno
Humboldt
Peterson
Muenster
St. Gregor
Naicam
Spalding
Lake Lenore
Watson
Leroy
L. Lenore

Cudworth
St. Benedict
Lake Lenore
Muenster
Watson
Leroy
Peterson
Saskatoony
Humboldt
Grayson
Regina
Balgonie
Sedley
Claybank
Little Britain

Heisler
Wainwright
Bashaw
Stettler
Consort
Trochu
Drumheller
Beiseker
Gleichen
Medicine Hat
Schuler
Raymond

0   100 200   400
Kilometres

60°
95°
120°
49°
95°
120°
49°

who join the monastic community for the Sunday Eucharist but otherwise lead lives of solitary prayer and reflection. This radical return to the roots of monasticism local Catholics find difficult to appreciate, having been convinced for more than seventy-five years that the monks of St. Peter's are primarily pastors and teachers.

The colony cannot be written off as a futile or failed dream. It is a thriving and wealthy rural area characterized by generosity, good community spirit and a law-abiding peacefulness, which makes it somewhat unexciting for local Royal Canadian Mounted Police patrols. The former colony remains closely connected with the monastery through its Catholic clergy (all of whom are monks), its high proportion of *Prairie Messenger* subscribers, and its recent but lively interest in a new adult religious education program centred at St. Peter's and involving eleven hundred registrations for five-week courses in its first two years of operation. Yet the original hopes of escaping the North American melting pot failed as the colonists could not and would not hold onto their language and culture. The dream of a "New Jerusalem" became, on the one hand, for the people of the area, a vision of sharing completely in the life of the province and nation, while on the other hand, for the monks, sights were set on an ideal far older than that of the German-American settlers of 1903.

Conclusion

That the vision of the "New Jerusalem" has not disappeared among the monks may be illustrated by a quick look at one of the apostolates of St. Peter's Abbey, *The Prairie Messenger*. Although the monastery is over seventy miles away from the nearest city and although the pastoral responsibilities of the monks involve only a small rural diocese, their weekly newspaper attempts to serve all of Saskatchewan and Manitoba, including the urban centres of Regina, Saskatoon, and Winnipeg.

This presumption in itself could be interpreted as simply the continuation of that marvellously strange combination of historical forces which saw a monastery succeed in leading and founding a German-American colony on the prairies. But such boldness is also prepared to live with paradoxes and polarity beyond the historical. *The Prairie Messenger*, shunning any regard for staidness and comfortable churchiness, shocks many of its readers and alarms a number of Roman Catholics with its independence of thought— apparent, over the years, in its willingness to promote government-sponsored universal health care; in its insistence on distinguishing socialism (much of which it was prepared to defend) from communism; in its strong sympathy for co-operatives; in its impatience with governments that failed to respond to minority concerns; in its eager espousal of church renewal and reform; and in its promotion of ecumenism, social justice, rural life, and environmental protection.

Given the paper's geographical context and the popular impression that religious journalism should be safe and quiet, such independence of thought may seem remarkable. But for the monks who own, publish, edit, and print the paper, there is little remarkable that they see in the goals or even the controversies involving *The Prairie Messenger*, and although some monks over the years have complained that the various monastic editors took too controversial or one-sided a stand, the community as a whole has never censored or censured the paper.

The ancient monastic vocation after all was a separation from the everyday structures and business of church and society, while the monastic heritage in its own rights is a critique of ecclesiastical and social realities. For the monks everything is to be seen in that all-encompassing vision of Benedict: a living harmony of God, humanity, and creation. The ancient dream of the desert still lives: that the Kingdom of God is being realized here and now. Thus whatever furthers the New Jerusalem should be fostered and encouraged, while whatever impedes or clouds that vision must be reformed or eradicated. It was this simple vision that had led the monks to help colonize a Saskatchewan settlement and today keeps them willing to try new pioneering ventures.

XII Hutterites: An interview with Michael Entz

Gail McConnell

The Waldeck Colony, where we spoke with leader Michael Entz and some members of the colony, is a typical Hutterite colony or commune, familiar at least by sight to residents of the prairie provinces. The buildings of the colony—the apartments for married couples, the dormitories for unmarried young people and children, the communal dining hall, kitchen, laundry, nursery, school, and farm buildings—are clustered together for the convenience of the communal life. There is not necessarily any separate church building, as the community and daily life itself are both church and worship. However, formal services are held regularly on Sundays and on every weekday evening in a convenient gathering place.

The typical prairie Hutterite colony is at one and the same time a social group, a church or congregation, and an economic unit. The population of the group may range anywhere from eighty to two hundred persons, half of whom may be fifteen years or under. As a group reaches the upper end of that range they will begin to make plans for the establishment of a "daughter" colony, which will receive assistance from the senior colony until they are in their turn self-supporting and self-governing.

Among themselves, Hutterites speak the "low" German of their south German homeland from which they fled over 400 years ago. However, they learn English in the day-school and from visitors, who are generally welcome.

In the course of an afternoon's conversation, in an atmosphere of friendly mutual enquiry, Michael Entz put forward for us some of the living tradition of the Hutterian way. Some of what he had to say follows.

Children at the Hutterite colony near Waldeck, Saskatchewan.

The typical prairie Hutterite colony is a social group, a church or congregation, and an economic unit. The population of the group may range anywhere from 80 to 200 persons, half of whom may be 15 or under.

"When I talk with people, I tell them it's the best life in the world. There's a lot of people who wouldn't agree, but some people would. There's nothing like security—security and satisfaction—inner peace. You've got a good chance to have that in a colony. That's one of the most precious things I think you can have—peace with yourself and with your God.

"In the outside world there are too many temptations. As the writer of John's epistle cautions us, 'For all that is in the world, the lust of the flesh and the lust of the eyes and the pride of life, is not of the Father but is of the world.' (I John 2:16) You can easily fall there, do things that are not quite right, not in accordance with your beliefs. It's easier to maintain what you believe in within the colony. You have more watch. Pete watches me and I can watch Pete. We can be a source of inner strength for each other. I think on the outside you haven't got this. You're more scattered all over, you're more by yourself, there's nobody to see you so much. I think you do things a little easier than if there's two or three people beside you all the time. You've got to have watchmen around you in order to be a good Christian. It's a narrow path; we call it a narrow path to heaven.

(Matt. 7:14) And it's got to be narrow, if you want to enter the gates of the New Jerusalem.

"The most basic tenets of our life are community life and community of goods. We follow the basic organization of the first Christian Church. 'And all who believed went together and had all things in common. And they sold their possessions and goods, and distributed them all as any had need.' (Acts 2:44-45) We also practice the doctrine of nonresistance 'by turning the other cheek.' (Matt. 5:39) We're a pacifist people. And I think it's these two principles that have driven us from country to country over the last 450 years.

"We also believe in adult baptism, that is, a 'believer's' baptism (Mark 16: 16). This has been a tough principle for our forefathers to face. I think that's why they suffered so much persecution at the hands of the Roman [Catholic Church] authorities.

"I think it's one of the tenets of our faith, too, to remain aloof from the world. As Paul said to the early Christians who found themselves in the midst of loose-living Corinthians, 'Therefore come out from them and be separate from them says the Lord.' (II Cor. 6: 17a) We don't want to get mixed up with outside society too much. We're in this world, but not of this world. That's what we believe in, and we don't want to get too deeply involved in it for fear we might harm our consciences by doing this.

"Our teachings are based mainly on the New Testament. We look on the Old Testament as being a shadow of the New. I think what was prophesied in the Old was fulfilled in the New. The 'New Jerusalem' would be a vision of heaven, then. No one can attain it on earth; you'd have to be perfect, and nobody's perfect. (Phil. 3:12) That's the way we look at it, anyway, and that's what the Bible teaches; the New Testament. We always hope to attain it someday, but we have to live here on earth just as good as we can so we'll be worthy to enter into the New Jerusalem in the life after life.

"The Hutterite way is not the only way, but I think it's the most complete path. But when Christ said the people will come from all corners of the earth to enter this New Jerusalem, I think he was referring to a lot of people who are really trying to do the best that they can.

"I think living the Hutterite way of life is probably not meant for everyone. We've been called to do this, and, I think, to God's special grace, but I don't think it's practical as a world order. It'd be very difficult to get this going all over the world.

"There are limitations to the acceptance of the Hutterian Brethren in Saskatchewan, and one recent attempt at exclusion was quashed in the courts. Hutterians have been asked by the government of Saskatchewan not to found new colonies in close proximity to established ones, a requirement not unlike the former Alberta "forty-mile limit." The court case arose out of an attempt on the part of the Rural Municipality of Whiska Creek to prevent the establishment of a Hutterian colony in the municipality. In 1977 the Waldeck colony purchased land near Vanguard, Saskatchewan, and shortly after the sale the R.M. passed a by-law requiring the R.M.'s permission to erect more than one home on a quarter-section. The Hutterites applied for permission, were refused, and went ahead and built anyway. They were charged under the *Municipal Planning and Development Act* with building without the permission of the R.M. In the subsequent court case the by-law was set aside, and the Vanguard colony is now established.

"This system—I mean sharing goods—has probably existed from the time of Christ, although we just haven't got the records of it. But it was reborn in 1528 as a direct effect of the Protestant Reformation and Martin Luther's teachings. I think people were so fed up with the system that they just went into doing the right thing, and it just kept on going.

"Now twice in our history the community life has been abandoned. The first time, I think, the armies just went back and forth, back and forth, and reduced the communes to poverty until they just had to go out as individuals. But they never lost contact with their sermons. We still have the old sermons they were preaching 300 to 400 years ago.

"The second time was after they had escaped into Russia. They established the community life for a few years, then they lived among the Mennonites there, on individual farms and villages. But they never had inner peace—that's what we always hear. And it just started to stir and churn in them, to get back to the old way again. When they came over to America from Russia they just started up the community system again, sharing the goods one hundred percent and we've been doing it over a hundred years.

"There's two kinds of communism in the world. There's a Christian communism and there's a secular communism, like there are communist countries in Russia. They're the very reverse of our communism. Their communism preaches what's thine is mine, I'll take it from you, where we believe that what is mine is thine. We give and share. I think that's the big difference. This is a Christian belief, and theirs isn't. A co-op farm like they had here in Saskatchewan for a number of years is different again. They just help each other out as a co-op, but still everybody took his own worth. I guess the government owns it [the Matador] now. When we first came here (the last member of the co-op is still on the land) he came over two or three times and inquired to see how our system works. 'It must work different than ours, ours doesn't work,' he said. It worked all right when the oldtimers were still together, after the war; they were veterans. But with the younger generation coming up it just doesn't work. I think it's because it wasn't based on a scriptural basis. It wouldn't work here if we didn't believe in the Bible New Testament teaching. You do it conscientiously. I think the other way you don't.

"It's a great life, I tell you. I wouldn't trade it for any outside. You're happy, content. A lot of outside people think it's a little bit stringent or rigid. It isn't that. We're free. I think it's a real democratic system we've got.

"All the major decisions of the community are made by the voting members of the congregation, that is, by the baptized male members. This group votes on all positions of responsibility in the community, from the two most important positions—those of "spiritual leader" and of "householder" or colony manager (always held by men) to the positions held by women—supervising the kitchen, the garden, the laundry, the infant's school and so on. Positions are held for life, and no position carries any special privileges with it. The leader, for example, is not exempt from ordinary work within the colony because of his position." Michael Entz points out that "history has proven" that the colonies break down when they get to be too large. As a result the tradition of establishing "daughter" colonies has become firmly established.

In spite of the lifetime terms of office, the Hutterian way militates against the development of rigid hierarchical structures. The offices of the minister of the Word exist solely to help order the communal life, and "not as domineering over those in your charge, but being examples to the flock." (I Peter 5:3) Moreover, there is no impulse to extend the structure beyond the individual colony to encompass the whole of the Hutterian Brotherhood under one "rule." However, in Canada a more formal association known as the Hutterian Brethren Church was formed and recognized as a church by the federal government in 1951. The elders from each colony, or "Christian commune" as Michael Entz suggested they might be called, usually meet together once a year to discuss matters of common interest. Differences of practice that may appear major to an outsider can develop among the groups without destroying the common sense of being "Hutterite."

When the Hutterites came to Canada from the United States at the end of the First World War they were already divided into three distinct groups, known among the Brethren by the names of the elders who had led them from Russia to the United States in the 1870s. They were the "Schmiedeleut," or "blacksmith people," so named because their elder, Michael Waldner, was a blacksmith by trade; the "Dariusleut," named after their leader, Darius Walther; and the "Lehrerleut," so called after the profession of their leader, Jacob Wipf, who was a teacher.

The Waldeck Colony is of the Lehrerleut or "teacher's people," and they and the Schmiedeleut or "smith's people" differed from the Dariusleut for many years over the payment of taxes. The Dariusleut refused to pay taxes until recently, according to Mr. Entz, because part of the taxes were going to the military. Both the tax-paying and the non-tax-paying groups had arrived at their decisions in a typically Hutterite way—by discussion and sifting scripture until a consensus was reached. Michael Entz describes the Waldeck Colony's conclusions:

"We thought the Bible taught us to render unto Caesar the things that are Caesar's. You have to have law and order in a country. We believe that the higher powers, that government, is an ordination of God and you can't sustain a government without having law and order, and therefore you have to have police, you have to have the uniform, and you have to have the sword too. The Apostle Paul teaches that, in Romans 13:1. Hutterite people couldn't be in government. But still we think that government is in this world because man sinned, and that's why God has ordained government."

A similar sifting process took place before the use of farm machinery and trucks was adopted by the colonies in 1950. However, the Hutterites are not infinitely tolerant of differences among themselves, nor are they always willing or able to accomodate the outside world. The Hutterites who took up individual landholdings after settling in the United States, the "prairieleut" as they are called, were cut off from further contact with the main body of the communal societies. The three groups mentioned above, the Dariusleut, the Schmiedeleut and the Lehrerleut, left the United States because of the American government's imposition of the draft on their young men in the First World War. Two died in prison while refusing to wear the uniform, and the Hutterites turned to Manitoba in settler-hungry Canada.

In Canada persecution of the Hutterites has been non-existent or limited to attempts to control their access to land. Today there are colonies in all three of the prairie provinces. Colonies were established in Alberta from South Dakota settlements and, when Alberta established what is known as the "forty-mile limit" (now rescinded) in an attempt to prevent new colonies from settling close to old ones, many of the Brethren moved to Saskatchewan. Since 1953, thirty-five colonies have been established in Saskatchewan. Although all the colonies are agricultural communes, there is no requirement from the Hutterites' point of view; that is, there is no scriptural base, for pursuing farming rather than some other occupation. According to Michael Entz:

"We'll do anything just to maintain our principles, whether it be farming or factory work, or anything else, it makes no difference. Our forefathers, they were not only farming, they made wagons and knives, and they had a factory. They had all kinds of things going for them. Maybe there were small gardens and things. But they never owned land, they just rented."

The Hutterites refer to their "forefathers" frequently and without affectation. They live daily with their words—sermons and statements of faith going back to the early sixteenth century, many of them written in prison—and believe firmly in the importance of maintaining their traditions in the protection of their faith. One cannot understand the modern Hutterites without being aware of their history.

Jacob Huter, from whom the Hutterian Brethren in Canada and the United States take their name, was an Anabaptist from the Tirol in southern Germany. He was put to death by fire for his beliefs at Innsbruck in 1536. The Anabaptist doctrine, which emerged in the articles of the Schlietheim Confession of 1527, endorsed four main points: adult baptism; the use of the ban, or excommunication; the observance of communion as a remembrance rather than a sacred mystery; and separation from the world.

The label "Anabaptist," applied to the religious movement from whom the Hutterians, or Hutterites, emerged as a separate sect of communal Christians, was invented by their enemies. The term means, roughly, "those who baptize again." It was descriptive as well as opprobrious, in that the new adherents were Christians who had been baptized as infants, and were now being re-baptized as adults to affirm their commitment to a new life. A modern analogy might be the use of the term "born again Christian," which is used literally by some and ironically by others. With the Hutterites, however, and with some other survivors of the "radical fringe" of the Protestant Reformation—in Canada notably the Moravian Brothers and some Mennonite groups—baptism remains a commitment which only an adult can undertake, as it represents a conscious commitment to the Christian faith and to the Christian life as defined by the group.

In the years succeeding the brutal suppression of the "Peasants'

War" of 1524 to 1525, the Anabaptists were associated with the uprisings by the authorities in the German states, and suffered in the continuing suppression of dissent to which both church and state lent their hands. In spite of their shared intellectual roots in Zurich, the Anabaptists were outlawed by the Zwinglians and the Lutherans as well as by the Roman Catholic establishment. Their insistence on ordering their own religious affairs within their congregations, and on electing their own religious leaders, was too radical for the Protestant reformers. No state would tolerate groups within its borders who put their consciences above national loyalty, and in particular refused to bear arms.

Not every hand was against them however. Moravia provided a haven for the "bruderhof" (household) people, as they were called by some. Here, in the latter part of the sixteenth century, the Hutterites enjoyed a temporary "golden age." Before the end of the century there were between sixty-five and eighty-five "households" or colonies established in Moravia and in neighbouring Slovakia, providing refuges for adherents still escaping from the German states. Huter himself had been captured by the authorities on one of his many rescue and missionary trips to southern Germany.

One of the Hutterian tenets most familiar to western Canadians, that of community of property, was established during one of their moves within Moravia itself. A group of about 200 fled Nikelsburg rather than have their protector, Liechtenstein, take up arms on their behalf. They had been led by Hans Hut (who had died in Augsburg prison in 1528) and had accepted his preaching of uncompromising nonresistance and the nonpayment of war taxes. In their flight, as a practical measure, they pooled their resources, yielding their belongings to common ownership in the interest of group solidarity and survival.

The "golden age" was a brief period in the four and a half centuries of the Hutterites' history, hardly long enough to be termed an "age," and not, in itself, entirely peaceful or free from persecution. However, it was the high point of their missionary zeal, and the period during which the rules of their community life were established. The records of the decisions taken and the practices established at that time, copied and recopied by successive Hutterian congregations, along with the statement of faith composed by the early leaders and the scriptures, especially the New Testament, form the basis of the Hutterite way of life as it exists today in North America.

Victor Peters, in his "A History of the Hutterian Brethren 1528-1958," summarizes the process in this way:

Jacob Huter institutionalized the brotherhood community, where private property in any form was considered a cardinal sin; Peter Riedemann formalized the structure and provided all its aspects with scriptural sanction; Peter Walbot, through his school system, created a medium for indoctrination that bound succeeding generations to the community more firmly than rules and regulations; but Ehrenpreis instilled into the Hutterian system 'the milk of human kindness' in a measure that made the austere Hutterian life practicable and contributed to its survival.

Ehrenpresis was a leader of the brotherhood in the middle of the seventeenth century, after the congregation had been forced to leave Moravia and was once again under great pressure to abandon the communal religious life. Before his death in 1662 he wrote a small book, or "Ein Sendbrief," subtitled (in English) "Brotherly Community, the First Commandment of Love," in which he developed the view that "true community" is not the result of force and pressure, but the voluntary surrender and integration of the individual, his total submergence in the "Gemeinschaft." "Ein Sendbrief" is to this day found and read in practically every Hutterian home, and is an important resource for the communal life. In explaining the lack of need for police in a Hutterite colony, for example, Michael Entz automatically referred to the "Sendbrief" in saying, "We are put together with love. Or we should be."

It is worth remembering today, when state-supported public education is the norm in Europe and North America, that the principles of general education—the rules for the conduct of schools and schoolteachers, including the physical care of children—laid down by the Hutterites in Moravia in the late sixteenth and early seventeenth centuries were far in advance of their time. In their brief "golden age" the colonies' schools were often hosts to the children of their non-Hutterian neighbours, who were anxious to obtain for their own children the benefits of the Hutterite training in literacy and in manual skills.

For the Hutterites, the basis for insistence on universal (and communal) education was and is religious. The commitment to the faith and to the community taken at baptism is to be a personal choice, guided by scripture and Hutterian religious writings, to which all believers must therefore have access. Moreover, because all members of the community must be able to contribute to the "gemeinschaft" to the extent of their capabilities, each must be trained in a trade or skill. The Hutterians have not changed their view of education and thus, although in Canada they have accepted

HUTTERITE SETTLEMENTS

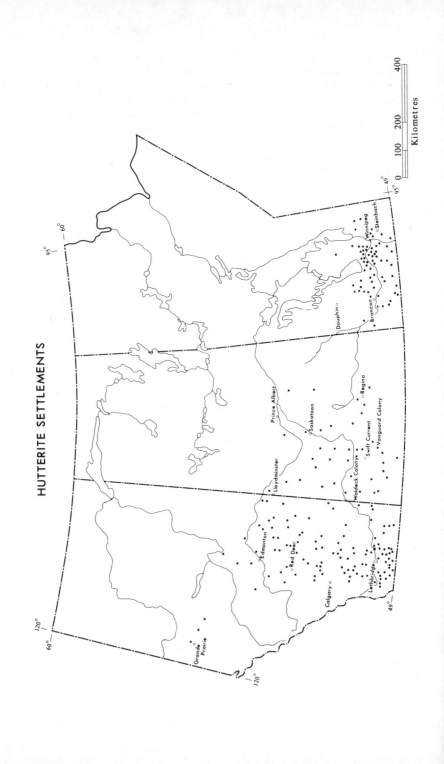

Anne Smart

Paul Entz demonstrates the durable and efficient machinery manufactured by members of the Waldeck colony.

Because all members of the community must be able to contribute to the "gemeinschaft" to the extent of their capabilities, each must be trained in a trade or skill.

provincial education requirements in addition to their traditional schooling, they have developed little or no interest in "higher" education.

The end of the Hutterian community in Moravia came in the 1620s with the establishment of Ferdinand II as emperor and the outbreak of the Thirty Years' War. The Protestant nobility who had protected the Hutterites left or were executed, and an order was issued from Vienna to drive the "Ababaptists" out of Moravia. Over the next one hundred and fifty years, until a "few score" surviving Hutterites fleeing out of Wallachia appeared in eastern Russia, the brotherhood's history was one of persecution at the hands of religious authorities and the common lot of noncombatants caught in the paths of advancing and retreating armies.

Ironically, according to Peters, the air of order and prosperity, lent to the "bruderhof" households by the communal life, was their undoing as much as their religious beliefs. Their willingness to share all that they had fostered the belief that they had more than others, that the households had hoards of food, or money, amassed by the labours of the group. From being islands of peace they became the targets of the hungry and dispossessed, as well as of the scavenging armies, and of officials in search of the means to pay the levies. The households disintegrated, physically and morally, under the impact of these attacks, and some even took up arms to defend themselves.

In Russia, the remnant, along with the Mennonites, found a haven for over one hundred years. However, the threat of enforced military service moved them to emigrate, first to the United States between 1874 and 1879, and then, in 1918, once again under nationalistic pressure to accept military service, to Canada, where they now flourish in relative peace.

XIII   Conclusion

B.G. Smillie

O Jerusalem, Jerusalem, killing the prophets, and stoning those
who are sent to you. How often would I have gathered your
children together as a hen gathers her brood under her wings
and you would not!   Behold your house is forsaken and
desolate. (Matthew 23:37-38)

Jesus' lament over Jerusalem, a lament which sensed the
impending destruction of the city by the Romans in the cataclysmic
period between 30-70 A.D., makes a striking elegy for the main
theme of this book. A nostalgic lament is voiced by each writer as
each expresses a deep sorrow for a religious heritage that seems to be
doomed to either genocidal assimilation or to an attenuated
existence with geriatric future.

On the other hand there is something remarkably tenacious
about the eulogized past. The strong urge for a simpler life in contrast
to the plundering nature of the present in the name of progress is
reflected in the Indian-Metis religious formation based on a circle
that includes the whole human race in which needs and wants are
held in balance. The same longing for simplicity is visible in the
German-Catholic Colony and Abbey at Muenster where in the midst
of a highly successful farming operation and in addition to a weekly
newspaper with a national reputation, five hermits live a life of
solitary prayer and reflection. French Roman Catholics have a "*je
me souviens*" awareness of struggle for survival in the west as they
seek to retain the simple memory for New France of "French and
Catholic."   Mennonites moving from Saskatchewan to Northern
Alberta and British Columbia and from there to remote parts of

Latin America represent the same search for simplicity in a world suffocating in graveyards of used cars and gadgets.

There are also in these religious communities islands of cooperation shaped by the early church, which "had all things in common." (Acts 4:32) The Hutterites' remain the most visible lasting cooperatives. James McCrorie looks back to the cooperative spirit of the early farm movements and suggests that if that spirit is not regained, the family farm will have a "future with no future." The Doukhobors who stand on the edge of becoming a cultural anachronism are seeking to find their roots in a religious revival in which their original symbolic acts of burning weapons of war can be re-enacted in a cooperative peaceable society.

But perhaps the most challenging question for the pioneer churches as they look back on their past, particularly those established in positions of influence, is what will they learn from their history? Will they be left with a fading euphoric memory of the pioneer religious settlement, or will the vision of the "New Jerusalem" as a symbol of a new goal help them revitalize their outlook? Will Anglicans begin to see themselves not only "as part of a long procession of history and tradition transcending locality and time" but also as a Canadian church called to shed its trappings of British cultural religion? Will the Jewish community, which has suffered so much at the hands of cultural Christianity, recapture its tradition of the biblical prophets as it seeks to shed its upper-middle-class image and identify with the downtrodden in its fight for social justice. Will Ukrainians, both Catholic and Orthodox, spread their influence beyond their own kith and kin and become tribunes of all oppressed racial minorities? Will United Church people develop the same love for religious and cultural beauty that they now show for social justice? Will Lutherans branch out from doctrinal orthodoxy and bring the same diligence they apply to theology to the social and political issues that are beginning to press on them? Nor are these merely rhetorical questions. There are signs of metamorphosis of a different type of religious outlook.

Invariably when religious groups want to explain a new dimension forming in their religious lives they speak of a "new spirit" quickening in the community. Hebrew scripture refers to this spirit as *ruah* (wind). The early Christians describe their own birth as a church as the spirit breaking in "like a rushing mighty wind" (Acts 2:2). The same language of the power of the spirit may be used to describe the new boldness in religious circles born of a feeling that the human race cannot be left to lemming-like self-destruction. So we find churches, along with other religious groups, that take on the cause of native and aboriginal rights against the power of multinationals; that link uranium mining with nuclear proliferation; that question the right of Canadian banks to prop up the economy of repressive regimes in South Africa and Latin America; that seek the removal of advertising that misleads and encourages waste; that question the tax structures which allow a few Canadians to collect salaries that reinforce a grossly unequal distribution of wealth. One way of describing this phenomenon is to express it as a movement of the collective spirit.

Paradoxically, the new spirit is bringing politically-oriented religious groups closer to their colleagues who have been more artistically and liturgically oriented. Such enjoyment and celebration may be discussed under the metaphor of the dance. On the other hand those religious groups who have been noted for the beauty of their liturgy, their music, and their art are learning more about the hurting bleeding world that stands so near to the brink of nuclear suicide and are recognizing the need for more political involvement. This political toughness may be discussed using the metaphor of the race.

The New Jerusalem as a Dance

G.K. Chesterton, the British author and literary critic, in considering people on a journey says some look upon the pilgimage as a dance and others as a race.

In describing the pilgrims in Chaucer's *Canterbury Tales*,[1] Chesterton explains that they seem to be totally absorbed in the company of one another. As they journey to the shrine of Thomas á Becket and tell their stories, they epitomize medieval morality which emphasized that everything must be in balance. There was always movement but the movement was around a central theme. In a dance there are many variations, points out Chesterton, and the good dancer weaves the many alternatives into an exciting pattern.

The dance theme is an appropriate simile for those who stand in the Catholic tradition. Dancing suggests, for instance, the world of arts in its many variations. On the prairie, even a casual observer is struck by the contrast between the beauty of Anglican, Roman, and Ukrainian Catholic and Orthodox places of worship and the plain, granary-like Protestant churches. The colourful liturgy of Catholic and Orthodox worship also captures the artistic imagination. In particular, the Ukrainian religious experience has brought to the fore a cultural richness in dance, arts, and crafts which should provoke in all Canadians a gratitude for a religious heritage where the New

Jerusalem was widely celebrated in the poetic spirit of the Psalmist who speaks of the holy city as "the joy of the whole earth." (Psalm 48:2)

The dance tradition does have its shortcomings. Its religious roots in the faith of its believers can become reduced to colourful empty ritual and its theology may be unequipped to shape a theology for the disadvantaged.

In Canada, culture in its broadest sense is an upper-middle-class tradition which may be seen as dominantly apolitical. That cultural activities draw on the upper and middle classes for support is obvious to anyone visiting the ballet, the art galleries, the symphony, or the cultural ethnic museums. Although there is a certain romantic quaintness celebrated by ethnic groups who desire to perpetuate the cultural events of the pioneer era, there is also the impression of a patronizing re-enactment of museum drama. This is particularly serious where the religious roots have been allowed to wither. No longer are these groups the uneducated, exploited, uncomplaining farm labour force settled in an inhospitable climate. In general, they have moved up in the economic structure of the dominant society in Canada. These pilgrims whose theology has been built on the dance continue to provide cultural heritage with a capital "C."

The early pioneers, motivated by a strong faith in God's guidance, wished to establish settlements in the west that would reflect God's righteous kingdom by providing justice for all. When this strong motivation is primarily directed towards the maintenance of cultural distinctiveness, the early zeal for an equal sharing of God-given resources and benefits is lost and the political will to bring about a just society may become limited to lobbying for cultural grants from politicians for arts festivals.

A major shortcoming of the religious dance tradition has been its inability in the past to shape a theology that addresses itself to the conditions of disadvantaged people. In reviewing the strong impact of the Progressive movement on Canadian society it may be seen that Protestants in the tradition of the race have done better for the disadvantaged. Protestant leaders were at the forefront in fighting for justice for farmers, labourers, women, and European immigrants. The theological motivation that informed this struggle came from the Social Gospel which had little impact on Catholic leaders.

The religion of the dance, therefore, lives under the accusation of being apolitical and of catering to elitist culture. Nevertheless, its permanent contribution to theology is its emphasis on the beauty of creation. The dance-oriented pilgrims (as illustrated by Chaucer) advocated religious expression which does not take life too seriously, and their attitude may be useful in humanizing more politically oriented theology. We have already seen that the crusade mentality of the Social Gospel tended toward an overly self-righteous moralism in which God's plan became equated with the reform programme of the Protestant Zealots. The good humour of the dance orientation combines a mixture of mercy and judgement. At the end of this chapter, the importance of this contribution is examined more closely.

The Journey to New Jerusalem as a Race

According to Chesterton, at the end of the medieval period the pilgrimage turned from a dance into a race. He graphically describes the change in theological outlook by comparing Chaucer's *Canterbury Tales* with John Bunyan's *Pilgrim's Progress*. Chesterton explains that the pilgrim of Chaucer is as genuine as the pilgrim of Bunyan, but the Canterbury pilgrim is not in such a hurry as the hero of *Pilgrim's Progress*. For Pilgrim, life is a race to beat all the wily temptations of the devil. In the race outlook exemplified by Bunyan, the goal takes on magnetic power to attract the runner.[2]

Saskatchewan Archives Board

The Rev. C.T. Melley (Anglican) on his motorcycle which has been fixed with a special front wheel fitted to run on railway tracks, 1917.

Chapelle du Convent Jesus-Marie de Gravelbourg, Saskatchewan.

G.K. Chesterton suggests that running a race is more dominant in Protestant theology while the dance is played out in the drama of Catholic worship.

Bunyan's description captures Paul's call for self-discipline for the Christian in the race of life. Talking about his experience, Paul says:

> Do you not know that in a race all the runners compete, but only one receives the prize? So run that you may obtain it. Every athlete exercises self-control in all things. They do it to receive a perishable wreath, but we an imperishable. Well, I do not run aimlessly, I do not box as one beating the air, but I pommel my body and subdue it, lest after preaching to others, I myself should be disqualified. (1 Cor. 9:24-27).

Is there a potential for a more just society along the lines of that built by those whose theological pilgrimage to the New Jerusalem has been via the route of the race? Certainly the competition involved in running a race has caused many Protestant groups to put a great amount of energy into establishing their denominational version of the Kingdom of God on the prairie. Witness the zeal with which

Lutherans poured energy and money into establishing their branch of Lutheranism. Mennonites, in their missionary endeavours, were frequently motivated "to save the heathen from their sinful life." This motivation has provided an impetus for Protestant missionaries to rescue the perishing. It has also provided the very practical emphasis on service evident in the Mennonite Central Committee. Furthermore, if the early prairie settlers had not possessed a strong belief that their particular group was the most faithful representative of the kingdom that God wished to establish, there would not have been the benefits of competition!

One example of Presbyterian and Methodist competition in the pioneer period has an amusing twist. The late Dr. R.D. Tannahill, former Professor of Church History at St. Andrew's College and United Church Archivist in Saskatchewan, recounted the story of the first Canadian Pacific Railway train out of Moose Jaw going south and west to Assiniboia in 1908. An agreement had been reached between the Methodists and the Presbyterians that they would not compete for church membership in the small frontier prairie towns that were opening. The decision as to whether they would be Methodist or Presbyterian was to be determined by which denomination got there first. As Rev. Oliver Darwin, Superintendent of Methodist missions in Southern Saskatchewan, stepped aboard the day coach of the first train, he saw Rev. Peter Strang, his counterpart in the Presbyterian church, already aboard. Quietly, Darwin got off, went up to the front of the train and got into the baggage car so that he would be the first off at the first town. But when the train reached the first town, Oliver was mortified to find that Strang had beaten him to it because Strang had been riding on the "cow catcher"! Telling the story, Dr. Tannahill added, "I think the story may be apocryphal!"

When the question is seriously asked as to whether the Christian life as an athletic competition has provided a theological outlook conducive to producing an equitable society, then the answer is both "yes" and "no."

The "yes" side of the race theology is that Protestants have left an indelible mark in the fight for social justice through their commitment in following the apostle Paul's call for self-discipline in the race. The Pauline outlook on the Christian life as a race was strongly reinforced in many forms in the Protestant spirit on the prairie. For example, the progressive political tradition had a strong champion in Edmund Oliver, quoted earlier in this book. This church historian entitled his history of the Canadian church, *Winning the Frontier*. He envisioned the urgent need to build a cooperative kingdom based on a well-educated public. While chaplain to the forces in France in the First World War, Oliver became President of Vimy Ridge University, a programme developed by the Canadian army for educational upgrading of soldiers. In a letter written home to his wife, he expressed the race-like urgency: "... for if we don't hurry, our pupils may get shot before they get educated."[3]   Oliver's cooperative kingdom was built with confidence in the role of the church as an agent of this progressive kingdom. In the midst of the depression, he defined this role:

> ... [the church] must be concerned for the hungry, the naked,
> the shelterless and the stranger, the underprivileged and the
> ignorant, the exploited and the worthless as well as for the
> righteous who need no repentance and the whole who need no
> physician.[4]

Although there is a hint of condescension in the concern voiced for the suffering, there is also compassion in this idealism. Along with other leaders in this progressive tradition, Oliver demonstrated social passion and urgency about the task.

But some historians, particularly among Canadian liberal academics, have criticized these religious leaders for distorting orthodox protestant theology and for their naive optimism, which they say distorts the facts of history.[5]

I have said that the Social Gospellers who stood with most Protestant groups in identifying life as a race promoted the image of a God active in the immediate building of His kingdom in the cities and towns of the prairie. They were optimistic and they were naive, but the academic liberals who unduly emphasize facts are "usually the promoters of social conformity."[6] Invariably, the person who says "let the facts speak for themselves" is in a position where the facts selected are legitimized by those in power. The most transparent current form of controlled manipulation can be seen in instances where political opinions are based on the Gallup Poll which has produced broker politics through which the most vociferous economic and regional interests are placated. The noisiest lobbyists who have developed enormous power are the multinational companies who are rewarded with tax holidays and subsidies if they set up industry in the vast hinterland of Canada.[7] [8] With tax rebates and development funds, these companies hold the different regions of Canada for ransom, threatening to leave thousands of people without jobs as they move to the sweat shop labour markets of the Third World.[9] The result of this manoeuvring is that the resources of the country are raped by foreign owners (mostly American) and regional inequalities become permanent because there is no cause above the personal greed of the economically powerful who determine policy.[10] Frank Scott's poem on Mackenzie King satirizes the politician who incarnates this causeless political outlook, in which political expediency becomes a way of life for governing the nation.

W.L.M.K.

How shall we speak of Canada
Mackenzie King dead?
The Mother's boy in the lonely room
With his dog, his medium and his ruins?

He blunted us.

We had no shape
Because he never took sides,
and no sides
Because he never allowed them to take shape.

He skillfully avoided what was wrong
Without saying what was right,
And never let his on the one hand
Know what on the other hand was doing.

The height of his ambition
Was to pile a Parliamentary Committee on a Royal Commission
To have "conscription if necessary
But not necessarily conscription"
To let Parliament decide—
Later.

Postpone, postpone, abstain.

Only one thread was certain:
After World War I
Business as usual,
After World War II
Orderly Decontrol.
Always he led us back to where we were before.

> He seemed to be in the centre
> Because we had no centre,
> No vision
> To pierce the smoke-screen of his politics.
>
> Truly he will be remembered
> Whenever men honor ingenuity,
> Ambiguity, inactivity, and political longevity.
>
> Let us raise up a temple
> To the cult of mediocrity,
> Do nothing by halves
> Which can be done by quarters.[11]

The ghost of Mackenzie King is alive and well in the body politic on the prairies. The three major political parties today pile up their political stance on the right and in the centre, timidly determining their policy with a Gallup Poll mentality. Certainly this is unlike the progressive religious politicians of the pioneer era who, with a great deal of optimistic confidence, built their hope for the political future on an ideal kingdom of justice and righteousness symbolized in the New Jerusalem! The political mediocrity reflected in those elected to office today (who "never do things by halves which can be done by quarters") lacks the religious race tradition of vision, boldness, and urgency so desperately needed to bring about changes for those who remain poor and defenceless.

What about the "no" side of the Protestant emphasis on the race? As indicated, the progressive political tradition was often guilty of self-righteous moralism which the Catholic tradition of the dance helped to ameliorate. But there is yet another negative dimension to the Protestant race outlook. This was a crass type of "boosterism" which came to the fore in the period of early settlement and found its home in the five prairie cities of Winnipeg, Regina, Calgary, Saskatoon, and Edmonton.[12] Alan Artibise, a Western Canadian historian, explains that "urban boosterism was both something more than a compendium of super salesmanship or mindless rhetoric, and something less than a precise ideology . . . its central theme was the need for growth; the idea that for a city to become "better" it had to become bigger."[13] This competitive growth attitude, reinforcing the atmosphere of a race, had its theological base in Anglo-Saxon Protestantism.[14]   Artibise elaborates that the "Protestants of relatively humble Anglo-Saxon origin who had come west from small towns and cities of the Maritimes and Ontario" formed the majority of boosters.   There was a high concentration of individualism in these western tycoons and a disdain for the disadvantaged and the poor. Booster-dominated cities "spent only a small fraction of their budgets on such community services as sanitation, health departments, or welfare—much less than was spent on promoting growth. In these areas "survival of the fittest" was the norm."[15]

It is not surprising that this secular version of Protestantism has its roots in a theology obsessed with expanding Christendom. This outlook, which assumes that the expansion of Christian enterprises is a sign of God's blessing, faces serious self-doubt today as possessive individualism, a by-product of this mentality, is greedily plundering the world's resources at a time when limits to growth offer the only hope of inheritance to future generations.

A Political Theology

In discussing the two metaphors describing pilgrims—one centered in worship and culture and symbolized in the dance, the other focused in the rigour of the race—both traditions can be seen as having had considerable influence on contemporary political theology. This influence is manifest primarily in the eschatological conviction that speaking about God must be in large part a political act. All religious groups who believe that God is concerned about the human condition are beginning to see God's involvement in the political structures that oppress people. Harvey Cox, a pioneer theologian of secular theology, explains:

> To say that speaking about God must be political means that it must engage people at particular points not just 'in general.' It must be a word about their own lives—their children, their job, their hopes, their disappointments. It must be a word to the bewildering crisis within which our personal troubles arise—a freedom in a society stifled by segregation.[16]

This new movement in political theology has certain advantages over the pioneer progressive movement based on the Social Gospel. There is not today the blind optimism that the forces of righteousness will be victorious. Partly through a recognition of the folly of theologically-approved militarism as seen through the critique of the German theologian, Karl Barth, the inadequacies of this "sunny side up" liberal optimism have been brought to light. Barth recognized that his teachers of liberal theology during the First World War, in trying to show that their theology was relevant to current events, were supporting the militarism of the Kaiser:

> One day in early August 1914 stands out in my personal
> memory as a black day. Ninety-three German intellectuals
> impressed public opinion by their proclamation in support of
> the war policy of Wilhelm II and his counsellors. Among these
> intellectuals, I discovered to my horror almost all of my
> theological teachers whom I had greatly venerated. In despair
> over what this indicated about the signs of the times, I suddenly
> realized that I could not any longer follow either their ethics or
> their understanding of the Bible and history.[17]

This realization brought Barth to oppose the liberal theology of his
teachers and instead to emphasize the transcendence of God in the
Biblical message. And by transcendence Barth meant God's
unwillingness to be co-opted by cultural religion.

A theological emphasis on transcendence does not mean
consigning God to a pie-in-the-sky outer-space kingdom; it means, as
Karl Barth explained, bringing God's words of judgement to the
oppressive political structures. This theological focus on
transcendence necessitates much stronger resistance to existing
conditions than that which has been provided by cultural religion
and which has in turn often been co-opted by mainstream capitalism.
Evident in the actions of the Canadian Council of Churches and the
Canadian Catholic Conference is a much greater willingness today to
take on Canadian political and economic power structures. The
prophetic tradition in the churches in Saskatchewan is seen in the
anti-uranium lobby in the province which is strongly anchored in the
churches who provide opposition to the three political parties and
their catering to uranium development, disregarding (or relegating to
second place) potential environmental hazards and the threat of
global nuclear arms proliferation.

Interesting (and exciting) is the festive dimension of these
church-related environmental groups. Political actions centre on
picnics in the park with protest songs and dancing which at the same
time retain the pressure of movement politics in that they are highly
visible lobbies against city hall and the legislative assemblies. Clearly
depicted here is a fusion of the dance and the race.

Another recent emphasis in current political theology is a greater
consciousness that God's concern is for all creation and not just for
human beings. The earlier progressive movement in politics built on
human progress has too often exploited nature for human greed. In
the first creation story in Genesis 1, human beings are given
"dominion" over every living thing that moves upon the earth. But

this "dominion" has been misinterpreted as "domination"—a license for industrial nations to exploit and ravage nature for selfish ends! Religious groups whose theology has been described through the metaphor of the dance have been less obsessed with progress. Indian and Catholic religions particularly have emphasized oneness with nature. Today, there is evidence of a new ecumenical spirit that combines both the dance and the race in its vision of the peaceable kingdom described in Isaiah 11:6-9:

> The wolf shall dwell with the lamb, and the leopard shall lie down with the kid, and the calf and the lion and the fatling together, and a little child shall lead them. . . . They shall not hurt or destroy in all my holy mountain; for the earth shall be full of the knowledge of the Lord as the waters cover the sea.

The vision of Isaiah which depicts this harmony of humanity with nature is reinforced by Jesus in his warning against the faithless apprehension of those who feel they have to do everything on their own:

> Consider the lilies of the field, how they grow; they neither toil nor spin; yet I tell you, even Solomon in all his glory was not arrayed like one of these. (Matt. 6:28).

But perhaps the most important aspect of contemporary political theology is its strong emphasis on the corporate nature of sin. Traditional theologies emphasize personal sin as being universal to all humankind. However, "to universalize sin is to trivialize it," says Dorothee Soelle, a German political theologian. Furthermore, "The Protestant consciousness of sin is innocuous and distresses no one in its indiscriminate universality for it identifies sin, not theoretically, but *de facto*, with a universal human fate comparable perhaps to smallpox which we are protected by vaccination (of Baptism)."[18] More accurately, says Soelle, sin is "apathy and collaboration." Jesus died as a result of corporate sin. Jon Sobrino, an El Salvadorean political theologian, defines sin as "that which brought death to the Son of God—and it is that which brings death to the children of God, to human beings; it may be sudden violent death, or, it may be the slow unremitting death caused by unjust structures. . . . Theology must take life as a whole—it must focus on the practical problems of the people in following Jesus and building up and realizing the kingdom of God in the face of their oppression."[19] Contemporary political theology is therefore bolder in naming the principalities and powers that oppress our society.

How does the church develop a style of life to meet this situation?

By moving away from establishment power it can learn how to be a non-status servant church. Instead of anxious preoccupation with whether or not church membership is increasing (and all the compromises that go with this type of statistical evangelism), Catholic and Protestant churches see themselves increasingly as a little flock. The Bible indicates that the flower of Israel's history revived when its political hopes of success were shattered by Babylonian captivity. The prophet Isaiah visualizes a remnant people with a new Messiah sprouting out of the broken dreams of King David, the son of Jesse:

> There shall come forth a shoot from the stump of Jesse and a branch shall grow out of his roots. And the Spirit of the Lord shall rest upon him. (Isaiah 11:1-2)

The style of life that develops out of the Biblical remnant theme is one with less worry about success and hence greater boldness in the venture. The new realization that comes as revelation is that God does not call us to be successful but faithful. In commissioning his disciples, Jesus uses the race-dance theme.

> Fear not, little flock, for it is your father's good pleasure to give you the kingdom. . . .Let your loins be girded and your lamps burning, and be like [people] who are waiting for their master to come home from a marriage feast, so that they may be open to him at once when he comes and knocks (Luke 12:32 and 35).

This race-dance outlook keeps the politically astute Christian from false optimism which paints a glowing picture of New Jerusalem that looks like a real estate advertisement. Because God remains active in the world, the politically-minded believer is also saved from cynicism which often becomes the stance of those who have been wounded many times in the battle for good causes, but who have not the faith.

Modesty about success will help to keep the pilgrims' eyes open to those who still see the New Jerusalem from afar. The outstanding international statesman, President Julius Nyerere of Tanzania, launched his poor East African country on the road to economic independence through the 1967 Arusha programme which centred on rural socialism and self-sufficient agriculture. Evidence of the success of this programme is reflected in the per capita annual income increase from $60 to $258 between 1967 and 1976[20] and in the increase in life expectancy from forty to forty-six.[21]   The slow improvement in the living conditions of these poor people has required both realism and hope, and the hope is reflected in Nyerere's own words about the Holy City. He says, "If you state that the New Jerusalem is where we're going. . . .Our friends should not be disappointed when they find we are still in the desert."[22]

The prayer of Ignatius Loyola may be used to remind people of the need to retain a tenacious hope for a better day (symbolized in the New Jerusalem) while they live in solidarity with those who still see Jerusalem from afar.

> Teach us good Lord to serve Thee as Thou deservest.
> To give and not to count the cost.
> To fight and not to heed the wounds.
> To toil and not to seek for any reward
> Save that of knowing that we do Thy will.

Contributors

Abraham Arnold   Lecturer, writer, and broadcaster on Jewish life in Canada. He is past Executive Secretary of the Jewish Historical Society of Western Canada, presently Executive Director of the Manitoba Association for Rights and Liberties.

Marjorie Beaucage   Of French-Canadian Metis family, born in Vassar, Manitoba. She studied at the Universities of Regina and Ottawa. For twelve years was a member of Our Lady of the Missions Order. She is presently working at the Native Women's Transition Centre in action training in Winnipeg.

Michael Entz   Born in South Dakota, U.S.A. Formerly an elder of the Waldeck Hutterian Brethren's colony, he is now leader of the Vanguard colony established in 1977.

Bede Hubbard   Born in England, his family emigrated to Saskatchewan. B.A. St. John's University, Minnesota. He has been a member of the Benedictine Order for eighteen years. Former editor of the *Prairie Messenger*.

Raymond Huel   Born in Gravelbourg, Saskatchewan. B.A. and M.A., University of Regina. Diploma in Civil Engineering. Ph.D. University of Alberta. Professor of History, University of Lethbridge.

Stella Hryniuk   B.A. and M.A., University of Manitoba. Ph.D. candidate doing research on Ukrainian Canadian Church History. Lecturer in Department of History, University of Manitoba.

Faye Kernan (Editorial Assistant). Born in Veregin, Saskatchewan of Doukhobor parents. B.Sc. (Pharmacy) University of Saskatchewan. Supervisor of the Pharmacy, Western College of Veterinary Medicine. Assistant Professor of Veterinary Clinical Studies.

Emma LaRoque   Born in Lac La Biche, Alberta. Cree-Metis. Professor of Native Studies (History), University of Manitoba. Author of *Defeathering the Indian*.

Gail McConnell   Born in Kirkland Lake, Ontario. B.A. University of Toronto. M.A. University of Saskatchewan. Former Publications Editor for University of Saskatchewan. Author of the Churchill River Enquiry Report. Free lance writer.

James McCrorie   Born in Montreal. B.A. and M.A. McGill University. Ph.D. University of Illinois. Professor of Sociology, University of Regina. Formerly Education Officer with the Saskatchewan Farmers Union.

Frank Peake   Born in England. B.A. University of Saskatchewan. M.A. University of Alberta. B.D. Huron College, London. He is an Anglican parish priest who has served pastorates in Alberta. Professor of History (retired), Laurentian University. Fellow of the Royal Society.

Ted Regehr   Born in Coaldale (largest Mennonite settlement in Alberta). B.A. Carleton University. Ph.D. University of Alberta. Head of the History Department, University of Saskatchewan.

Anne Smart   (Photograph coordinator). Born in Brooklyn, New York. B.A. Queen's University. Teacher of English at Conestoga College (Waterloo). Programme coordinator, Saskatoon Public Library.

Benjamin G. Smillie   Born in India of missionary parents. B.A. and M.A. University of Toronto. S.T.M., Andover-Newton (Mass.). Ed.D. Columbia (N.Y.). Coordinator of Institute for Saskatchewan Studies 1971-1980. A minister of the United Church of Canada. Professor of Church and Society, St. Andrew's College, Saskatoon.

Koozma Tarasoff   Born near Saskatoon of Doukhobor parents. His grandparents immigrated to Canada in 1899. B.A University of Saskatchewan. M.A. University of Alberta. Author of a *Pictorial History of the Doukhobors.*

Norman Threinen   Grew up in Saskatchewan and studied at Concordia College, Edmonton. Th.D. Concordia Seminary, St. Louis, Missouri. Served as parish pastor in Edmonton and Executive Secretary of Theology of the Lutheran Council in Canada. Founding Editor of *Consensus* (a Canadian Lutheran Journal of Theology).

Roman Yereniuk   Born in Salzburg, Austria. B.A. University of Manitoba. B.D. St. Andrew's College, Winnipeg. M.A. McGill University. Professor of Eastern Slavic Church History, St. Andrew's College, Winnipeg.

Notes

Preface

1. Howard E. Jensen, "Pelagianism," *An Encyclopedia of Religion,* ed. Vergiluis Fern (New York: The Philosophical Library, 1945), pp. 569-570. Pelagianism, based on the teaching of a fourth century British monk Pelagius, denied original sin, and insisted each person can work out their own salvation aided by Divine grace.

2. William E. Mann, *Sect, Cult, and Church in Alberta* (Toronto: University of Toronto Press, 1955), pp. 9-38. Mann traces the history of 38 sects, as well as mainline churches, who arrived in the flood of American immigrants who came to Alberta before 1930 and established themselves.

3. Susan Langer, *Feeling and Form* (New York: Scribners, 1953), p. 189.

I

1. Quoted by Alasdair MacIntyre in *A Short History of Ethics* (New York: Macmillan, 1966), p. 183.

2. Edward McCourt, *Saskatchewan* (Toronto: Macmillan, 1968), pp. 34-36.

3. Norman Cohn, *The Pursuit of the Millenium* (London: Secker and Warberg), pp. 40-58.

4. *Ibid.,* p. 42.

5. *Ibid.,* pp. 42-43.

6. *Ibid.,* p. 45.

7. Karl Marx and Frederick Engels, *Manifesto of the Communist Party,* ed. Lewis S. Feuer (New York: Anchor Books, 1959), p. 39.

8. Karl Marx, *Critique of the Gotha Programme,* in *Selected Writings in Sociology and Social Philosophy,* ed. T. B. Bottomore and M. Rubel (London: Pelican, 1963), p. 263.

9. J. S. Woodsworth, "Report of a Preliminary and General Social Survey of Regina" (Department of Temperance and Moral Reform of the Methodist Church and the Board of Social Services and Evangelism of the Presbyterian Church, Sept. 1913), p.

21. Cited by B. G. Smillie, *J. S. Woodsworth, Civic Pedagogue, 1874-1942* (unpublished Ed. D. thesis, Columbia University, 1970), p. 37.

10. J. S. Woodsworth, "The Holy City," *Hours that Stand Apart* (n.d., n.p.), pp. 26-27.

11. William Irvine, *The Farmers in Politics* (Toronto: McClelland & Stewart, 1920), p. 100.

12. Salem Bland, *The New Christianity,* introd. Richard Allen (Toronto: University of Toronto Press, 1973 (1920)), p. 87.

13. Vernon C. Fowke, *The National Policy and the Wheat Economy* (Toronto: University of Toronto Press, 1957 (1973)), p. 60.

14. Dominion Lands Act, Ottawa, 1872, Clause 37.

15. Isaac Watts, "We're Marching to Zion", *Sacred Songs and Solos,* ed. Ira D. Sankey (London: Marshall, Morgan & Scott, 1971) Hymn No. 823.

II

1. The degree to which monopoly capital as represented by the banks, mortgage companies, retail-wholesale chains, etc. has been able to successfully cope with co-operative alternatives is perhaps indicated by the modest share of the market co-operatives enjoy, and their corresponding tendency to accept the marketing leadership of their "betters."

2. The changes in question have to do with farm enlargement, intensive capitalization, the restructuring of transportation and marketing infrastructure—a development being vigorously opposed by the more radical farm organizations such as the National Farmers Union.

III

1. H. P. Beaver, *Church, State and the American Indian* (Missouri: Concordia Publishing House, 1966), p. 82.

2. Harold Cardinal, *The Unjust Society* (Edmonton: Hurtig Publishers, 1969), p. 54.

3. Elizabeth Graham, *Medicine Man to Missionary* (Toronto: Peter Martin Associates Ltd., 1975), p. 78.

4. *Ibid.*, p. 35.

5. Edward Ahenekew, *Voices of the Plains Cree*, ed. Ruth N. Buck (Toronto: McClelland & Stewart Ltd., 1973), p. 69.

6. *Ibid.*, p. 182.

7. *Ibid.*, p. 72.

8. T. C. Boon, *The Anglican Church from the Bay to the Rockies* (Toronto: Ryerson Press, 1962), p. 39.

9. Ahenekew, p. 13.

IV

1. An earlier version of this paper was presented before the interdisciplinary seminar in Canadian Plains Studies at the University of Regina in 1973 and subsequently published in A. R. Allen, ed., *Religion and Society in the Prairie West* (Regina: Canadian Plains Research Center, 1974).

2. R. Latouche, *Caesar to Charlemagne: The Beginnings of France* (London: Phoenix House, 1968), pp. 225-27.

3. G. Masson, *Early Chroniclers of Europe: France* (New York: Burt Franklin, 1971), p. 65.

4. H. H. Walsh, *The Church in the French Era: From Colonization to the British Conquest* (Toronto: Ryerson Press, 1966), Ch. VI.

5. Gallicanism was a series of political and theological doctrines directed against the claims of the clergy and papacy; Ultramontanism emphasized supreme papal authority in matters relating to doctrine and church administration. Thus, an ultramontane (one who looked beyond the mountains) was one who turned to Rome for guidance and direction and who tolerated no interference from the state in what were deemed to be ecclesiastical matters. For a more comprehensive discussion consult J. Hastings, ed., *The Encylopedia of Religion and Ethics* (New York: Scribner's, n.d.), Vols. VI, XII.

6. P. Benoit, *Vie de Monseigneur Tache, Archeveque de St. Boniface* (Montreal: Librairie Beauchemin, 1904), Vol. I, pp. 50-55. A. G. Morice, O.M.I., *Histoire de l'Eglise Catholique dans l'Ouest Canadien* (Nouvelle Edition; Montreal: Granger Freres, 1915), Vol. I, pp. 273-76. For an excellent English language survey of the activities of the Oblates consult G. Carriere, O.M.I., "The Early Efforts of the Oblate Missionaries in Western Canada," *Prairie Forum*, 4 (Spring, 1979), pp. 1-25.

7. Luke 4:18, "He hath anointed me to preach the gospel to the poor."

8. *Statutes of Canada,* 38th Vict., Ch. 49, s.11.

9. *Ibid.*, 40th Vict., Ch. 7, p. 11.

10. A. I. Silver, "French Canadian Attitudes Toward the North-West and North-Western Settlement 1870-90" (M. A. dissertation, McGill University, 1966), pp. 123-33. For a modification and refinement of Silver's views consult A. N. Lalonde, "L'intelligentsia du Quebec et la migration des Canadiens Francais vers l'Ouest canadien 1870-1930," pp. 163-85 and R. Painchaud, "French-Canadian Historiography and Franco-Catholic Settlement in Western Canada 1870-1915," *Canadian Historical Review* (Dec. 1967), pp. 447-66.

11. Silver, "French Canadian Attitudes," p. 171.

12. *Census of Canada,* 1891, Vol. I, Table II, p. 112; Table III, p. 221; Table IV, p. 328.

13. For statistics concerning the French and Catholic population of Manitoba, Saskatchewan and Alberta in 1901, 1911 and 1921 consult *Census of Canada* 1931, Table 35, pp. 716-20; Table 42, pp. 792-95.

14. *Journals of the Legislative Assembly of the North-West Territories,* 1891-92, pp. 110-11.

15. Les Cloches de St. Boniface, IV (15 sept., 1905), p. 240.

16. *Ibid.*, V (15 aout, 1906), p. 208.

17. Saskatoon *Phoenix* (July 2, 1909).

18. *Le Patriote de l'Ouest* (21 fev., 1923). Declaration de O. Charlebois, O.M.I., et P. E. Myre, ptre. miss.

19. *Ibid.*, (24 aout, 1911).

20. G. T. Daly, *Catholic Problems in Western Canada* (Toronto: Macmillan, 1921), p. 74.

21. R. Painchaud, "Les exigences linguistiques dans le recrutement d'un clerge pour l'Ouest canadien, 1818-1920," *Sessions d'Etude,* 1975, La Societe Canadienne d'Histoire de l'Eglise Catholique, p. 60.

22. Mgr. L. P. A. Langevin, O.M.I., *Memoire Confidentiel sur la Situation Religieuse et Statistique de la Population Catholique de l'Archidiocese de St. Boniface* (St. Boniface: n.p. 18 mai, 1911), p. 13.

23. Painchaud, "le recrutement d'un clerge," pp. 55-59.

24. G. W. Simpson, "Father Delaere, Pioneer Missionary and Founder of Churches," *Saskatchewan History,* III (Winter, 1950), pp. 5-6.

25. Langevin, *la Situation Religieuse,* pp. 4-5, 24.

26. Emilien Tremblay, *Le Pere Delaere et l'Eglise Ukrainienne de Canada* (Berthierville: n.d.), Ch. IX.

27. J. M. Reid, "The Erection of the Roman Catholic Archdiocese of Winnipeg" (M. A. Thesis, University of Manitoba, 1961), p. 13.

28. *Ibid.,* p. 56.

29. Painchaud, "le recrutement d'un clerge," p. 64.

30. H. Bourassa, *La Langue Gardienne de la Foi* (Montreal: Bibliotheque de l'Action francaise, n.d.), p. 9, 31.

31. T. Flanagan, *Louis 'David' Riel: 'Prophet of the New World'* (Toronto: University of Toronto Press, 1979), p. 81.

32. *Ibid.,* p. 175.

V

1. *Canada West and the Hudson's Bay Company* (London: the Aborigines' Protection Society, 1856), a Leaflet. For a further discussion see my essay, "Fur Traders and Missionaries," *Western Canadian Journal of Archeology,* III (1973), pp. 72-93.

2. E. M. Howse, *Saints in Politics* (London: George Allen and Unwin, 1953).

3. F. A. Peake, "Anglican Theological Education in Saskatchewan," *Saskatchewan History,* XXXV (1982), pp. 25-33.

4. Eugene Stock, *The History of the Church Missionary Society* (London: C.M.S., 1899), 3 volumes.

5. H. A. Seegmiller, *No Bought 'Em Tea: A History of the Colonial and Continental Church Society* (D. D. Thesis, London: Huron College, n.d.).

6. Helen Evans Reid, *All Silent, All Damned: The Search for Isaac Barr* (Toronto: Ryerson Press, 1969).

7. F. A. Peake, "David Anderson: Lord Bishop of Rupert's Land," *Journal of the Canadian Church Historical Society,* XXIV (1982), pp. 3-46.

8. F. A. Peake, "The Achievements and Frustrations of James Hunter," *Journal of the Canadian Church Historical Society,* XIX (1977), pp. 138-165.

9. David Anderson, *The Net in the Bay: Journal of a Visit to Moose and Albany* (London: Thomas Hatchard, 1854).

10. Reginald Heber (1783-1826) was Bishop of Calcutta for the last three years of his life during which time he laboured incessantly for the spread of the Gospel in India. He is also remembered for several hymns including "From Greenland's icy mountains" from which the quotation is taken and for a life and edition of the works of Jeremy Taylor.

11. Vilhjalmur Stefansson, *My Life with the Eskimos* (New York: Macmillan, 1951), p. 25.

12. *C. M. S. Archives,* July 31, 1847.

13. T. C. B. Boon, *The Anglican Church from the Bay to the Rockies* (Toronto: Ryerson Press, 1962).

14. There is a wide literature on this subject including, for example, E. R. Wickham, *Church and People in an Industrial City* (London: Lutterworth Press, 1957).

15. W. S. Darling, *Sketches of Canadian Life: Lay and Ecclesiastical* (London: David Bogue, 1849)

16. C. W. Vernon, *The Old Church in the New Dominion* (London: Society

for Promoting Christian Knowledge, 1929), p. 3.

17. F. A. Peake, "Anglican Theological Education in Saskatchewan," *Saskatchewan History*, XXXV (1882), pp. 57-59.

18. Harry Pick, *Next Year: A Romance of the Barr Colonists in Canada* (Toronto: Ryerson Press, 1928). C. Wetton, "The Promised Land: The Story of the Barr Colonists," *Lloydminster Times*, n.d., 1953. F. A. Peake, "Isaac Barr: Missionary Extraordinary," *Journal of the Canadian Church Historical Society*, VI (1964), pp. 1-11. Helen Evans Reid, *All Silent, All Damned* (Toronto: Ryerson Press, 1969).

VI

1. Karl Marx and Fredrick Engels, *German Ideology*, in *Selected Writings in Sociology and Social Philosophy*, ed. T. B. Bottomore and M. Rubel (Harmondsworth: Penguin Books, 1956 & 1978), pp. 35-37.

2. S. D. Clark, *The Developing Canadian Community*, 2nd ed. (Toronto: University of Toronto Press, 1968), p. 145.

3. Author Unknown.

4. The Hymnary, No. 669 Based on Psalm 100, Tune "Old 100th", (Toronto: The United Church Publishing House, 1930).

5. John Calvin, *Institutes of the Christian Religion*, Volume 2, Book III. Chapter 23. sect. 12 (Grand Rapids: Eerdmans, 1957), p. 235.

6. Richard Hofstadter, *Social Darwinism in American Thought* (New York: George Braziller, 1959), p. 5.

7. Josiah Strong, *Our Country: Its Possible Future and its Present Crisis* (New York: Baker and Taylor, 1885), p. 165.

8. James Woodsworth, *Thirty Years in the Canadian North West* (n.p. Methodist Church in Canada, Young Peoples' Forward Movement, 1909) pp. 124-125.

9. Carl Berger, "The True North Strong and Free", *Nationalism in Canada*, ed. Peter Russell (Toronto: McGraw Hill, 1966), pp. 3, 6.

10. Edmund Oliver, *The Religious History of Saskatchewan to 1935*, Volume 2, (page references are absent in the nine volumes) unpublished history in the United Church Archives, Saskatchewan, St. Andrew's College, Saskatoon. Edmund Oliver (1882-1935) was principal of the Presbyterian Theological College and after 1923 of St. Andrew's College. As well, he was professor of New Testament and Church History. He started his career as Professor of Economics at the University of Saskatchewan, giving the first lecture of the University (in October, 1908) in the Drinkley Building. He wrote this unpublished history on the tenth anniversary of the United Church of Canada. It is invaluable for its inclusion of information about the early history of western settlement through church reports, letters, government documents and for Oliver's understanding of church history.

In the preface to this unpublished history of the church in Saskatchewan, Oliver wrote:

> I consign this narrative to the Archives anticipating that it will not be read for many days to come. If at some future date some earnest student interested in the early history of Saskatchewan's religious development should happen upon this sketch written in the heart of the depression of the Thirties and in the midst of the Great Drought I would have him know that the courage of our ministers and of our people was adequate, and that the church was sympathetic to human need and contributed to the morals of the community as did no other institution.

11. Oliver, *History of Sask.*, Volume 1.

12. *Ibid.*

13. *Ibid.*

14. *Ibid.*, Vol. 4.

15. *Ibid.*, Vol. 3.

16. *Ibid.*, Vol. 1.

17. *The Rundle Journal* 1840-1848, Aug. 7, 1846. Ed. Hugh A. Dempsey (Calgary: Historical Society of Alberta, Glenbow Archives, 1977), p. 230.

18. *Ibid.,* p. 143. Letter dated December 25, 1843.

19. Oliver, *History of Sask.,* Vol. 1.

20. *Ibid.,* Vol. 2.

21. John Wesley, "On God's Vineyard," *Wesley Sermons* (London: Wesley Methodist Book Room, 1870), Vol. II, p. 624.

22. Charter and By-Laws of the Temperance Colonization Society. Lake Mss., University of Saskatchewan, Library. Cited by Alan F. J. Artibise, *Town and City,* (Regina: Canadian Plains Research Center, 1981), p. 240.

23. *Ibid.*

24. *Ibid.,* p. 241.

25. William P. Delainey and William A. S. Sarjeant, *Saskatoon, The Growth of a City, Part 1: The Formative Years, 1882-1960* (Saskatoon: Saskatoon Environmental Society, 1974), p. 2.

26. Artibise, *Town and City,* p. 243.

27. *Ibid.*

28. Oliver, *History of Sask.,* Vol. 2.

29. Woodsworth, *Thirty Years in the Canadian North West,* p. 183.

30. Oliver, *History of Sask.,* Vol. 2.

31. Rudolf Metz, *A Hundred Years of British Philosophy* (London: George Allen and Unwin, 1938), pp. 286-293.
Readers and students of the history of ideas may query the roots of the British Idealism which permeated the thoughts of missionaries, labour and agrarian leaders on the western Canadian frontier. Metz calls this the neo-idealistic tradition in British Philosophy. It was pantheistic to see God in every part of nature. The following verse (written by Hartley Coleridge and often quoted by J. S. Woodsworth in "My Religion") is an example of pantheism:

Sweet girl believe that every bird that sings,
And every flower that stars the elastic sod,
And every thought the happy summer brings
To thy pure spirit is a Word of God.

This philosophy was articulated mainly by the British T. H. Green (1836-1882) who carried on a battle with the utilitarian philosophers, Bentham and Mill. He insisted on a dialectic in philosophy that ran from Hume to Kant and Hegel. The combination of the empiricism of Hume with the idealism of Hegel brought these pioneers in the West to combine an idealistic hope with an accurate analysis of the current situation.

32. J. S. Woodsworth, "Our Immigrant," Winnipeg: Bureau of Social Research, Gov't. of Manitoba, Saskatchewan and Alberta, n.d., p. 1.

33. *Ibid.*

34. J. S. Woodsworth, *Strangers Within Our Gates* (Toronto: University of Toronto Press, 1909, 1972), p. xv. In the Introduction to this book, Marilyn Barber accused Woodsworth of being "a true representative of English Canadian nationalism when he assumed that Canada would achieve her highest destiny as an Anglo-Saxon nation, but he was less representative in his conclusions about the effects of immigration." But Barber does not elaborate on Woodsworth's later conclusions about immigrants. Instead, for the balance of the introduction, she provides a certain guilt by association because she gives examples of Methodists who saw their mission to be to "Christianize," "Protestantize," and "Canadianize" the immigrant. This labelling misrepresents Woodsworth's changing outlook on the immigrant.

35. J. S. Woodsworth, "Some Aspects of Immigration." *University Magazine,* April 1914, p. 193.

36. Oliver, *History of Sask.,* Vol. 5.

37. *Ibid.*

38. Elizabeth Smillie, "The Homesteads—for Women's Movement." (Essay, Trent University, March 23, 1980).

39. Oliver, *History of Sask.,* Vol. 9.

40. "Home Mission Report," *Minnesota and Dakota District Proceedings* (1892), p. 65.

41. *Ibid.*

42. Augsburg Confession, VII, *The Book of Concord* (Philadelphia: Fortress Press, 1959), p. 32.

43. For a discussion of Luther's doctrine of the two kingdoms see Karl

H. Hertz, editor, *Two Kingdoms and One World* (Minneapolis: Augsburg Publishing House, 1976), pp. 15-66; Ulrich Duchrow, ed., *Lutheran Churches—Salt or Mirror of Society?* (Geneva: Lutheran World Federation, 1977), pp. 3-9; Eric W. Gritsch and Robert W. Jenson, *Lutheranism. The Theological Movement and its Confessional Writings* (Philadelphia: Fortress Press, 1976), pp. 179-190.

44. William Hordern, "Interrelation and Interaction between Reformation Principles and the Canadian Context," *In Search of Identity,* ed. Norman J. Threinen (Winnipeg: Lutheran Council in Canada, 1977), pp. 19-32.

45. Martin Luther, "To the Christian Nobility of the German Nation Concerning the Reform of the Christian Estate," *Luther's Works,* American Edition, Volume 44 (Philadelphia: Fortress Press, 1966), p. 130.

46. George W. Sandt, *Theodore Emmanuel Schmauk, D.D., LL.D., A Biographical Sketch* (Philadelphia: United Lutheran Publication House, 1921), p. 279, cited in Karl H. Hertz, *Two Kingdoms and One World,* p. 142.

47. Norman J. Threinen, "The Stuermer Union Movement in Canada," *Concordia Historical Institute Quarterly,* 46 (Winter, 1973), 148-157.

48. *Ibid.,* p. 152.

49. Minutes, Manitoba and Saskatchewan Pastoral Conference, Winnipeg, February 18-23, 1914.

50. Proceedings, Manitoba and Saskatchewan District, June 24-30, 1925.

51. For a discussion of Lutheran involvements both during World War II and in the post-war see Norman J. Threinen, *The Convergence of Canadian Lutheranism, 1922-1972.*

52. Reinhold Niebuhr, *Moral Man and Immoral Society* (New York: Scribners, 1932), p. 221.

VII

1. Isaiah 2:3.

2. Psalms 135:5, 6.

3. Quotations from the Talmud cited in Joseph L. Baron, *A Treasury of Jewish Quotations,* ed. Thomas Joseloff, (New York and London: 1956), pp. 216-17.

4. Isaiah 44:28.

5. Baron, *Jewish Quotations,* pp. 216-17.

6. Revelation 21:2.

7. Revelation 3:9.

8. *Manitoba Free Press,* February 2, 1882, cited in A. A. Chiel, *The Jews in Manitoba* (The University of Toronto Press, 1961), p. 26.

9. Cardinal Manning's words published in B. G. Sack, Appendix to *History of the Jews in Canada* (Montreal: Harvest House, 1965), pp. 272-73.

10. Alexander Galt to Sir John A. Macdonald, January 25 and February 3, 1882, Macdonald Papers, Public Archives of Canada, Ottawa.

11. John Taylor to Marquis of Lorne, February 13, 1882, Macdonald Papers, Public Archives of Canada, Ottawa.

12. *Ibid.,* Macdonald to Lorne, February 20, 1882.

13. *Ibid.,* Macdonald to Galt, February 27, 1882.

14. *Ibid.,* Macdonald to Galt, February 26, 1882.

15. Isaiah 23:4; Ezekiel 28:21, 22; Joel 4:4-6.

16. *Hamelitz,* June and September, 1882. Cited in A. A. Chiel, *Jews in Manitoba,* pp. 37, 38.

17. Simon Belkin, *Through Narrow Gates* (Montreal: Canadian Jewish Congress and Jewish Colonization Association, 1966), p. 22, ft. 4.

18. *The New Standard Jewish Encyclopedia* (New York: Doubleday & Co., 1970), p. 85.

19. "Settlement of Russian Refugee Jews under Mansion House Committee," Dept. of Interior, Dominion Lands Bureau 73568 (1) R. G. 15 1A Vol. 87; Public Archives of Canada, Ottawa.

20. Belkin, *Through Narrow Gates,* Appendix #2, p. 212.

21. H. Landau quoted in letter from Alexander Begg, CPR agent in

London, to CPR Lands Commissioner in Winnipeg, in Dept. of Interior, Dominion Lands Branch files, 1886, #128731; Public Archives of Canada, Ottawa.

22. Resolution dated April 18, 1887 in Department of Interior Files; Public Archives of Canada, Ottawa.

23. Letters #14614, April 26, 1887 and #73586, May 3, 1887 from A. A. Ruttan, Asst. Sec., Dominion Lands office, Winnipeg, to Dept. of Interior, Ottawa, and from A. M. Burgess, Deputy Interior Minister, to W. D. Perley, MP, and H. H. Smith, Dominion Lands Commissioner, Winnipeg; Public Archives of Canada, Ottawa.

24. Report of Homestead Inspector R. S. Park to H. H. Smith, Winnipeg, July 19, 1887 #153854; Public Archives of Canada, Ottawa.

25. Cyril E. Leonoff, *Wapella Farm Settlement* (Winnipeg: Manitoba Historical Society and Jewish Historical Society of Western Canada, 1972), pp. 3-5.

26. Petition to Edgar Dewdney Minister of Interior, Ottawa, June 29, 1889 #212834, Dept. of Interior Files, Public Archives of Canada, Ottawa.

27. Letter, February 17 and 10-page memorandum February 15, 1892 from H. B. Small, Sec'y, Dept. of Agriculture, Ottawa to W. H. Baker, Clerk of Baron de Hirsch Institute, Montreal, in Institute files, Montreal.

28. Notice to Farmers, March 7, 1892, in Jewish Historical Society Archives, Winnipeg; D. W. Reidle letter, January 25, 1892 in Baron de Hirsch Institute files with Canadian Jewish Congress Archives, Montreal.

29. Leonoff, p. 16.

30. Abraham Arnold, "The First Rabbis in Saskatchewan " in *Western Jewish News* (Winnipeg: October 2, 1980).

31. Abraham Arnold, in Pictorial Supplement, "Contribution of the Jews to the Opening and Development of the West " (Winnipeg: Manitoba Historical Society and Jewish Historical Society of Western Canada, 1969), pp. 1-3 and fn. 2-6, pp. 13, 14.

32. *Jewish Times,* February 9, 1906, pp. 94-96; reprinted from *London*

Jewish Chronicle, cited in "Jewish Farm Settlements in Saskatchewan" by Abraham Arnold, *Canadian Jewish Historical Society Journal* (Spring, 1980), p. 37.

33. Arnold, "Jewish Farm Settlements of Saskatchewan," *Canadian Jewish Historical Society Journal* (Spring, 1980), pp. 37-39 and references fn. 60-66.

34. Hersh Wolofsky, "Laurier and Canada's Immigration" in *Canadian Jewish Yearbook,* 1941-42, p. 93; and *Jewish Times,* May 31, 1907, p. 217.

35. Belkin, *Through Narrow Gates,* p. 78.

36. Irving Abella and Harold Troper, "The Line Must be Drawn Somewhere: Canada and Jewish Refugees," *Canadian Historical Review,* LX, No. 2 (June 1979).

37. A. A. Chiel, *Jews in Manitoba, p. 78.*

38. *Ibid.*

39. The opposite of "Gan Eden," the Jewish version of heaven, is "Gehenna" or Hell. Gehenna comes from Ge-Hinnom, the valley of Hinnom, the "Accursed Valley" where the Canaanites sacrificed children to the man-eating God, Molech, in pre-Israelitic times. It was said to be located south of Jerusalem.

40. Nathan Ausubel, *Book of Jewish Knowledge* (New York: Crown Publishers, 1964), p. 496.

41. Cecil Roth and Geoffrey Wigoder, eds., *New Standard Jewish Encyclopedia* (Doubleday & Co., 1970), p. 636.

42. *Ibid.,* p. 637.

43. *Ibid.,* p. 530.

44. Ausubel, *Book of Jewish Knowledge,* p. 373.

45. J. L. Baron, ed. *Treasury of Jewish Quotations,* p. 349, 402.

VIII

1. The most complete and detailed account of this incident is given in Lawrence Klippenstein, "Manitoba Metis and Mennonite Immigrants: First Contacts," *Mennonite Quarterly Review,* 48 (Oct. 1974), pp. 476-88.

2. Frank H. Epp, *Mennonites in Canada, Vol. 1, 1786-1920: The History of a Separate People* (Toronto: Macmillan, 1974), p. 200.

3. P. J. Klassen, *The Economics of Anabaptism, 1525-1560* (The Hague: Mouton & Co., 1964).

4. Robert Friedman, "The Doctrine of the Two Worlds," in Guy F. Hershberger, ed., *The Recovery of the Anabaptist Vision* (Scottdale, Pa.: Herald Press, 1957), pp. 105-118. Robert Kreider, "The Anabaptists and the State," *Ibid.*, pp. 180-93. James C. Juhnke, *A People of Two Kingdoms, The Political Acculturation of the Kansas Mennonites* (Newton, Kansas: Faith and Life Press, 1975).

5. W. E. Keeney, *Dutch Anabaptist Thought and Practice* (B. DeGraaf: Neuwkoop, 1968). Harold S. Bender, *The Anabaptist Vision* (Scottdale, Pa.: Herald Press, 1944).

6. Hans J. Hillerbrand, "The Anabaptist View of the State," *Mennonite Quarterly Review,* 32 (April, 1958), pp. 83-110.

7. Denis V. Wieler, "The Political Thought of Anabaptism in the Sixteenth Century" (M.A. Thesis, University of Saskatchewan, Saskatoon, 1977).

8. Clarence Bauman, "The Theology of 'The Two Kingdoms': A Comparison of Luther and Anabaptists," *Mennonite Quarterly Review,* 38 (January, 1964), pp. 37-49.

9. Cornelius Krahn, *Dutch Anabaptism: Origin, Spread, Life and Thought, 1450-1600* (The Hague: Martinus Nijhoff, 1968), pp. 239-40. Johan Sjouke Postma, *Das niederlaedische Erbe der preuszisch-ruszlaendischen Mennoniten in Europa, Asien und Amerika* (Leeuwarden: Jongbloed, 1959), A. L. E. Verheydon, *Anabaptism in Flanders, 1530-1650* (Scottdale, Pa.: Herald Press, 1961).

10. J. Winfield Fretz, *Mennonite Colonization: Lessons From the Past for the Future* (Akron, Pa.: Mennonite Central Committee, 1944), and *Christian Mutual Aid: A Handbook of Brotherhood Economics* (Akron, Pa.: Mennonite Central Committee, 1947).

11. E. Randt, "Die Mennoniten in Ostpreussen und Litauen bis 1772"

(Doctoral Dissertation, Koenigsberg, 1902). W. Mannhardt, "Die Mennoniten under den preussischen Koenigen," *Gemeinde Kalendar,* 1902. *Mennonite Encyclopedia,* Vol 2 (Scottdale, Pa.: Herald Press, 1956), pp. 383-84.

12. David G. Rempel, "The Mennonite Commonwealth in Russia: A Sketch of its Founding and Endurance, 1789-1919," *Mennonite Quarterly Review,* 47 (Oct. 1973), pp. 259-308. The entire October 1974 issue of *Mennonite Quarterly Review,* Vol. 48, is devoted to articles dealing with the Russian Mennonite experience.

13. E. K. Francis, *In Search of Utopia. The Mennonites in Manitoba* (Altona, Man.: D. W. Friesen & Sons, 1955).

14. Frank H. Epp, *Mennonites in Canada, Vol. 1, 1786-1920* (Toronto: Macmillan, 1974), pp. 303-332.

15. *Ibid.,* pp. 283-302, 333-364. H. J. Gerbrandt, *Adventure in Faith* (Altona, Man.: D. W. Friesen & Sons, 1970), pp. 92-108, 253-78.

16. I. I. Friesen, "The Mennonites of Western Canada with Special Reference to Education" (M.Ed. Thesis, University of Saskatchewan, Saskatoon, 1934).

17. Adolph Ens, "Canadian Mennonite Relations with Government, 1900-1930" (Ph.D. Thesis, University of Ottawa, 1979).

18. Frank H. Epp, "The Migrations of 100 Years and Their Meanings," *Mennonite Reporter,* Nov. 25, 1974, p. 6.

19. Frank H. Epp, *Mennonite Exodus. The Rescue and Resettlement of the Russian Mennonites Since the Communist Revolution* (Altona, Man.: D. W. Friesen & Sons, 1962).

20. H. L. Sawatzky, *They Sought a Country. Mennonite Colonization in Mexico* (Berkeley and Los Angeles: University of California Press, 1971). J. Winfield Fretz, *Pilgrims in Paraguay, The Story of Mennonite Colonization in South America* (Scottdale, Pa.: Herald Press, 1953). H. Hack, *Die Kolonisation der Mennoniten im Paraguayischen Chaco* (Amsterdam: Koenigliches Tropeninstitut, n.d.).

21. Guy F. Herschberger, "Our Kingdom is in Heaven," in J. R.

Burkholder and Calvin Redekop, eds., *Kingdom, Cross and Community* (Scottdale, Pa.: Herald Press, 1976).

22. J. S. Woodsworth, *Strangers Within Our Gates* (Toronto: Ryerson, 1909).

23. J. T. M. Anderson, *The Education of the New Canadian* (Toronto: Dent, 1918), p. 79.

24. Kurt Tischler, "German Canadians in Saskatchewan, 1900-1930" (M.A. Thesis, University of Saskatchewan, Saskatoon), p. 94.

25. Norman Priestly served as Secretary of the United Farmers of Alberta and was the United Church minister at Coaldale, Alberta, in the 1920s when a number of Mennonites moved into the area. When these Mennonites established their own German Saturday School, Priestly had the building closed and placed under police guard, and urged that no more Mennonites be allowed into the country and that those already in Canada be forcibly assimilated. B. B. Janz to T. O. F. Herzer, 10 March, 1928, *Canadian Pacific Railway Papers,* Box 46, File 520, Glenbow-Alberta Institute Archives.

26. For a more extensive discussion see the as yet unpublished Chapter 2 of Frank H. Epp's "Mennonites in Canada, Vol. 2." A copy is in the possession of the author. See also, Paul Peachey, "Our Social Ministry in the Gospel," *Mennonite Quarterly Review,* 29 (July 1962), pp. 227-35. Guy F. Herscheberger, "Our Citizenship is in Heaven," in J. R. Burkholder and Calvin Redekop, eds., *Kingdom, Cross and Community* (Scottdale, Pa.: Herald Press, 1976), pp. 273-85.

27. When Frank H. Epp, a prominent Mennonite journalist, historian and educator entered politics he prepared a statement entitled "One Mennonite in Politics, A Personal Statement in Response to Many Inquiries." A copy is in this author's possession.

28. A. Ross McCormack, *Reformers, Rebels and Revolutionaries. The Western Canadian Radical Movement, 1899-1919* (Toronto: University of Toronto Press, 1977).

29. Dave Fransen, "New Mennonite Approaches to the State," *Mennonite*

Brethren Herald, January 30, 1981, pp. 31-32.

X

1. The two major Ukrainian churches, Orthodox and Greek-Catholic, belong to the family of Byzantine-rite churches. The Church of Ukraine traces its origin from the ancient church in the Kievan-Rus' state which adopted the Christian faith from Byzantium. The Orthodox Church professes the fullness of Revelation which is expressed through Holy Tradition and embodies the whole spectrum of doctrine, church government, worship and art. Here are included the books of the Bible, the Creed, the decrees and canons of the seven ecumenical councils, the writings of the Holy Fathers, canon law, liturgical worship and holy icons. The Ukrainian Orthodox Church, as a national church, also acknowledges the decision of its local councils (*sobor*), the writings of its fathers and saints, and the specific and particular practices and traditions of the Ukrainian people. The Ukrainian Catholic Church (known also as the Uniate, Ruthenian or Greek-Catholic Church), established at the Union of Brest (1596), acknowledges the dogmas and teachings of the entire Roman Catholic Church. Although maintaining the Byzantine-rite, the Ukrainian Catholic accepts the decisions of all twenty-one councils and the teachings on the Immaculate Conception, purgatory, and papal infallibility (when speaking *ex cathedra*). Lastly, the church acknowledges the see of Rome as the spiritual and administrative centre for the entire Catholic Church. Both churches in their internal life are closely related by their common roots emanating from Byzantium. Therefore, the differences in the liturgical life, church language, architecture, customs and traditions are quite minor. A comprehensive treatment of the development of the Ukrainian Church is found in *Ukraine: A Concise Encyclopedia* (Toronto: 1971), Vol. 2.

2. A general study of Ukrainian history can be found in Michael Hrushevsky, *A History of Ukraine,* ed. O. J. Frederiksen (New Haven: Archon Books, 1941), and D. Doroshenko, *A*

Survey of Ukrainian History
(Winnipeg: Trident Press, 1975).
Revised edition.

3. The exact number is difficult to
ascertain because of the variety of
names under which they were recorded
in Canadian records—Galicians,
Bukovians, Austrians, Poles,
Ruthenians, Russians, Ukrainians, etc.
See W. Darcovich and P. Yuzyk, eds.,
*A Statistical Compendium of the
Ukrainians in Canada,* 1891-1976,
Series 31.

4. *Gemeino elexikon Der im
Reichsrate Vertretenen Konigreiche
und Lander* (Vienna: 1907).

5. It is of interest that many of the
family Bibles and Prayer books of the
pioneers reflect this. For example, the
days of births, deaths, marriages as well
as planting and harvesting were
recorded in the covers of these books,
often giving their relation to the church
liturgical year. Among the early
popular works published in Canada
were the religious almanacs
(Kalendar).

6. *Resurrection Matins,* Paschal
Canon, VIII Song, Irmos.

7. *Ibid.,* IX Song, Irmos.

8. *Ibid.,* I Song, Tropar.

9. This hymn which permeates the
entire Resurrection celebration as well
as those of the period until Pentecost, is
not limited only to the liturgical cycle
but is sung in the homes of the faithful
throughout the same period.

10. This is best illustrated in the icon of
the resurrection known as the descent
of Christ into Hades. Here a radiant
and triumphant Christ reaches
downward to Adam (in some icons to
both Adam and Eve), the first man, and
pulls him upward, symbolically
granting life eternal.

11. On the celebration of *Provody* on
St. Thomas Sunday (first Sunday after
Easter) and during the Paschal period,
the practice in Ukraine and in Canada
was to assemble in the cemetery after
the Holy Liturgy. Each grave was
decorated to resemble a banquet table,
covered first by an embroidered cloth,
then appointed with place settings of
fruits and breads. As the family stood
by the graves, the priest walked amidst
the graves and blessed each one with
Holy Water. The faithful broke bread

and shared their fruits with friends and
neighbours, requesting the priest to say
special prayers for those that had
departed.

12. The symbolism of the liturgy is well
illustrated in the classic work of
Nicholas Cabasilas, *A Commentary on
the Divine Liturgy* and Nikoli Hohol
(Gogol), *Meditations on the Divine
Liturgy.* Both books have been
published in many western languages
in a number of editions.

13. The moving experience of the
beginning of the liturgy is recorded by
Rev. Nesto Dmytriw. In 1897, upon
arrival in the Dauphin area, he recalls
the celebrations as follows: "Late in the
evening . . . I began to hear confessions.
The next morning it was impossible to
celebrate the liturgy outdoors; hence it
was necessary to improvise an altar in
the house. The small home was jammed
with worshippers. Hearing the first
words of the liturgy—'Blessed is the
Kingdom . . .' they gave way to their
tears like little children." See N.
Dmytriw, "Canadian Rutheria" in H.
Pinuita, *Land of Pain, Land of
Promise* (Western Producer Prairie
Books, 1978), p. 47.

14. The iconographic plan of an
eastern Christian church building
clearly emphasized the entrance into
eternity of the faithful. The Church
interior in its dome has the icon of
Christ Pantocrater (the Judge); in the
vaults of the dome, the evangelists; in
the apse of the Church, the icon of the
Mother of God; on the walls of the
building is the hierarchic development
of the saints, teachers, martyrs, and
holy men and women of the church.
Thus here is gathered the entire Church
triumphant to which are added the
living believers.

15. Maria Adamowska, "Beginnings
in Canada" in Piniuta, *Land of
Promise,* p. 74.

16. The readings of the lives of the
saints was very popular in the homes of
the Ukrainian pioneers and was
practiced on a regular basis.

17. Many of these editions can still be
found in the archives and libraries of
churches and cultural institutions
across western Canada. A number of
these are now found in the various
major Ukrainian library holdings in
Canada.

18. In the liturgical celebrations of the Eastern Church, the cross is always referred to as "the life-giving cross" or "triumphant cross."

19. After their homes, the first structure built by Ukrainian settlers in Canada was the Church whereas settlers of other cultures might have built the jailhouse and tavern prior to a church.

20. A good account of the role of the priest in Galacian Ukrainian society can be found in J. P. Himka, "Priests and Peasants: The Uniate Pastor and the Ukrainian National Movement in Austria, 1867-1900," *Canadian Slavonic Papers,* XXI (March 1979), pp. 1-14.

21. *Collecteana S. Congregationis de Propaganda Fide seu Decreta Instructionis Rescripta pro Apostolious Missionibus 1907,* II, p. 303, no. 1866.

22. V. J. Kaye, *Early Ukrainian Settlements in Canada, 1895-1900* (Toronto: University of Toronto Press, 1964), pp. 1851-56.

23. Zhovkva, *Misionar,* 1899.

24. The efforts of Bishop Langevin of St. Boniface and other Roman Catholic clergy on behalf of the Ukrainians has been described in several works, particularly in G. Comeault, "The Politics of the Manitoba School Question and its Impact on L. P. A. Langevin's Relations with Manitoba's Catholic Minority Groups," (M.A. Thesis, University of Manitoba, 1977).

25. See the introductory chapter in P. Yuzyk, "The Ukrainian Greek Orthodox Church of Canada to 1951" (Ph.D. Thesis, University of Minnesota, 1958).

26. Reference is made here to the early writings of J. S. Woodsworth in which Anglophone condescension towards the Ukrainians and other immigrants was evident. However, after 1914, Woodsworth retreated markedly from this position.

27. O. Martynowych, "Village Radicals and Peasant Immigrants: The Social Roots of Factionalism among Ukrainian Immigrants in Canada, 1896-1918" (M.A. Thesis, University of Manitoba, 1978).

28. Biographies of these men in F. Swyripa, *Ukrainian Canadians: A survey of their portrayal in English language works* (University of Alberta Press, 1978).

29. In its title, the church used "Greek" to signify the Byzantine rite and the term "independent" to differentiate it from the Roman Catholic Church.

30. For example, the liturgy of St. John Chrysostom, the seven sacraments, the Nicene Creed, vestments and church interiors were to be maintained. By 1911, the Church had 72 congregations, 40 church buildings and 19 full time ministers. Yuzyk, *Ukrainians in Canada,* p. 95.

31. For further reading on the development of the Ukrainian Orthodox Church, see *Ibid.,* and O. S. Trosky, *The Ukrainian Greek Orthodox Church in Canada* (Winnipeg, 1968).

32. The prelates after Bishop Budka (1912-1927) were Bishop Basil Vladimir Ladyka (1929-1956) and Bishop Maxym Hermaniuk (1956-present). The Church consists of five eparchies—eastern Canada (Toronto), Manitoba (Winnipeg), Saskatchewan (Saskatoon), Alberta (Edmonton), and British Columbia (New Westminster).

33. The present Metropolitan of the Ukrainian Orthodox Church is Andrew Metiu, (1975-present). The church has 3 diocese—Toronto (eastern), Edmonton (western) and Winnipeg (central).

XI

1. *Le Canada ecclesiastique* (Montreal: Beauchemin), the former annual directory for the Catholic Church in Canada, as late as 1954 listed St. Mary's in Regina as a German parish; however, no Saskatoon city parish was ever so designated. More recently, Rev. K. J. Schindler, C.S.S.R., "Die Deutschsprachigen katholischen Kirchengemeinde in Kanada, Teil 2," in the *German-Canadian Yearbook,* Vol. 2 (Toronto: Historical Society of Mecklenburg Upper Canada, 1975), pp. 276-84, describes three contemporary urban Catholic parishes in Western Canada as German speaking. They are St. Joseph's in Winnipeg, St. Boniface in

206   Visions of the New Jerusalem

Calgary and St. Boniface in Edmonton.

Msgr. George P. Aberle mentions the "large number" of German Catholic immigrants in Winnipeg, *From the Steppes to the Prairies* (Dickinson, N.D.: 1963), p. 189, and James B. Hedges adverts to help made by the Winnipeg offices of the Volksverein Deutsch-Canadischer Katholiken (not the Verein Deutsch Condischer Katholiken, as the footnote in Hedges incorrectly states) for settling 30 German Catholic families on 30,000 acres of land near the city, James B. Hedges, *Building the Canadian West* (New York: Macmillan, 1939), pp. 376-77. However, according to 1956 population statistics for the whole Archdiocese of Winnipeg, there were only 4,033 German Catholics in a total Catholic population of 524,086; Emilian Milton Tramblay, *The Epic of St. Anne in Western Canada* (Battleford, Sask.: Marian Press, imprimatur, 1967), p. 6.

XIII

1. G. K. Chesterton, *Chaucer* (London: Faber & Faber, 1964), pp. 154-85. I am indebted to Rev. Bob Haverluck for drawing my attention to this Chesterton description.

2. *Ibid.,* p. 161.

3. Edmund Oliver to his wife, January 1, 1919, University of Saskatchewan Archives, cited by G. L. Barnhart, "E. H. Oliver: A Study of Protestant Progressivism in Saskatchewan, 1909-1935" (M.A. Thesis, University of Regina, 1977), p. 90.

4. Edmund Oliver, "The Religious History of Saskatchewan to 1935," Vol. 1, (unpublished history in the United Church Archives, St. Andrew's College, Saskatoon, Saskatchewan).

5. Ramsey Cook, "A Prairie Prophet," a book review of Anthony Mardiros, *William Irvine, The Life of a Prairie Radical,* in *Canadian Forum,* Vol. 59, No. 695, pp. 35-37. Cook, in a critical review of a biography of William Irvine (farm leader, minister, quoted earlier), accuses the biographer, Anthony Mardiros, of glossing over the theological inadequacy of Irvine. Cook suggests that Irvine, along with other Social Gospel leaders, had a

"theological education that must have been of a very low intellectual order." Quoting Norman Cohn, *The Pursuit of the Millenium,* pp. 309-310, Cook also suggests "that all these theologians who follow a utopian tradition are self-appointed prophets of the powerless and are drawn from intellectuals and half intellectuals—the farmer priest turned freelance preacher was the commonest type of all." In supporting Cohn's criticism of utopian eschatology, one can only assume that Cook shares Cohn's conclusions that this mentality degenerates into the totalitarianism of a Hitler or Stalin. Cohn's criticism of the Crusade mentality used for Cook's objection to "half-baked religious ideas," appears to be a cover to justify Cook's own politically quiescent Protestant orthodoxy which legitimizes the weak Liberal Government in Canada and which leaves the country in its political and economic bondage to American multinationals!

6. Alfredo Fierro, *The Militant Gospel* (New York: Orbis, 1975), p. 92.

7. Robert Chodos, "The Great Canadian Dree Machine," *Corporate Canada,* ed. Rae Murphy and Mark Starowicz (Toronto: Lewis and Samuel, 1972), pp. 140-52. Chodos explains that through a system of political patronage, large multinationals like I.B.M., I.T.T., Michelin Tire, Westinghouse and Procter and Gamble have received large grants from the Department of Regional Economic Expansion (DREE). This department was established to provide stimulus for companies to set up factories and insure jobs in underdeveloped areas of Canada. DREE's performance shows that it has given large subsidies but has been unable to insist that companies stay in areas where they set up factories.

8. Harold E. Bronson, *The Two Superpowers* (Saskatoon: Liberation Books, 1980), p. 77. Perhaps the clearest example of the federal government's impotence in controlling foreign take-over is the setting up of the Foreign Investment Review Agency FIRA in 1974. An editorial writer, Ian Urquhart said, in *MacLeans* (July 11, 1977) that an agency that was intended as a "watchdog has become a lap dog." Between 1974-1976, FIRA approved 84% of the take-overs and 90% of the take-overs between 1977 and 1979.

Seventy-five percent of these take-overs have been by American companies.

9. Latin American Working Group and Canadian News Synthesis Project, "The Cost of INCO's Goof," *The Last Post,* January, 1978, pp. 10-11. On October 20, 1977, INCO laid off 3,450 workers in its nickel mining operation in Sudbury. Falconbridge laid off 4,000 in September of that year. The reason given by both companies for these layoffs was a depressed international nickel market. But Falconbridge at the same time invested 500 million dollars in copper mines in the repressive regime in Chile. INCO, at the same time as its Sudbury layoffs, was opening up new mines in Indonesia and Guatemala. "The scandal is not in the coincidence of the foreign start-ups with domestic cutbacks. Rather it is the decision of these companies to use Canadian generated capital for investment in countries where labour is cheap because it is severely repressed by brutal dictatorial regimes."

10. John Deverell and the Latin American Working Group, *Falconbridge,* (Toronto: James Lorimer, 1975), pp. 12, 22, 71, 76. A classical example of how the economically powerful in foreign countries determine policies of Canadian companies is the Falconbridge mining company. The recent controller of Falconbridge is the wealthy family enterprise of Howard B. Keck who bought out a British and South African consortium through holdings in the Canadian Bank of Commerce. It is this group which shows that, while American multinationals appear to be transnational, they are prudentially nationals. Through United States political power they have been able to develop large contracts. The Howard Keck connection to Lyndon Johnson was through the oil magnate Robert Anderson who, as Secretary of the Navy in successive American cabinets, was able to insure navy contracts. John Connally, appointed to the Falconbridge Board in 1973, was one more repeat of American political influence on the Canadian economy. He was the prime engineer of the economic blockage of Chile after the election of Salvadore Allende. Connally, as Secretary of the Treasury, was also U.S. representative to the World Bank. With this portfolio he was

able to encourage the stranglehold of that country through withholding credit. He strongly supported the setting up of the Domestic International Sales Corporation (DISC) in the U.S. which encouraged American companies with branch plants in Canada to repatriate their operations to the United States and take advantage of an indefinite tax deferral by expanding direct control of their foreign operation from the U.S. With this record, how could Canadians remain unperturbed? Perhaps our impotence lies partly in that we have no say in who Falconbridge appoints to its Board of Directors.

11. F. R. Scott, "W.L.M.K.," *The Blasted Pine, An Anthology of Satire, Invective and Disrespectful Verse,* selected by F. R. Scott and A. T. M. Smith (Toronto: MacMillan, 1957), pp. 27-28.

12. Alan F. J. Artibise, "Boosterism and the Development of Prairie Cities, 1871-1913," *Town and City,* ed. Alan F. J. Artibise (Regina: Canadian Plains Research Centre, 1981), pp. 210-235.

13. *Ibid.,* p. 211.

14. *Ibid.,* p. 213.

15. *Ibid.,* p. 21.

16. Harvey Cox, *The Secular City* (New York: MacMillan, 1965), p. 256.

17. Karl Barth, *The Humanity of God* (London: Collins, 1961), p. 14.

18. Dorothy Soelle, *Political Theology* (Philadelphia: Fortress Press, 1974), p. 89.

19. Jon Sobrino, *Christology at the Crossroads* (New York: Orbis, 1978), p. xvii.

20. *The World Almanac and Book of Facts* (New York: Newspaper Enterprise Association, 1976).

21. *World Mark Encyclopedia of the Nations,* 5th ed., Vol. 2, p. 330.

22. David Martin, "President Nyerere talks to David Martin about poverty and progress," *The New Internationalist,* 1967. Special Issue Julius Nyerere.